RIP IT UP!
RIP IT UP!
RIP IT UP!

ROCK & ROLL RULEBREAKERS

BY DENISE SULLIVAN

Backbeat
Books
San Francisco

Published by Backbeat Books
600 Harrison Street, San Francisco, CA 94107
www.backbeatbooks.com
Email: books@musicplayer.com
An imprint of the Music Player Network
United Entertainment Media, Inc.

Distributed to the book trade in the U.S and Canada by
Publishers Group West 1700 Fourth Street, Berkeley, CA 94710

Distributed to the music trade in the U.S. and Canada by
Hal Leonard Publishing P.O. Box 13819, Milwaukee, WI 53213

Cover Design by Richard Leeds
Text Design and Composition by Leigh McLellan
Front Cover Photo of Talking Heads: David Corio/RETNA
Back Cover Photo of Peter Case: Courtesy of Vanguard Records; Photo by
    Anthony Artiaga

Library of Congress Cataloging-in-Publication Data

Sullivan, Denise
    Rip it up! : rock & roll rulebreakers / by Denise Sullivan.
        p . cm.
    Includes bibliographical references and indexes.
    ISBN 0-87930-635-1 (alk. paper)
    1. Rock music—History and criticism. 2. Music—Social aspects.
    I. Title.

    ML3534.S88 2001
    781.66—dc21   2001025186

Printed in the United States of America

01 02 03 04 05   5 4 3 2 1

contents

contents

To Louie Beeson, Buz Renard, Alan Robinson,
and all the other angels.

And in the waking dreams our societies
permit, in our myths, our arts, our songs,
we celebrate the non-belongers, the
different ones, the outlaws, the freaks.
What we forbid ourselves we pay good
money to watch, in a playhouse or movie
theatre, or to read about between the secret
covers of a book. —Salman Rushdie,
The Ground Beneath Her Feet

fREE-THINKERS ARE DANGEROUS.

Rock and roll was never about extolling the seemingly comfortable and often deceptively homey virtues of the status quo. It was, real rock and roll was, always the often anguished—sometimes joyful—howl of teenage alienation. Rock and roll belongs to teenagers (of whatever age); so does alienation. And real rock and roll is what Sullivan is talking about here; not Foreigner, not Kansas, not Journey, not Pat Boone, not Pablo Cruise.... She's not talking about gentlemen, or even slobs, earning a wage in order to keep an exorbitant lifestyle going. She's not talking about studious musician/technicians playing towards superhuman perfection. She's talking about the real thing—an inspired ability to move people, even move People. And that's revolutionary.

In 1965, I was the freshman class president at a state university on the East Coast. It seemed perfectly normal to me—already having grown my unruly hair long, sporting a big ol' beard and smoking pot daily—to book The Fugs, post-beatnik/pre-hippie East Village outrageousness, for the freshman class dance. The captain of the basketball team/Young Republican fraternity grind thought it was just as perfectly normal to threaten my life for exposing his bobby-socked girlfriend to those hirsute freaks singing about a Coca Cola douche. It was right then and there that I saw the power of rock and roll, and it was right then and there that I knew what I wanted to do instead of growing up.

After my freshman year, I imposed upon the Young Republicans of my university an almost unrelentless barrage of what must have been a total nightmare to their Establishment sensitivities: The Doors, The Who, the Jefferson Airplane, Sun Ra, Country Joe and the Fish, Cream, Muddy Waters, Big Brother and the Holding Company, Jimi Hendrix, the Grateful Dead, Otis Redding...what an assault! I was always too stoned to make a deal with the Velvet Underground when I'd go see their shows at the Dom—I saw every one of them—although I did manage to convince Velvets openers Jackson

Browne, Tim Buckley, Sandy Bull, and John Hammond to come out to the distant suburbs and play at my school.

This was the soundtrack of that period's Revolution. We were going to end racism, end the war in Vietnam, end the control power elites held over our young lives. Turns out it's an ongoing battle. When the liberationist consciousness-expanding sounds—and ideas—of Frank Zappa, Janis Joplin, Pink Floyd, and early Elvis were replaced by the slick and pathetic careerist commercialism of Styx, ELO, REO, later Elvis (music your parents or 9-year-old siblings could enjoy), and lifestyle free-form FM radio was co-opted by pre-programmed, advertiser-friendly AOR dreck, I ran off to Morocco, Afghanistan, Nepal, and Bulgaria.

The early '70s ushered in some really reactionary times. But eventually, the favorite son of the Far Right Establishment, Nixon, was dragged kicking and screaming from the White House while the embers of the underground were being stoked and kept alive by Lou Reed, the Stooges, MC5, the NY Dolls, Patti Smith, then Tom Verlaine, Richard Hell and, finally, The Ramones, who exploded into a receptive, plowed-up underground like four manic Johnny Appleseeds who left punk bands everywhere in the wake of their now legendary exuberant, jaw-dropping shows, shows that put the fun and rage back into a rock and roll anesthetized by uninspired musicians and falsely inspired producers. The Ramones turned rock on its head—just when it was most sorely needed—in what *The New York Times* once called "a joke that conquered the world." Suddenly one didn't need to try to compete with Jeff Beck in order to get up on a stage anymore.

But in these matters between people, it seems nothing ever is like decisive forever. The battles just rage and rage. They get fought over and over again. Sullivan has lived through—and participated in—the battles that took place in her lifetime and understands the tactics, the strategies, the significance, and the futilities. If she isn't strictly, coldly objective, she is committed, passionate, prescient, knowledgeable and, thankfully, inspired. Like her protagonists, she's a freethinker; and, like them, she's dangerous.

how many times have we heard the stories of how people's lives were changed by the appearance of Elvis Presley or the Beatles on *The Ed Sullivan Show*? I won't be retelling that tale from my vantage point because I didn't see the broadcasts back then; but without a doubt, the Beatles and Elvis from those moments forward, would help define rock and roll, popular culture and youth rebellion. There are definitely days I wish I were old enough to have witnessed the most revolutionary televised moments in rock and roll history—as ultimately they would significantly impact me. But no matter what age we are, those of us whose lives have been charged and inspired by rock and roll and its rulebreaking spirit all have similar, defining rock and roll memories—the times we recognize as points where we crossed the line.

The most enduring passion of my childhood was listening to the radio, playing records on my phonograph, watching musicians on television and, when I was old enough, going to concerts. It was my entire world, and I still derive comfort, strength and happiness from a good song or album side. Like many of us who felt as if they hadn't been issued a guidebook to life, rock and roll—with its twang, its rumble and its beat, its cowboy code of ethics and its way-out style—informed my taste and my value system, sometimes for the better and sometimes for the worse. It helped give access to feelings I might otherwise not have had. And it gave me a sense of community and some kind of direction, particularly at times when I had none. For all of that, I'm grateful.

I only ever remember being interested in music that was extraordinary, outside and different from that which was enjoyed by my peers. During the Summer of Love, I was six years old when I insisted my mother buy me Jefferson Airplane's *Surrealistic Pillow*. I chose the record because I saw the thrill my teenage cousins got when they played the Airplane, the Chambers Brothers, Cream, and later, the Beatles' white album at family gatherings. (Years later, I learned it was because they were stoned out of their minds, but after all, it was the '60s).

Along with the album, I got my first record player at White Front, an old-fashioned discount chain store. The turntable was essentially a glorified, version of the Close and Play; I took it and my record into my bedroom and closed the door for the next 12 years. Here was where I would spend the majority of my time, making discoveries, conducting experiments, floating in ecstasy on a rock and roll high.

I felt certain I was the only one experiencing this music on some kind of higher level; as it turned out, I was way wrong. In 1967, the Jefferson Airplane was known around the world as the prime movers of the San Francisco Sound. Yet among the kids on my block, they were hardly the stuff of conversation so I *was* alone in my thrall. The Airplane compelled me at first because they looked like freaks (right on!) and had a girl in the band and her hair looked like mine (when you're a kid, that's no small thing). Though I couldn't articulate the pull they had for me then—maybe still can't—the feeling that zoomed through me when I blasted the dangerous sounding "3/5 of a Mile in 10 Seconds" was something I'd never felt before and I wanted to feel it again and again. For one thing, the song had the phrase "blowin' my mind" in it, and though I wasn't sure what it meant, I knew it couldn't possibly be good. "Take me to a simple place where I can easily see my face…and all the other freaks can share my cares." These lyrics along with the incessant cymbal crash, psychedelicized blues riff and swirly guitar lead planted themselves in my subconscious. And though at the time, those words and sounds were just plain scary to me, their secret powers pulled me deeper into the beautiful and chaotic rock and roll fire.

Behind closed doors, I had my first taste of the idea that rock and roll was intrinsically linked to breaking rules. I learned—thanks to television—that somewhere, they were burning Beatles records (it was around the time John Lennon said the Beatles were more popular than Jesus); Jim Morrison was getting hauled off to jail; and generally, kids who listened to rock music ended up getting busted for smoking marijuana (as seen on *Dragnet*).

Rock and roll—the Beatles in particular—might as well have been God to me. So how come something that made me feel so good was perceived as bad by parents, the authorities, and the media? It was terribly confusing. But over the years, I discovered that the most interesting people to me—the people who played music, listened to it, enjoyed it, and talked about it—were just a little bit…other…and so I decided to join their gang. And that's how I found out that rock music had the power to shape and transform lives—just ask any former hippie or punk rocker and they'll tell you so. I was taught by them that what was and wasn't acceptable to the norm didn't matter—that I could do what was right for me. Sometimes it turned out OK and other times it didn't. But like the song said, "It's my life and I'll do what I want."

Today, I know my experience was not unique. I had brothers and sisters all over the world that would eventually devote their lives to writing about music, listening to it, and playing it precisely because there was no option for them but to do so. It's probably no coincidence that the artists whose work I am most passionate about today are not only misunderstood visionaries but also, most of all, rulebreakers. They have conducted careers and lived lives in a fairly untraditional, iconoclastic fashion. They've passed the point of caring so much that they couldn't care less. You can hear it in their songs and see it in their eyes.

At some point in their careers, the artists collected here made a singular contribution that set them apart—whether it was the way they squeezed a note out of their instrument, told their stories in a song, or kept their vision intact when those around them caved. Their work has inspired others to act. And despite whatever kind of successes or failures may have been thrown their way, they have endured.

I've learned elemental lessons on perseverance, integrity, human frailty, kindness, joy, forgiveness, anger, passion, love, freedom, and faith through these artists' words and music. I attribute the fact that those ideas and emotions ever reached me to rock music's numinous nature. It's that super-natural aspect of the singer and the song that continues to fascinate me.

The connection to a song or an album can come from something very simple. The Kinks' *Sleepwalker* was my soundtrack to falling in love as a teenager. Years later, I realized I had also fallen in love with the Kinks; their music helps keep that sweet memory eternal for me. Studying the Kinks as a historian, I learned that the Kinks brothers, Ray and Dave Davies, were troublemakers and rulebreakers from the start. No wonder I loved their music.

When punk rock and new wave came along during my adolescence, I felt an instant rapport. For the first time in my life, music spoke more directly to my generation than to the Baby Boomer generation before us. (It wouldn't be until the '80s and '90s that my generation and bands like Camper Van Beethoven and Teenage Fanclub would actually make music that reflected exactly

who we were.) From the abrasive sound of it to the shocking new look of it—
punk rock music was all about upsetting the status quo. Like many music
lovers of my generation, I gravitated to it. When I had the opportunity to interview some of the most legendary figures of that era—Elvis Costello, Talking Heads and Television's Tom Verlaine—there was no way I was going to
pass up the opportunity to talk to the people whose music literally shook the
world and rocked my own. They were my people—and I understood them—
or so I thought. What I found out is that my connection to that place and time
in music made it difficult for me to be entirely objective about it. That said,
my connection to the new wave artists and the rest of the subjects whose his-
tories I've chosen to delve into here make this a somewhat subjective collection of rock and roll rulebreakers—simply because I've singled them out
according to my own code, interests, and space and time limitations. As fans,
we all have our own lists.

As women of my generation, Shonen Knife are among the artists at the
top of my list of rulebreakers; they make me smile every time I think of them.
They went boldly where few women had dared to go before. Shonen Knife
became a rock band even though they couldn't play—at all. Their courage to
forge ahead inspires me when I come to a creative bridge. Yet my admiration
for them is bittersweet. My would-be girl band attempted to get off the
ground about the same time Shonen Knife did, but regrettably, we gave up
because we couldn't play either (which is why, some would say, I am a music
journalist!).

The sibling duo Sparks was a band I admired from afar in the '70s. Their
quirky music was lost on me but their album covers, among the finite number of sleeves that could be flipped through in record stores in those days,
had a magnetic attraction for me.

In matters of heart and home and in their dedication to the music, the
two couples profiled here, Julie and Buddy Miller and Chuck Prophet and
Stephanie Finch, have taken roads less traveled as well as roads well-worn
in rock and roll and have found themselves in the enviable position of having it all, if there is such a thing. Let them be an inspiration to those who
still think anything is possible in love and a life in music.

Peter Case has shifted between the roles of rock bandleader and singer-
songwriter more than once in his long career, as if to illustrate that if one is
meant to do something, they will eventually do it all. Case's traveling folk

singer blues speak to the wayward side of me that is constantly seeking but rarely finding. It is often in quiet moments that phrases from Case's lyrics miraculously give voice to what is happening in my heart when my head can't quite figure it out.

Master storytellers and crafts people like Charlie Louvin, Wanda Jackson, Utah Phillips, Sonny Curtis and Jerry Allison of the Crickets, Ike Turner and Ramblin' Jack Elliott showed me that no matter what life hands you, no matter what mistakes you make, no matter how old you are, there's no reason not to keep on playing. Most importantly, without them, rock and folk as we know it today would not be as rich.

Ann Magnuson, Jason Pierce of Spiritualized and Julian Cope remind me that often the best rock music comes from people who are not only impossible to categorize, but who are a bit eccentric, if not certifiable. It's exactly what makes them great. When I'm afraid to accept the wacky part of others and myself, the music and artists on the fringe inform me of all that's good about that quality. It shows a particular strength of character to be OK with one's weirdness, foibles, and uniqueness—and to continue to do the unexpected and move forward in complete harmony. If rock and roll wasn't founded in part on the idea of otherness—of doing the opposite of what's expected and breaking the rules—while a community of like-minded individuals watch your back and cheer you on, well then perhaps I don't understand rock and roll at all.

Denise Sullivan
San Francisco, CA

talkin' 'bout my generation

post punkers

Beethoven
Teenage Fanclub
Camper Van
Beethoven
Teenage Fanclub

Camper Van
Beethoven
Teenage Fanclub

lthough it's been 20 years since its official inception, post-punk music, along with the bands that followed the new wave era, has for the most part gone undocumented. Those mostly British and American groups of the '80s—the Plimsouls, the Replacements, Dinosaur Jr., Sonic Youth, the Smiths, Hüsker Dü, Jesus and Mary Chain, Soul Asylum, Dream Syndicate, the list goes on forever—formed the foundation for the grunge and alternative rock sound of the '90s, the most significant shake-up to occur in rock and roll following punk rock's disturbance of rock's status quo in the mid-'70s. Only a handful of that generation of bands became superstars and sustain their careers today, but really only R.E.M., U2, Red Hot Chili Peppers, and Metallica are exceptions to the rule that most bands born in the '80s also died in the '80s—both literally and artistically.

Camper Van Beethoven was one of the bands that collapsed under the weight of artistic differences, record company woes, road weariness, drug addiction, and adult lives in transition; Camper was neither a democratic nor a diplomatic bunch, and in the end, ten years after their breakup, the members dissected the circumstances which led to the band's long and painful demise—one of the great band losses of my generation.

Teenage Fanclub, on the other hand, has yet to experience the dark nights of the rock band (and God willing they won't ever have to) as they've quietly survived the changes that traditionally destroy bands. The Fanclub's three principal singers and songwriters—Gerard Love, Norman Blake, and Raymond McGinley—keep their very similar artistic visions on track by operating as a true democracy. Midcareer, the members of Teenage Fanclub were occupied with the business of making records and conducting their personal lives and relationships without a whole lot of fanfare. They've also managed to keep their subtle humor intact (a quality way too rare in alternative rock).

Two very different situations, to be sure. Yet both of these bands' experiences and their music speak to my generation precisely because like myself, they were children in the '60s and early '70s. The members of Camper Van Beethoven and Teenage Fanclub came of age in the early '80s, and their personal and career achievements and disappointments mirror many of their listeners' young adult experiences; the bonus is that their respective journeys have been charted and set to music.

As late Baby Boomers/pre-Generation-Xers, we seem to be a generation, albeit an unrecognized one, unto itself. Overshadowed by the achievements, hopes, and failures of true Baby Boomers and eclipsed by the Gen-X media phenomenon, our "generation" has produced very few visible media figures. Two of the more illustrious people in our age bracket, John F. Kennedy Jr. and Princess Diana, died tragically. There is no singular voice, let alone group, that represents our views in politics, the media, the arts, or popular culture in general. Technically, there is not enough of a span of years to define those of us born between 1960 and 1970—give or take—as a generation, but our experiences reveal that we just don't fit with either the Boomers or the Gen-Xers.

We were the last wave of children before the age of technology. We grew up without computers in the classroom; we had records, not CDs; very few of our homes were equipped with VCRs; we played Pong and later PacMan. We were the children who weren't old enough to do anything about the tumult of the late '60s and early '70s, although we were profoundly affected by the horror of a war that unfolded before us every night on television (the first time in history that had ever occurred). Not old enough to fully comprehend what was happening, Vietnam, protests, race riots, assassinations, and the women's/gay/civil rights movements all occurred before most of us hit puberty. Many of us were from the first generation of broken homes and were left wondering what the hell was going on. No wonder we were confused. Years later, our music, our writing, and our visual art would begin to uncoil our legacy and reflect our fascination and confusion with the rapidly changing world. One of the things that allowed our freedom of expression was punk rock.

Hungry for something to call our own, our blank generation naturally glommed on to punk when it emerged in the mid-'70s. Although it wasn't truly the rock and roll of teenagers—it was made for the most part by people a bit older—it definitely wasn't music for Boomers. It addressed the stress of the confusing times as well as the inherent angst of adolescence. It would be another few years before we were old enough to have something that was truly ours, and that's why the bands that formed in the '80s—at least those directly impacted by punk's aesthetic—live large for us. They *were* us. And they provided the soundtrack to our coming of age.

Camper Van Beethoven was an '80s college radio phenomenon. Started by school chums, the group first came together in sunny Southern California, then retreated to the Northern California beach town of Santa Cruz, known for its free-thinking hippie population, long after the peace and love generation had taken day jobs. Scotland's Teenage Fanclub debuted in 1989, and although the group belongs to the same generation as the members of Camper, it took them a few extra years to get their wings as a band. They, too, were a college and alternative radio favorite out of the box. Also coming together at college-age, the members of the Fanclub grew up in the northern industrial Scottish capital city of Glasgow, where they remain based.

Although they would abandon their formal studies for rock and roll, the members of both bands were well-schooled in their respective specialty areas of music—Camper was based in traditional music and the progressive rock sounds of King Crimson, Pink Floyd, and Can; Teenage Fanclub were expert in power-pop and the jangle rock of the Beatles, Byrds, and Buffalo Springfield. But both Camper and the Fanclub injected punk rock into their mixes, as they belonged to the first generation of bands whose lives had been profoundly changed by punk. It was the musical foundation of their sounds until they found their own, yet clearly, they were especially attracted to the freedom implied by the unwieldy, anything-goes genre.

Camper Van Beethoven and Teenage Fanclub were among the cynical but happy young adults of the Reagan/Thatcher era. As the go-go '80s exploded around them, the musicians passed their time by slacking—playing music, hanging out in record shops, going to see bands and generally goofing off—while their peers sought more economically viable or traditional careers for themselves. The themes of happiness and sorrow and loves lost and found rang through their songs, although they would only be precursors of what was to come. This was music by young men with an innocence not quite lost. Although some of them had grown up quickly, there was still a naive, idealistic quality to the music of these bands, even though for the young adults in Reagan/Bush America and Thatcher's England, life could feel like a heavy burden.

From a business perspective, Camper began by following the D.I.Y. model set by fellow Americans R.E.M. and, until their demise, it served them well. For as long as they could, they kept their management and record label in the family, and their circle of business associates was of the homegrown variety. The Fanclub didn't have too many role models, coming from Scotland, home to only a handful of acts with anything resembling an American profile, but they had a mentor in a visionary record label chief, Creation's Alan McGee, and a head start on America with a signing to the prestigious indie label Matador, followed by the '90s-hot DGC. Both bands were critically lauded and charted high on the college and modern rock radio charts, although neither became anything close to a household name (except in some select households!). Yet among bands and music connoisseurs, they are duly noted as influential and exceptional; Camper having influenced '90s chart toppers like Counting Crows and the alternative-Americana sound and the Fanclub wielding a strong influence over '90s Brit-pop and its apparent kings, Oasis. In both cases, there is an ahead-of-their-time component to their music. Finally, neither band ever had anything to do with fashion. In their decidedly anti-fashion clothing choices, they became fashionable, helping to make thrift store finds, Levis, T-shirts, tennis shoes, and Doc Martens the preferred dress of understated, noncommercial alternative musicians everywhere. The idea of stage clothes was anathema to them, as it was with most post-punk–era bands.

Both Teenage Fanclub and Camper Van Beethoven are among my favorites in the history of rock music. CVB revitalized guitar rock in the San Francisco Bay Area in the mid-'80s. Teenage Fanclub helped keep the power-pop/jangle rock, guitar-based sound alive in the early '90s. Without the persistence of bands based in the four-chord, guitar, bass, and drums tradition, the entire contemporary music world might have found itself awash in synthesizer, techno, and fabricated studio sounds. Camper also added an element of rural tradition to their music with instruments like fiddle and mandolin, a sound that would not become firmly entrenched in mainstream rock until well into the '90s as more acts incorporated organic American and world music sounds into the rock and roll patchwork.

When Camper set the story of the Patricia Hearst kidnapping to music, one of those inexplicable, confusing '70s events, people our age pricked up their ears; when they covered Black Flag, Sonic Youth, and the Clash, we got that, too. When Teenage Fanclub dropped clichés like metal groupies and pet rocks into their songs, they sang to *us* about *them* with a nod and wink; when they railed against MTV's *120 Minutes* and radio formats in their songs, we were right there with them. As a mini-generation we'd finally been noticed. It may have been at the cost of our music being used for marketing concepts like grunge and themes to television commercials, but at least we'd found a voice to comment on it.

And so it was over. And with time passing came adulthood and the responsibility that goes with it—the kind many of us managed to avoid, escape, or put off by banding together in the underground subculture that the college and alternative radio scene provided. But the sounds of Camper Van Beethoven and Teenage Fanclub play on, to the tune of our memories of the times. No, the world did not change dramatically with the coming of Y2K or 2001 as it was represented in the film of the same title when we were children, nor did it end with the push of the button as they told us it would. The Cold War is over and it looks like we'll live to see middle age. But we still need each other—to gain perspective, to tell our stories, and to give each other a sense of belonging. I guess every generation is like that, but that's why the music of my generation resonates extra hard with me. We have *our* bands. They aren't your Elvises or your Beatles, nor are they your Nirvanas, N.W.A.s or even Becks. They're somewhere in between—just people our age, singing the songs of our lives.

camper van beethoven

> If you see me sittin' 'round and thinkin' the same old thoughts over and over again/or going back to old ways I long ago abandoned/please tell me, never go back. —*"Never Go Back,"* Camper Van Beethoven

"**t**he band, by all appearances, at least from what people tell me, is vastly influential, but I have no paycheck to show for it," says former Camper Van Beethoven bassist, Victor Krummenacher. "Not one."

Welcome to the world of cult rock. In the mid-'80s Camper Van Beethoven was perhaps the most important college-rock band in the days before alternative music had a name; at that time Hüsker Dü were near a breakup and the Bob Stinson-less Replacements were ceasing to be relevant. CVB topped critics polls, released records on its own Pitch-a-Tent label, and toured with a then-potent role model for young bands, R.E.M. But a less-than-amicable breakup in 1990 forced the Campers into separate corners. Frontman David Lowery retreated to Richmond, Virginia, to form Cracker. Krummenacher, with original violinist Jonathan Segel, pursued various local projects with lesser degrees of financial success. But in December 1999, Krummenacher and Segel joined Lowery in Richmond to complete tracks on an archival release, *Camper Van Beethoven Is Dead, Long Live Camper Van Beethoven.* The initial call came from Lowery, who asked Krummenacher and Segel if they would be interested in selling the material released on the pair's own label, Magnetic, on the Pitch-a-Tent Web site, making the Camper catalog, its offshoots, and related projects available on one easy-to-navigate site. In the long term, the band's plan is to regain the rights to its own recorded material (some of which is still in the hands of EMI, Camper's last distributor). And as Lowery was simultaneously readying a two-disc compilation of Cracker hits, rarities, and new material, *Garage D'or,* for release, he realized he needed a band to take the show on the road. "Cracker has done these sort of Rolling Blunder Revues with Joan Osborne and Adam Duritz," explains Lowery from his studio. "We play some of their songs, they play one of our songs, they do a duet. So we thought, 'Why don't we do it again with Victor and Jonathan?' It's basically a Cracker show. I would not call it a Camper reunion—we all sort of shrink back from that."

Call it what you will, but as it turned out, during a ten-day tour in early 2000, Krummenacher filled in on bass with Lowery's band, which includes guitarist Johnny Hickman; Segel added a song or two; Krummenacher and Segel opened the shows with their old guitarist Greg Lisher—"the reclusive Syd Barrett of Camper"—with Joey Peters on drums and Chris Xefos on bass; their old sideman, David Immerglück, joined them in San Francisco and L.A. The men trod the same boards for the first time in over ten years to play a few songs from the Camper songbook. The only one missing was drummer Chris Pedersen, and that's because he lives in Australia.

"We had a party the night before we were going to put all that stuff together [for the new record] here at the studio, and somehow a rumor got started that me, Victor, and Jonathan were going to play a reunion," says Lowery. "The thing was, we weren't planning to play, and the party was ultimately shut down by the police and fire departments. But we'd been in the basement rehearsing songs, thinking we could prevent a riot. We'd started talking about it."

Time, explains Krummenacher, is the other great facilitator for the new beginning, or what therapists might describe as an opportunity for closure to a bad ending.

"It took a long time," explains Segel. "David kicked me out of the band. He and our manager conspired to keep me from being able to tell my side of the story until it was kinda too late. And a different side of the story had already come out in the press in 1989. That was pretty upsetting. I had worked on demos for *Key Lime Pie* and didn't work on the record. When I finally heard the record, I was so shocked at how great it was—I really wanted it to be fucked up. But it was the best one they had made and it really upset me. It was at that point that I buckled down and wrote David a letter and said, 'This is the greatest stuff you've done—the best songs you've written.' Unfortunately, when I sent that letter, that was when Victor and Chris had decided they couldn't play with him anymore—in the middle of that tour in Sweden—so by the time he got the letter, he thought that I was being sarcastic. And so he was really pissed off at me for another year!"

"I certainly take responsibility for the fact that my walking probably made the band break up," says Krummenacher, who de-Camped in the middle of a European tour in 1990.

"So you're responsible for Cracker!" Segel sniggers. Constant conspirators, Krummenacher and Segel settle into the corner of a Vietnamese restaurant to gulp noodles and imperial rolls and recount the beginning, middle, and coda to their band's convoluted story. While they are at it, they manage to take some swipes at Lowery, but any true contempt for him or his white-boogie, MTV-successful band has all but vanished. In fact, Krummenacher and Segel say they're fans of Lowery's work, in particular Cracker's 1996 album, *The Golden Age*, which they characterize as "brilliant." They like what they've heard of the new material too, which harkens back a bit to the orchestral, experimental days of Camper's denouement—in fact, they know of one song that's resurfaced for the new Cracker recordings.

"One of the things I like about Camper is that the legacy is so muddled and completely confusing," says Krummenacher. "People say things like, 'I saw you in 1992 when I was a senior in high school,' and I tell them we broke up in 1990. Or they say, 'I saw the Monks of Doom—that was David Lowery's band after Camper broke up,'" referring to the jazz/experimental/prog rock band composed of Krummenacher, Lisher, Pedersen, and Immerglück that played concurrently with Camper and after. "Nobody knows the history unless they're intimately tied to us, and even then it's completely confusing because we're all such motherfuckers, we all have completely different ideas about what actually occurred. I'm kind of at a point where I think that's fine."

Lineage, legacy, and *family* are words that crop up repeatedly when the former Campers address the band's history. Like the Grateful Dead (to whom they were sometimes compared for their folk-based melodies smershed with dripping psychedelia; both bands' fans favored the twirling dance), the band has a mixed-up family tree that has remained at once interwoven and fractured throughout the years. Krummenacher and Lowery began making music together around Riverside and Redlands, California, in the summer of 1983 at Lowery's parents' house. Pedersen and Chris Molla joined when the group moved north to Santa Cruz, picking up Lisher and Segel in 1985.

The magical CVB collective: left to right: Krummenacher, Pedersen, Segel, Lisher (foreground), and Lowery

David Immerglück remembers that in the hippie enclave of Santa Cruz, the band wasn't entirely understood. Chris Pedersen had initially described them to him as "nauseating" and "a travesty." "Three weeks later he told me he was going on tour with them and they were coming to San Francisco. I had to check it out. I thought they were great. For some reason they reminded me of Mott the Hoople," he remembers.

Self-described as "surrealist absurdist folk," their merging of punk, folk, ska, and world music was truly a revelation. It was Segel's violin that would prove to be the band's hallmark at a time when alternative rock had yet to be invented, and indie rock was still shy of roots music or traditional instruments; not since Kansas had the violin been such an integral part of a band's identity and sound. Camper released *Telephone Free Landslide Victory* on their own imprint, Pitch-a-Tent.

The rerelease of the debut the following year for Rough Trade made the Top 10 in the 1986 *Village Voice* annual Pazz and Jop Poll on the strength of songs like "Take the Skinheads Bowling," which anyone with a college radio station within earshot had heard by then, as well as their cover of Black Flag's "Wasted," the naive melody, "The Day That Lassie Went to the Moon," and an ode to old band mate, Bill McDonald, "Where the Hell Is Bill?"

The band was among the hefty crop of American groups that formed in the wake of the guitar rock revival spearheaded by R.E.M. Krummenacher related a story to me in 1994 about how after one of R.E.M's 1985 Santa Cruz gigs, the band went backstage and pressed a copy of their *Telephone Free Landslide Victory* into the hands of the then god-like band.

"We were pretty surprised to hear from them a few days after we saw them. Michael Stipe called David from a phone booth in the desert to say how much he liked the record. We thought it was a prank. After many calls to the R.E.M. office and getting shrugged off, [R.E.M.'s manager] finally acknowledged that yes, Michael was into the band and that we should talk about touring together in the future."

But there was more to Camper than the novelty ska hook of "Skinheads." There were real songs with melodies sprinkled with Eastern European folk, punk, pop, progressive rock, and psychedelia. Lowery's disaffected vocals and willfully obtuse lyrics were another main component. Perhaps best of all, these slacker kids from a California beach town were the embodiment of what young people throughout America were feeling during the bleak Reagan years—they were so completely disenfranchised that their only option was to poke fun and party.

"Nobody can accuse us of not having had a good time, but that was a dark time in a certain way as far as a historical perspective," says Krummenacher. "Darker than it is now. People were dying and we said, 'Fuck it, it's all kind of crazy, let's have a good time.' I think that was part of the whole period of the last vestiges of punk rock. People got way serious and way more negative when things were getting better. Nirvana comes out when Clinton gets elected? I don't buy it."

Keeping house in Santa Cruz, the band sharpened its act in San Francisco clubs like the now-defunct V.I.S., Chatterbox, and the Farm with near-manic regularity. It frequently invited simpatico acts like Cat Heads, Donner Party, American Music Club, and friends like Spot 1019 and the White Fronts to open shows. For a brief time, it even helped to create a bona-fide guitar-rock scene in San Francisco.

Two releases followed in quick succession for Rough Trade: The second and third albums with their confusing titles, *II&III* and *Camper Van Beethoven*, were both released in 1986, and made the *Voice* poll again the following year. The band took its country and hillbilly influences and ran with them on "Abundance," "Sad Lovers Waltz," and Sonic Youth's "I Love Her All the Time," but their engaging punk/psychedelic journey, "(We're a) Bad Trip," was the one beloved by college radio. By that time, guitarist Molla had left the fold (he's since become a children's music recording artist).

On the self-titled third album, the band threw a reverent version of Pink Floyd's "Interstellar Overdrive" into the mix, confounding and delighting the critical crowd even further. "Joe Stalin's Cadillac" took the Balkan/folk/punk thing to its limit—it was time to grow and zone-in on what they did best. For the band's major-label debut for Virgin, *Our Beloved Revolutionary Sweetheart* (coincident with the label's U.S. relaunch in 1988), it took a more serious tack. Once confined to low-budgets and small studio facilities, the band could stretch out now, and it did, employing most of the available emerging technology. The recording suffers from some '80s studio annoyances like processed drums, but more successfully, it showcased Camper's humor, matured skills as musicians, and ability to incorporate disparate elements from all kinds of music and turn it into something entirely its own. "Eye of Fatima" is a swinging rock song, no doubt about it—the song's "Part II" is full-on prog rock. "One of These Days" is plain, sweet pop, and "Turquoise Jewelry," with its horn stings, is typical Camper quirksville. By now, the traces of ska and polka that had driven the early records were almost completely gone (well, "Tania" has that Eastern European flavor), but the band had retained its folk roots and turned them into something bigger—like Fairport Convention gone wacky. Yet there's a dark tension to almost every song, the overall melancholy a portent of things to come.

By the time of the release of *Our Beloved Revolutionary Sweetheart* in 1988, trouble was brewing. "We did a ton of shows with them in and out of California and also did a six-week tour all over the place with 'em," says Spot 1019's Jim Lyons. "That's where all the trouble started…a summer tour for *Revolutionary Sweetheart,* pretty much exclusively in college towns," he says. *Rolling Stone* had just included CVB in its summer "hot" issue, and the gigs were filled with "squeaky-clean college kids"—according to Lyons—but these were minor annoyances compared to the existing pressures within the ranks. The bands engaged in the usual pranks and stupidity offstage, but sometimes the letting off of steam got aggressive and the shenanigans turned ugly. One night culminated in a concussion for Lowery after Lyons chucked a full can of ginger ale at his head; Lyons thought he'd accidentally killed the singer. Hysteria ensued; though it seems like pretty mild stuff, at the end of the tour, a break was called.

"I came back after we'd taken a month off," recalls Segel. "David looked at me and said, 'I can't work with you anymore.' He told the rest of the band, 'He's out, or we break up the band,' and the rest of the band was thinking, 'We'd like to keep our jobs.' And I'm saying, 'I'd like to stay in the band.' I couldn't maintain my position at all." I had just put out this double album art rock horror called *Storytelling* and was starting a solo career, so I kinda needed some support. I didn't think the aesthetic tensions were things that couldn't have been resolved, and I thought that would've made for much more interesting music anyway."

Krummenacher shakes his head regretfully. "But there was no compromise offered."

"It's the five-way marriage thing," suggests Segel. "You live with people all the time and you have to deal with their personalities and psychoses …"

"And all the buried stuff people have about their own public images and their own perceptions of themselves enter into it, too. One thing about working a job is that at the end of the day, you get to go home. The thing about being in a band is that at the end of the day, you get to go back to the hotel with the rest of the band," adds Krummenacher. After the split, in addition to playing his own music, Krummenacher got a full-time job as an art director.

"Rock music has changed dramatically in the ten years since we broke up," he continues. "I've watched so many people pay such a price to the great rock-god monster, and I'm tired of seeing it. Friends of mine who are younger, in bands who are going out for the first time or the tenth, they're making less money than I ever made at it. And I wonder why they're doing it. One thread I can divine is that a lot of musicians are just running away. I've used music that way, too."

"Plus, the job, the creative-based career-thing… [entertainers] are insecure; they have to prove to themselves and to the rest of the world that they're creative rather than just being secure in their own creativity at flipping a burger," says Segel.

"I think that it's important to bring up that David was discovering that he worked best when he was being the captain of his own ship," says Krummenacher. "Camper was really founded on a different guise, and we deluded ourselves into thinking that it was more of a democracy than it really was. I don't think the delusion or the reality were bad things; it was just a matter of us growing. David does in fact work best when he's in charge of what he's doing. Of course, because I was in the band and wanted to be part of a democracy, I was like, 'Oh no!' I think David realized he was a good songwriter and that his confidence was growing."

"As much as no one wants to admit it, democracy breeds mediocrity," says guitarist Immerglück. "Initially they were a beautiful model for splitting things evenly, but it's a bad thing to dilute a vision when you're trying to make music."

By the time the band's swan song, the tragically beautiful *Key Lime Pie*, was released in 1989, the band hit another wall when tensions between Lowery and Krummenacher reached fever pitch. Although the record was by far the best the band had produced—classic-sounding production, with Lowery's songwriting in the A+ category—the record was unfairly treated by the underground with a "they've-got-a- big-label-and-a-video" backlash. However, the album is well-worth reassessing as "Sweethearts," "When I Win the Lottery," and "I Was Born in a Laundromat" are all outstanding slices of alternative-folk/psych-rock. But with Morgan Fichter having replaced Segel by this time and Immerglück touring with them, the original CVB magic was gone.

"I left because Camper had run its course for me," says Krummenacher. "But the band wasn't functioning very well anyway. The family had kind of broken down. I think if we had put more effort into it, we could've worked things out, but we didn't, and a lot of that was because I didn't want to. I was coming out at the time and I was in a headspace where I needed to go and be me, away from the band." Coming out as a gay man to his bandmates was the least stressful part of Krummenacher's departure. "Most of them dealt

Time Line

1983   An early version of the band forms in Redlands, CA

1985   First album is released as the lineup is solidified in Santa Cruz, CA

1986   *Telephone Free Landslide Victory* charts on *Village Voice* year-end poll

1987   *Camper Van Beethoven II & III* and self-titled third album also rate on the *Voice's* year-end poll

1988   Victor Krummenacher, Greg Lisher, Chris Pedersen, and David Immer-glück release *Soundtrack to the Film: Breakfast on the Beach of Deception* as Monks of Doom and record and release albums throughout the rest of Camper's career and afterward

1988   *Our Beloved Revolutionary Sweetheart*
Jonathan Segel no longer a member of CVB releases first solo album, *Storytelling*, and continues to record as a solo artist and with former band-mate, Krummenacher for another decade

1989   Final album, *Key Lime Pie*
Victor Krummenacher leaves the band and Greg Lisher and Chris Peder-sen follow

1991–2 David Lowery forms post-Camper band Cracker and releases debut

1995   Victor Krummenacher's Great Laugh releases *Out in the Heat*

1998   Victor Krummenacher releases *St. John's Mercy*

1999   Victor Krummenacher, Jonathan Segel, and Eugene Chadbourne release *Revenge of Camper Van Chadbourne*

2000   Lowery, Segel, and Krummenacher reconvene for the making of *Camper Van Beethoven Is Dead, Long Live Camper Van Beethoven*; Lowery's Cracker tours with Victor Krummenacher's band, including Jonathan Segel and Greg Lisher as support act. All four former members perform Camper Van Beethoven material on a short tour.
Cracker releases *Garage D'or*, a greatest hits package
Greg Lisher releases solo debut, *Handed Down the Wire*
Jonathan Segel releases *Paper and Scissors*
Victor Krummenacher releases *Bittersweet*

with it really well, though I never did tell David. If I had, I think he would've been fine with it. But I was also pretty strung-out too, which I managed to keep pretty well hidden from everybody. The thing about doing a lot of drugs is that if you want to maintain that, you go to the easier situation, rather than confronting it. We had people from the label offer to help, but I wasn't trustful that it would've worked out—that David would've worked on it. Now I wonder if he would have. I never gave him that benefit. But for better or worse, I wasn't ready to deal with saving the band at that point. The irony is that we were writing a lot of songs; there was really good music going on at the time. Going back and listening to those live tapes, the band was absolutely at the height of its power, without question. I was just miserable." Segel and Krummenacher didn't speak for a year or so after Krummenacher's departure. But for the last eight years they've collaborated on their Magnetic label, releasing records under the name Dent and other aliases, and working independently on solo offerings like Krummenacher's *St. John's Mercy* and *Bittersweet* and Segel's band, Jack and Jill.

"I'm really into the fact that I did these records and they sold one or two thousand copies through the Web site to people that genuinely wanted them," Krummenacher says. "I do it virtually as a hobby—like building a model railroad. It's my thing and I do it the way I want to do it, how I want to do it." Segel frequently finds work scoring independent films and playing with New York downtown musicians, like Elliot Sharpe and John Kruth. Following the Cracker dates, Segel and Krummenacher were reunited with their old pal Eugene Chadbourne for some acoustic Camper Van Chadbourne dates; a live album, *The Revenge of Camper Van Chadbourne*, released late in 1999, was well received by the group's longtime friends at college radio.

Of course Lowery had his Cracker, and in the late '90s, he revived his Pitch-a-Tent label, which has released recordings by Kitty Snyder, Lauren Hoffman, and Koester, among others. He's also done production for obscure experimentalists like Germany's F.S.K. and mainstream acts like Joan Osborne and the Counting Crows.

"I only wish that having a career and having a legacy didn't come along with so many expectations from other people," says Lowery. "I have a hard time dealing with that after 16 years…people like Adam Duritz and Eddie Vedder…both those guys were really freaking out on fame and stuff like that, but it's not really that, it's the expectations. Being famous is kinda fun, except

Lowery, Krummenacher, and Segel (left to right)
during the last days of Camper Van Beethoven

for the stalkers and Camden Joy." Lowery's last reference is to *Boy Island*, a novel by Joy (aka Tom Adelman), a former music journalist who gathered his facts for his book while covering Camper's breakup for the *L.A. Reader* in 1991; he also toured with Cracker as a journalist and wrote an unpublished biography of Camper. In *Boy Island* (coincidentally published during the Camper "reparations"), Joy tells the story of a musician struggling with his sexuality while on tour with "David Lowery" in a post-Camper milieu, the Gulf War its historical backdrop. Lowery and Krummenacher, as well as Lowery's Cracker band mate, Johnny Hickman, Lisher, Immerglück, and Fichter, all get name-checked in the book.

"It's a shitty book and I feel a little co-opted," says Krummenacher. "It's a very bizarre thing to read a book that's part fact and part fiction that definitely has real aspects of your life in it. I don't think much of it, but Jonathan wishes he was in it."

"When I did all the interviews with Tom Adelman when he was writing a Camper book, one of the things that pissed me off was having been written out of history," says Segel. "I don't believe that rewritten history is not real history; even though it's a fictionalized novel, it is real. That's why I think Tom's a fuckin' asshole for doing that in that book. Because he doesn't realize the extent to which he's creating a factual past by fictionalizing something that was actually a real story. Ten years after talking to him about that, he did it again."

In defense, Joy says, "I was trying to create a context where this stuff could be understood 30 to 40 years from now, when all the references had fallen away. To me, that couldn't just be a fact-finding mission. It had to be told in a setting that took liberties. The history isn't fictionalized; it's a fictionalized perspective. I had this raw material…all the stuff about them is true. And all the stuff about Lowery and Hickman is true. All of that is true."

"I [sent] an e-mail to the publisher," says Lowery. "It's really fiction. To tell you the truth, up until about halfway through the book, to me it was really funny, and I kept forgetting that it was sorta me in there, a fictionalized me. The thing that disturbs me is he wanted to get to the point where rock journalism and stalking his favorites were mixed together." Such a postmodern approach is not entirely alien to the Campers, particularly the way in which they've handled their own work for their archival album *Camper Van Beethoven Is Dead, Long Live Camper Van Beethoven.* "I feel this new material is somewhere between making music and archiving things," says Lowery. "It's very modern and very of the age. It's not postrock, it might be pre-rock."

"We went back and took old tapes and actively screwed with them," says Krummenacher. A lot of the live stuff had Morgan playing and Jonathan manipulating the tapes, so it was kind of a cool revenge."

Long Live CVB is in fact a wonderful pastiche of sound with real songs and rarities. An orchestral version of *Key Lime's* "All Her Favorite Fruit" stands beside the outstanding live performance medley "S.P. 37957" ("Hava Negila" meets Led Zeppelin) among other sonic delights.

"In a lot of ways, maybe it's what Camper would've been doing now," suggests Lowery. "It started out as an interesting contractual puzzle. We were trying to figure out what stuff we have the rights to—a certain late period and a certain early period of Camper—and there were some live things and there were some unfinished things, but there wasn't a whole record—it required us to put it together. Nowadays, with all this technology and what you can do with samplers and computers…singing to one song and then putting it on top of another one and seeing what happens…that's sort of the essence of trip-hop, and I think that's what coming out in those new songs."

"Yeah, it's very forward-thinking," says Krummenacher. "I played the record for Immerglück, and he said, 'My God, nobody could get away with this kind of outside music—nobody could come on the scene and get away with this anymore!'"

"David is adventurous and excited about music; he's spontaneous and willing to go there if it's working, without any preconceived notions. He'll have an idea in the studio and the next thing you know, you'll be plugged in and on the record," adds Immerglück, who's worked with Lowery in the studio in more recent, post-Camper incarnations.

Krummenacher: "It's like what Can has done—gone back, had several people that play together go back and screw with their own legacy. The word *postmodern* comes up way too much, but it's a very postmodern way of dealing with the legacy. It's a very interesting kind of recap to it."

"Once we got it to this point, we decided to make a bigger deal out of it," explains Lowery about the "reunion" disc and accompanying Cracker/Camper tour.

And so, with the Camper family circle only slightly broken (Molla and Pedersen aren't onboard this model of the Camper Van) the former members of Camper Van Beethoven began rehearsing for their upcoming tour in the California desert, a stone's throw from where it all began for them.

In the week preceding the gig at which the former members of Camper would appear, the local San Francisco press rallied, officially welcoming the band back to the place Segel and Krummenacher agree is the group's spiritual home. The *San Francisco Bay Guardian* ran the cover line "Ghost band: Camper Van Beethoven rises from the dead—sort of." A subhead read, "Never go back. Well, OK, maybe go back, but Camper Van Beethoven will not reunite at Slim's." A version of this chapter ran in the *SF Weekly* with the cover line "A kinda, sorta Camper Van Beethoven reunion." The *San Francisco Chronicle* called it an "informal reunion"; the online version of the newspaper *The Gate* made multiple references to Cracker van Beethoven and muddled most of the facts. But the major media outlets practiced responsible journalism based on firsthand interviews with Lowery and the former members of Camper Van Beethoven. Lowery was incensed.

"I'm very disappointed in the San Francisco press for turning this into a Camper reunion," said Lowery from the stage of Slim's in San Francisco on the night of February 10, 2000. "I'd really appreciate you hardcore Camper fans not harassing the Cracker guys.... Fuck you and your fuckin' San Francisco ass.... Sorry to mention this, but apparently you're a bunch of assholes."

In *Boy Island*, Joy describes a moment, presumably based on one of his "true" Cracker tales, when Lowery got on stage and lambasted an *L.A. Weekly* reporter in similar fashion. *Never go back*, indeed.

Jennifer Joseph, a former member of the San Francisco band the Furies, and part of the scene that existed in San Francisco during Camper's heyday, witnessed the nonreunion spectacle. "These guys can still play, and too bad David Lowery can't transcend his ego to allow them to play. If Crosby, Stills, and Nash can go on tour with Neil Young.... It's absurd that David Lowery has to yell at his audience. I was embarrassed for him, quite frankly."

Says Krummenacher, "I think he felt he was losing control of the crowd that night, so he lashed out. I think that what he feels—and part of me agrees and part of me scratches my head—that it's better to have a reaction that's bad than to have a nonplussed show. He wasn't getting the kind of response he gets in Charlottesville, Virginia, or in D.C., these all-out Cracker towns. In San Francisco you're just not going to get that, because his legacy precedes him here. A hard thing for David to accept is that we don't own the legacy anymore. The legacy belongs to other people. They interpret it and we get to deal with it. And he wants to control it, and I understand that, but you can't control people's impressions."

I note that people's preimpressions were pretty darn good: two shows had sold out and there was an anticipatory air—a palpable feeling of goodwill in the room—until the audience was provoked by the singer.

Krummenacher counters, "There are certain sides to the whole evening, and the whole question that I'm kinda more in agreement with David than I kinda would've anticipated, especially from his standpoint: He's a songwriter, he's had two bands, he writes songs. Whether or not he changed his songwriting deliberately for Cracker, he'll deny it to this day, but I think we all know he made some decisions about it.

"Sure, I had a lot of complaints that night. Friends were completely not into it, like 'He's the same asshole he always was. Fuck him. Fuck the whole thing.' But that, too, was part of the whole thing. Sometimes it's just nuts and kinda dysfunctional. Camper frequently had weird scenes. That was as authentic a Camper experience as anything. Whether that qualifies as entertainment or not—I don't think it necessarily does—but it's part of us."

Recommended Recordings

Telephone Free Landslide Victory (Rough Trade/IRS, 1985)
This self-described "surreal absurdist folk" album is the stunning debut that took the college radio world literally by storm with its keen sense of humor and deft juxtapositions of international folk music, punk rock, country, and ska—with violin. It contains the classic, "Take the Skinheads Bowling."

Key Lime Pie (Virgin, 1989)
Key Lime Pie showcases a fresh and more even-flowing songwriting approach by Lowery, while the by now accomplished band maintains and refines the original psychedelic, folk, and punk leanings that won them fans. Some of their most enduring songs, like "Sweethearts" and "When I Win the Lottery," live here. Just as the band had found its voice, ironically, this was its swan song.

2

TEENAGE FANCLUB

"I'm an optimist, but I always carry an umbrella." —*Norman Blake, Teenage Fanclub*

they aren't the bratty Brit-pop kids who invaded the States in the mid-'90s, nor are they the paisley and buckskin-jacketed Americans who revived guitar rock in the early '80s. Nope, Teenage Fanclub reinvented jangle rock in the early '90s all by their wee Scottish selves. "Ain't That Enough?" they ask in one of their songs. Well, sometimes yes, and sometimes no.

Oasis' Liam Gallagher once called them the "best band in the world"; producer David Bianco said, "Unless you're dead, you can't help falling in love with them." In 1991, they toured Europe with the *Nevermind*-era Nirvana, appeared on *Saturday Night Live,* and their record *Bandwagonesque* was voted by critics among the best of that year. Although they've only been around since the dawn of the '90s, the Glasgow band's underappreciated brand of guitar rock is so beautifully timeless, you'd swear it was created by some old geezers.

"We're old enough to remember punk rock, but we've also kept open enough minds to explore things that we were told back then were uncool—like Neil Young, Buffalo Springfield, and Bob Dylan," says Teenage Fanclub's Raymond McGinley in his thick Scottish accent.

McGinley is one of the group's three singer-songwriter guitarists. Like the Beatles, McGinley and band mates Norman Blake and Gerard Love all contribute songs and trade lead vocals; they tackle three-part harmonies and deliver them in a distinctly American accent; drummer Paul Quinn hasn't done a number—yet. But unlike the other British foursome, the one thing that doesn't come over crystal clear within the Fanclub's ranks is who sings what—perhaps owing to the fact that they operate as a unit rather than as a caricature of a rock band. Could it be not declaring a frontman has contributed to their lack of star power?

"A lot of people have said it's hard to distinguish our voices. For us, it's really easy!" says Blake. "We all play on each others' tracks, and I suppose we have the same influences. We've been playing together for a long time, so we all take something from each other when it comes to writing songs."

"There are some chordal/guitar things that we always try to do, and the harmonizing; I suppose that does kind of create our own sound," says McGinley.

The group didn't set out to be a sparkling American-style pop band, the kind that fans of the Byrds and Big Star find themselves drawn to, nor do they perceive themselves that way. But they *were* high on America from the get-go, having found on their first-ever American tour that they had more in common with American independents and classic artists than their little brothers in the British Isles' Brit-pop brat-pack who make music similar to their own.

"In a way we belong with some of those New York bands like Sonic Youth and Yo La Tengo rather than the British bands," says McGinley. "We grew up in America. When we first toured we slept on people's floors and got to meet real Americans, saw the country, and people took care of us. We feel very at home there."

"To be honest, most of the groups we like at the moment are American groups," says Blake. "I like Daniel Johnston. I like that Jonathan Richman is a guy that still makes records. I love his lyrics. I think Yo La Tengo are a really good band. They don't get covered in this country. There's almost like an anti-American climate. There's Halo Bend and Calvin Johnson, Sebadoh and Lou Barlowe, Pavement. We're playing in Glasgow next week and we're taking the Palace Brothers. They've never played there before. I think it annoys the British music papers when we say most of the groups we like are American. There aren't as many good groups here as there are in America," says Blake, adding in his typically droll manner, "It's a bigger country. Of course, rock and roll is American."

Teenage Fanclub formed in the late '80s in the Glasgow suburb of Bellshill. Blake, formerly of the BMX Bandits, met McGinley on the club scene. At the time, McGinley was spending his days finishing up an engineering degree at the University of Glasgow, while Blake was working in a music shop. Their

Teenage Fanclub: Grand Prix winners in power-pop. Left to right: Paul Quinn, Norman Blake, Gerard Love, Raymond McGinley

first collaboration, the Boy Hairdressers, was short-lived, and soon they'd recruited bassist Gerard "Gerry" Love, an engineering student from the University of Strathclyde. Their first drummer, Francis MacDonald, left the fold before the first recordings and was replaced by Brendan O'Hare.

The debut single, "Everything Flows" and an album, *A Catholic Education*—released in America on the prestigious indie label Matador—kept pretty close company with the grunge sound of the day: They were both quickly recorded endeavors with New York musician/producer Don Fleming and played up the droney, guitar-heavy sounds that were popular with independent rockers on both sides of the Atlantic. But they would prove to be atypical releases in the band's catalog of purer, glimmering pop material (though the records weren't without their fans in the indie-rock under-ground). The group followed a No. 1 U.K. indie single, "God Knows It's True," with "So Far Gone" and "The Ballad of John and Yoko"; it made for a nice transition while also foretelling the Fanclub's future as a developing hook-and harmony-driven band. In 1991 came the Fleming-produced *Bandwag-onesque*—its critical reception that year was eclipsed only by DGC label-mates Nirvana. The record had incredibly strong melodies and a mellow, wall-of-guitar sound; the critics gushed. The record also helped to solidify the group's reputation as a smart pop band, in no small part due to its over-whelming resemblance to a lost album by the ultimate cult band Big Star. Had the Memphis group lived to hear punk rock, they may have sounded like Teenage Fanclub did on *Bandwagonesque*. The Scots' vocals were pure power-pop, but the guitars were filtered through the sound of SubPop.

"The reason this whole Big Star thing happened was because this writer who's now dead, Paul Lester, interviewed us and asked who we like, and we said, 'Big Star,' and he asked, 'Who are they?' We explained, 'Alex Chilton…from the Box Tops…and he still didn't know who they were!" says Blake. "A few months later we brought out *Bandwagonesque* and he did a review saying it was a rip-off of Big Star! We *were* listening to the Big Star records a lot at the time," he admits. "Especially the first one; there's a real kind of optimism and an amazing sound—a real spirit and a lot of soul."

Blake could be referring to his own band with that description, as it is the essence of the Fanclub's sound.

On *Bandwagonesque*'s opening six-minute opus, "The Concept," an in-credible instrumental coda is filled with squeezed-out, sour guitar notes; it's a sound that the band would phase out as quickly as it had phased it in, but at the time, it sounded so right. "December" is almost an amalgam of the Big Star songs "September Gurls," "Thirteen," and "Way Out West"; "I Don't Know" could be an outtake from Bram Tchaikovsky's epic debut power-pop record. It's incredible that Teenage Fanclub released a record so completely outré at the dawn of the '90s; no wonder it caught people off guard and agog.

"We just weren't prepared for that kind of press," says Blake. "I don't think *Bandwagonesque* was a brilliant album. A couple of influential peo-ple liked it and it built from there. We were kind of flavor of the month for a time."

So in response, although not deliberately, the band delivered an over-labored third album when *Thirteen* was released in 1993. It was only a couple of years into the Fanclub's career, and the band was already feeling the hangover of hype and diminished expectations. They railed against the music industry in songs like "120 Minutes," "Commercial Alternative," and "Radio," but it was a project that failed in the band's eyes.

"We took a dip. When we went to record *Thirteen*, we felt pretty jaded," says Blake. "We weren't together as a band. I think it was a reflection of what we were feeling. It took us eight months in the studio, and we don't really work well that way. It wasn't fun making that album. We still play the songs live, and I think we play them better than how we recorded them. One thing I like about *Bandwagonesque*, I think we sounded like we were enjoying ourselves. We didn't really have that on *Thirteen*. We didn't really believe in ourselves." By the time the tour to support the album was finished, drummer Brendan O'Hare was asked to leave.

"Basically what happened was that Brendan lost interest. We were having arguments. He wasn't showing up for rehearsal for the new record. So we said, that's it. It's over. He didn't take it too well at the time," explains Blake. "He was never too interested in playing the drums. When we were jamming,

Time Line

1989	Teenage Fanclub forms in Glasgow suburb Bellshill
1990	Debut EP, *Everything Flows*
1990	*A Catholic Education* (Matador)
1991	*The King* (Creation), a U.K. rarity of odds and ends
1991	*Bandwagonesque* (DGC)
1993	*Thirteen* (DGC)
1995	*Grand Prix* (DGC)
1997	*Songs from Northern Britain* (Creation/Columbia) Oasis' Liam Gallagher calls the Fanclub "the best band in the world"
2000	*Howdy*

The optimistic Norman Blake rocks the world with his songs from Northern Britain.

Brendan would pick up a guitar instead of drum along. If we hadn't fired him, we wouldn't have made [the next] record. Raymond and Gerry and I really changed after that last tour, and Brendan didn't really come with us. We got our belief back, but at that point, he wasn't really interested anymore."

O'Hare was replaced in 1994 by a hometown chum, drummer Paul Quinn. "When Raymond and I were doing the demos that became *A Catholic Education,* Paul sat in and played drums. When we were looking for someone, he was the obvious guy, because he was out of a job. He played with the Soup Dragons, but he left the group because he didn't get paid any money. He's happier now. He fits in with the band—we've known him a long time," says Blake.

With the lineup secure, the band set about recording its midcareer master stroke, *Grand Prix.* It didn't so much rival *Bandwagonesque* for sweet melodies and heartfelt lyrics as take the Fanclub one step closer toward exploring other kinds of pop songs and sounds (including horns and strings), and some wild, let-er-rip guitar in the tradition of Neil Young (one song was even called "Neil Jung"). Another sweet pop song was titled "Verisimilitude." Were these guys just being too clever for their own good, willfully consigning themselves to the cult rock bin? It certainly wasn't a consideration in their minds, as they went into the studio with a confidence Blake says was unequaled on previous excursions.

"We made the album at the end of the summer at the Manor, an amazing 14th-century house. It once belonged to Richard Branson, and *Tubular Bells* was made there, and so was *Never Mind the Bollocks.* So this place had a real history and it was in an amazing part of Oxfordshire. The weather was great and there was a great atmosphere in the studio," says Blake. " And there's a certain amount of belief in the playing."

The band had finally reached full flower. But just then, its U.S. live appearances tapered off. Despite having found its footing as a terminally faithful and accomplished pop band, critics and fans, not to mention their record company, had nearly forgotten them; its progress was rarely charted and its evolution, for the most part, was left undocumented and unwitnessed, save for a brief U.S. tour opening for Weezer. Ironically, the band had just made the best album of their career and were especially pleased with the newfound focus. The record was released in the midst of the insurgent wave of new Brit-pop bands, who had an appeal of their own.

"I think the difference between us and most of the British groups that are around, like Oasis, is they say they are the best group in the world ever. And we never did that. We've never bought into that at all. We think that's rubbish. We want to be liked because we make good records, not because we take cocaine and punch people out in discotheques," says Blake.

"I think it's pretty sad, because it's unfashionable to be frank and to write love songs," he continues. "We've got what we call an indie background here—what you call commercial alternative. Maybe we're out of time, maybe people don't want to listen to love songs anymore. It's more fashionable to write about how messed up you are on heroin. You know, I don't use heroin, so I can't write songs about how messed up I am on heroin."

The situation at home wasn't much better. "We're very aware that in Britain, the press wants to discover something new every week or they want to create a scene. I think basically, the British music press are hung up about British groups not being successful in America," explains Blake. "It's kind of weird that a group like Menswear that hadn't yet made a record were on the cover of both music papers, and they're talking about the guy's cheekbones and that he wears a funny jacket or something. They're more interested in people who make outrageous statements than people who write songs. I think it's just the way it is. It's kind of sad, really."

While the Fanclub were never going to get any acknowledgment for looking cool, it's not as though they paid zero attention to grooming. Like their peers in American indie-rock, they chose anti-fashion as their statement; T-shirts, jeans, and trainers were standard issue, as if to say, "we don't care about being cool," and thus, they *were* cool—and everyone knows cool counts for a lot in rock. In the early '90s, Blake took to wearing a beard—not a goatee—with his adidas; a full beard was pretty much unseen on trend-barometer MTV (not that the band was being seen on MTV, either). Blake said the band members had changed—not only with age but with attitude. With it came a slight shift in musical direction—less rough around the edges—and the songs were more directly about matters of the heart and the more philosophical aspects of pairing up and breaking up.

"I've been reading lots of Raymond Carver recently. I'd like to write songs the way he writes short stories. They seem really human. He gets the way people interact with each other," he says.

So as the Brit pack beat each other up in bars and on the charts, the Fanclub had no trouble keeping themselves busy, although they may've been officially out of the papers. Ever since their early gambit, "The Ballad of John and Yoko," carried them straight into the hearts of sophisticated listeners, they continued to augment their studio output with live rarities and EPs, most of which included a choice cover or two: Neil Young's "Don't Cry No Tears" was an early side, as was Phil Ochs' "Chords of Fame," followed by the Velvet Underground's "Femme Fatale." They recorded an acoustic EP of new and old songs, *Teenage Fanclub Have Lost It*, in McGinley's living room. And then in 1997, a new record deal with Creation/Columbia yielded *Songs from Northern Britain*—a precious gem in the Fanclub's power-pop crown.

Fixating on elongated, swirling guitar parts (check "Mount Everest," please!) harmonies, and over-the-top, sweet chord changes, the album went for the ultimate timeless sound and captured it on the Neil Young–like "Start Again" and the Byrdsy "Ain't That Enough," There was a touch of the Beatles in everything, but it never sounded contrived, just natural. Again, the subject was home and hearth—it was a sort of "goin' up the country" album, with room to indulge the lyricists' habits of dropping references to the stars, space, and the occult.

Like *Grand Prix,* the bulk of the songs from *Northern Britain* were made in a studio inside an English manor house. "Since we'd done the last record that way, there wasn't so much novelty to it," says McGinley. "'What a great place…look at the countryside…wow.' It was like, 'Great, another place in the country, like last time.' But it had an effect. Recording in that environment, you're sort of cut off from everything else. If we recorded in New York instead of Ridge Farm in Surrey, it would be a whole different sound." Three years later, the band refined and quieted its sound even further on its most pensive record to date, *Howdy.*

"Some people want to draw conclusions about us that are a little obvious. They say we write songs about relationships—because they know that we have girlfriends and wives—and then they'll go and say things about us in the press like, 'His mood changed visibly when his girlfriend arrived at the studio.' It nearly makes us throw up. People want to represent us as sincere young songwriters, but there's more to us than that," says McGinley. "We don't do things so people will think we're great. We aren't even that aware that people have an opinion about what we do," he says. "When we go back to Glasgow, people say, 'There's those guys in that band—who cares,' y' know?"

There's nothing like the good folks at home to keep a band humble, even one that holds the informal title, Best Band in the World.

Recommended Recordings

Bandwagonesque (DGC, 1991)

> The Fanclub cannily incorporate sensitive jangle rock and Big Star–inspired love songs with grunge guitars. Widely considered by critics to be one of the best recordings of 1991, it contains some of their shiniest pop moments: "What You Do to Me," and "December."

Grand Prix (DGC, 1995)

> Honing their love of the Byrds, the Beatles, and Buffalo Springfield to a fine point, Teenage Fanclub turn in what is arguably their finest pop/wall-of-guitar recording to date. It includes guitar-intensives like "Neil Jung" and the thrilling harmony-rich versions "About You" and "I'll Make It Clear."

the strangely beautiful stories and songs of siblings

brothers and sisters

The Kinks
Sparks
The Louvin Brothers
Shonen Knife

The Kinks
Sparks
The Louvin Brothers
Shonen Knife

many musicians have said that their careers in music began as children at home, whether they were born into musical families or insisted that their parents buy them their first musical instruments. In turn, they entertained (or annoyed) the troops with their newfound passion. When it comes to sibling acts, childhood beginnings are almost exclusively the case; brothers and sisters who sing and play together belong to a unique group of musicians who've chosen to share their musical visions, aspirations, triumphs, and disappointments with a member of their family. Although the results are often mixed, and there can be consequences when creatively collaborating with a close family member, brothers and sisters are capable of making a beautiful noise together.

There's a long tradition of sibling acts, particularly brothers, in popular music. From the Everly Brothers and the Allman Brothers to the Black Crowes, brotherly singing, songwriting and playing duos and groups are most noted for the ethereal, sometimes eerie interplay between their voices and instruments. Sometimes their vision for their music—not to mention their personalities—are curiously opposed. The resulting tension can fuel the mystical qualities of brotherly bands. Other times, the strange juxtapositions can work to the detriment of the music. One sibling's contributions can also begin to overtake the other's. But, for family acts, the ties that bind, coupled with the inherent tension, inevitably make unique music.

While brother acts are notorious for misbehaving and not getting along with each other (just think of the Gallagher brothers of Oasis), sisters are usually known for their harmonies (that have been practiced since childhood), which underscore what they can deliver when they work together as opposed to apart. Less known for brawling than perhaps just plain lack of interest, there are certainly fewer sister acts out there, although the ones who broke through tended to be important—just look at rock's Shangri-Las, the Bangles, and Heart, or folk's Roches and McGarrigles—groups that left an indelible imprint on their respective music.

Country music has its own sibling and family acts, from the legendary Carter Family to the contemporary Judds and Dixie Chicks. The story of country music duo the Louvin Brothers has been well documented. Generally considered the most influential brother act in traditional American music history, their influence extended beyond the gospel-inspired country world they inhabited. They're particularly admired within the back-to-basics, neo-roots-rock movement known as alternative country or No Depression.

The Louvins came from a long line of sacred harp singers, and were inspired by the other brother acts of their day, like the close-harmony, old-time country of the Delmore Brothers and bluegrass' Monroes. The Louvins broke ground in country music with a unique high-tenor harmony sound, which they honed as the guest act at local Alabama radio stations. The brothers were for the most part inseparable as performers, except for periods when the younger brother, Charlie, was called to serve during World War II and the Korean War. Although they struggled for acceptance before finally breaking through in the mid-'50s, their career was essentially over by the early '60s. Yet their impact on country and country-rock music is almost unparalleled. They had a profound effect on the music of other country-rock legends in the '70s, in particular Emmylou Harris and Gram Parsons, which in turn spread their influence even further. In a 1997 interview with surviving Louvin brother Charlie, he spoke of his difficult relationship with his brother Ira, who was known to be a bit of a loose cannon during his short life.

When the Louvins started they were sacred singers; although they soon began singing secular songs, they never gave up sacred music and managed to carve out a career in both worlds, making records that crossed over. When the world's attention turned toward rock and roll, the Louvins didn't change their sound to fit in, as did a number of other country acts, with different degrees of success and failure. Instead, they stayed close to home and tradition on the Grand Ole Opry stage, never forsaking the twang. When Ira's alcoholism began to get in the way of the brothers' career and the demand for their music finally waned, the pair parted ways, but they pressed on as solo musicians. At the age of 73, Charlie Louvin belonged to the rare group of country and blues septuagenarians still making regular concert appearances.

Trouble was the middle name of brothers Ray and Dave Davies. Their notorious feuds are what finally ended their time together as the founding members of the Kinks, although for 30 years their fights never seemed to get in the way of their music. Among the handful of vastly influential rock acts to emerge from Great Britain in the early '60s, their only rivals in brotherland were perhaps the all-American Beach Boys (who had an edge on them, numbers-wise and of course a magnificent talent in Brian Wilson).

The Davies were the only boys among eight children—their six sisters were older and began having children themselves around the time Ray and then Dave were born, adding to the chaos in the extended Davies household, which occupied two side-by-side units in London's Muswell Hill district. The sisters were all music lovers; they played piano, and their country and rock and roll record collections informed their brothers' tastes from an early age, as did the girls' passion for ballroom dancing. Between the whirring 78 player, the family piano, and Dad's banjo playing, there was always some form of music in the Davies household; once a week they played music together. It was the brothers' second-eldest sister, Rene, who nurtured Ray's interest in the piano, and his brother-in-law helped him learn the guitar after Rene died on Ray's 13th birthday. It would be a couple more years before the boys would play together in a band.

When Dave was 14, he and Ray began playing as a duo, inspired by the guitar-intensive sounds of the Ventures and Chet Atkins. After they formed their band in 1963, Ray took on the role of hit-crafter, writing such successful songs as "You Really Got Me," "All Day and All of the Night," "Tired of Waiting for You," "A Well Respected Man," "Dedicated Follower of Fashion," "Sunny Afternoon," and ambitious concept albums like *Arthur* and *Schoolboys in Disgrace,* among others (the list goes on). Dave was always at his side, playing his signature, distortion-heavy metal guitar and supplying highly evocative parts to fit whichever of the many styles his brother was dabbling in at the time. Concurrently, Dave was also writing his own music, most significantly the Kink standards "Death of a Clown" and "Love Me Till the Sun Shines," both of which bear his downbeat stamp. Dave even tried on and off to pursue a solo career. Then, at the end of the '90s, both Ray and Dave took on high-profile solo projects amid what was looking to be an ideal time for a Kinks revival. Ray had published a science-fiction autobiography, *X-Ray*, and his stage show about his life as a Kink, *20th Century Man*, was touring the country; he talked of making his solo debut. Dave had his first double-disc anthology in stores and his own autobiography on the shelves, *Kink*. The Kinks catalog had been reissued (again), not long after they'd cut *To the Bone*, a double acoustic set that critics named among the Kinks' finest in a long line of career retrospective albums. But by 1997, the brothers weren't speaking. Yet the Kinks' collective work lives on record, on video, and increasingly in television commercials (the most surreal being the cult favorite "Set Me Free" in a car ad). But don't count them out yet.

On the flipside, there hardly seems to be a pair of brothers in music happier with each other than native Californians Ron and Russell Mael of Sparks. Nor is there another group like them. Their symbiotic career has spanned three decades and "like 75 trends," says songwriter and straight man, Ron (once famous for his Hitler moustache). He and Russell, the singer and "good-looking one," as they like to say, formed their group Halfnelson straight out of UCLA in 1971. They'd had no real musical inclination as children—although Ron had taken piano lessons—and actually gravitated more toward sports. At the time they formed their band, they were working as catalog models. Since then—which was at the height of the crunchy-granola, rootsy L.A. singer-songwriter era—the brothers, dressed in their glam-rock finest and delivering their sublime pop, have made a career out of running against the grain, never working apart. They've met stateside recognition on and off again throughout their career, but early on, they were exiled to the U.K. Their record company at the time, Bearsville, perceived that they might be better understood overseas, and they were right. The group had also exhausted their resources at home; they'd been banned from their hometown rock venue, the Whisky-a-Go-Go on the Sunset Strip, for playing "too loud." Over the years, their music has remained better understood and appreciated by European audiences.

In the '70s, Sparks' pop operettas, such as "This Town Ain't Big Enough for the Both of Us" and the pre-new wave bounce of "Happy Hunting Ground," among others, bore the hallmarks of innovative, complexly melodic art rock.

But they soon tired of the rock band paradigm, and switched gears. While the Bee Gees had made millions off the high gloss disco of *Saturday Night Fever*, Sparks went for a different kind of dance sound, working with techno innovator Giorgio Moroder. The resulting album, *Number One in Heaven*, helped to define a more enduring club sound that was ultimately more influential than the brothers Gibb; with Moroder, the Maels experimented with electronica nearly 20 years before the genre was given a name. They have never bowed to trends (although for a period in the early '80s, their offbeat style happened to coincide with new wave). Over a span of 30 years, the pair has released 18 albums, with clever titles like *A Woofer in Tweeter's Clothing*, *Kimono My House*, and *Gratuitous Sax and Senseless Violins*, in beautifully rendered, hyper-real photo sleeves, all of which have influenced dance, punk, metal, and experimental bands. For a group with such theatrical lyrics and music, there is very little drama in the Sparks story, nor in the relationship between the brothers. Their skewed yet traditional sense of pop melody and their juxtaposition of traditional themes with the bizarre is all part of Sparks' charm. Their self-contained bubble is seemingly impervious to outside influence.

The same could be said of never-say-die sisters Atsuko and Naoko Yamano of Shonen Knife, a group that came roaring out of Osaka, Japan, in the '80s with a primitive, innocent rock sound. The first all-female Japanese punk-pop band to catch the underground's attention in a big way, Shonen Knife was the first postpunk Japanese rock group to get taken seriously outside of their home country before a later '90s wave would cross over. Part of the same postpunk generation of musicians that spawned Cris and Curt Kirkwood of the Meat Puppets, Tommy and Bob Stinson of the Replacements, and William and Jim Reid of the Jesus and Mary Chain, the Knife, like Sparks, have never kowtowed to trends. With no formal musical training and a national, cultural, and family influence that just said no to nonconformism, the Yamano sisters kept their musical identities hidden until it could no longer be avoided (their pictures started showing up in the papers and people started noticing). Mrs. Yamano was particularly worried when her barely young-adult girls negotiated their way home from gigs late at night, wielding "unladylike" and cumbersome equipment.

Singing in English and Japanese or an entertaining amalgam of both ("Pretty Little Baka Guy"), Shonen Knife is dedicated to the D.I.Y. punk rock ethic as well as to themselves as women and citizens of the world.

They incorporate everything from '60s psychedelia to reggae into their singular mix. Naoko is the chief songwriter, Atsuko the drummer. Despite some hurdles like not knowing the foggiest about their instruments when they formed, record label snafus, and even the loss of a principal founding member, bassist Michie Nakatani, the Yamanos remain dedicated and determinedly "of the Knife."

Family members playing together as musicians is a tradition that will remain as long as there are brothers and sisters. Anywhere there are kids hanging around a house, musical instruments, and a place to play them, a band will be born. The challenge for future sibling superstars is to avoid the pitfalls of their figurative brothers and sisters before them—either stylistically (such as the disposable pop of the Osmonds, Nelson, and Hanson) or behaviorally (such as the feuding Fogertys of Creedence Clearwater Revival and the aforementioned Gallaghers of Oasis).

In the case of the Louvins, their brotherly connection was severed due to Ira's drinking and subsequent death; for the Davies, persistent bickering created a rift that may never heal. The Maels' and the Yamanos' stories illustrate the rewards and strength of conviction that comes from toughing out the good and the bad together. Although their stories vary in degrees, what can't be denied is the complexity and power of sibling ties. None of these musicians had a choice in who their sibling would be, but they did have a choice in their band mate. These groups choose to exercise their musical gifts as a family. Clearly, they were born to make music together—their way.

RAY AND DAVE DAVIES

THE KINKS

"I know someday we'll find a way. We'll be ok.
'Cause I'm your brother." —*Ray Davies*

"I'm fucking sick of the whole thing. I'm sick up to here with it," announced the Kinks' Ray Davies from a London stage in 1973. Davies had recently attempted to take his own life once again by downing a bottle of uppers, and as the story goes, later that evening he checked himself into a hospital dressed as a clown. During triage he announced, "My name is Ray Davies and I'm dying." After a few hours, his brother Dave, who by his own admission had already survived his own period of being "mentally in very bad shape," went and checked Ray out of the hospital. He and his wife nursed Ray back to health.

That was just a part of the real-life soap opera known as the Kinks' career in the mid-'70s. In 1998, Velvel Records reissued four entries from the disturbed Davies family album—1975's *A Soap Opera, Schoolboys in Disgrace*, 1977's *Sleepwalker*, and 1978's *Misfits*. Dogged by multiple label deals, out-of-print selections, mismanagement, and misplaced royalties, it was part of the plan at Konk, the Kinks' custom label, to set the record straight, and celebrate one of the great dysfunctional family relationships in showbiz. With additional liner notes, photos, and obligatory bonus tracks, Kinks kompletists (the "k" is a time-honored Kinks gimmick) will note that this is at least the third time these recordings have been released. But who's counting? Bridging the gap between the last of their early '70s concept albums, and their late '70s U.S. revival, it's an interesting aside to four decades of Kinks theatrics.

Dave Davies' guitar sound, which defined both the Kinks and "You Really Got Me," was discovered by accident when he started poking around with a razor blade on the speaker of his cheap amp set up in the Davies' family sitting room in Muswell Hill. That song, with its distorto, heavy-metal guitar riff—often imitated, never duplicated—topped the British charts and hit the U.S. Top 10 in 1964, setting the pace for a string of hits in the mid-'60s. So imagine Dave's state of confusion ten years later when brother Ray, the band's chief cook and resident malcontent, insisted on embarking on yet another band morale-deflating, critically ill-received concept album. 1975's *A Soap Opera* would be about a "rock star" who lives his life backwards and becomes a "normal" guy.

Ray had conceived the idea during the making of *Preservation Act 2*, an unwieldy double-record concept album that followed *Preservation Act 1*, an unwieldy single-record concept album conceived in the wake of Ray's famous "sick of it" speech. By that point, the once tidy sense of melody—the hits with the hooks—that drove the Kinks' early years was but a memory. The melodies were verging on improvisational jazz and show tunes; the stage shows to support the *Preservation Act* albums, with their requisite costumes and touring personnel, resembled a small circus. For his part, Dave claims he was reconsidering his membership in the band; the rest of the group craved normalcy.

"I felt that could easily have been the swan song for the Kinks. That period when Ray was experimenting a lot and not really knowing what direction he wanted to take as a writer, I felt the band wasn't very cohesive, there didn't seem to be any spirit, and we were kind of going through the motions a little bit," recalls Dave. "Having said that, on reflection, it's quite an interesting album, *Soap Opera*. It was a chance for us to experiment a little bit differently with the stage production. It gave us a chance to sort of dress up in silly clothes and wigs and things and it was quite fun actually to tour with it. It had an interesting side effect to it."

Dave, that former cape and kinky boot wearer, is speaking from his part-time Los Angeles home, where he pursues an interest in yoga and monitors two Web sites, davedavies.com and spiritualplanet.com. A softspoken man, he talks quite openly of the days when Ray had retired the hook-laden hits and was "disappearing up his own ass," as he says. But maybe Ray wasn't the mad hatter everyone made him out to be in 1974. *Soap Opera*'s opener, "Everybody's a Star (Starmaker)," has the same pomp and swagger as the best glam tracks from the era, from T. Rex's "20th Century Boy" and David

Sleepwalker-era *Kinks. Left to right: Jim Rod-*
ford, Mick Avory, and Ray and Dave Davies

Bowie's "Diamond Dogs" to Roxy Music's "Prairie Rose." Ray had a knack for capturing the zeitgeist in song. And boy, could he roll his eyes better than any of those other queen bitches.

"It's a very tongue-in-cheek, satirical look at the rock and roll of that period—how people take themselves too seriously," explains Dave, as if the concept of his brother having a major meltdown in public needed explaining. "There was a lot of phoniness to rock and roll—there always had been in the music business and showbiz. They make a lot of money, they build themselves up, their ego tells them they are incredible people, and they're really just ordinary people who have talent. The glam rock thing was a particularly superficial period, although it was fun." Dave thinks the best-realized songs on the album are "Holiday Romance" and "Ducks on the Wall."

"My tastes in music have always been very broad," he explains. "I always liked [Holiday Romance] because it was harkening back to the early '40s and '50s, Brighton Rock and all these kinds of influences of growing up in England, Ramsgate and these seaside resorts we'd go to, candy floss and cuddling on the beach, stuff like that. It had a nostalgic vibe for me personally, which I had very fond memories about as a child.

"A lot of Kinks music is political and social, but the root of the Kinks' music is like folk music. It delves back into our past and our family. Ray and I are two boys in a family of eight and I'm the youngest. My family was very musical. My dad used to like to go to vaudeville and see comedians and play banjo, and my sisters liked everything from Perry Como to Fats Domino. It was really quite a cacophony of influences growing up, which luckily, I think we drew on a lot throughout our own careers."

Time Line (Conceptual Projects Only)

1968 First conceptual recording, *Village Green Preservation Society* (dislocation in the face of a shifting environment/collapse of the British Empire)

1969 *Arthur* (displacement again—in this case Arthur's relocation to Australia after WWII)

1970 *Lola vs. Powerman and the Money-Go-Round, Part One* (an indictment of the power structure of the music industry)

1971 *Percy* airs (U.K.-only television program)
Muswell Hillbillies (boys from humble beginnings make good)

1972 *Everybody's in Showbiz* (an examination of life as a touring band)

1973 *Preservation Act 1* (Mr. Flash as capitalism coming to wreak havoc on the village green)

1974 *Preservation Act 2* (Mr. Flash rules, but vigilante forces succeed in preserving the village green)

1975 *Soap Opera* (rock star plays a regular Joe who imagines himself to be a rock star)
Schoolboys in Disgrace (based on experiences from Dave Davies' school days)

Among their British Invasion peers—the Who, the Stones, and the Beatles—the Kinks stood alone. The Who had the angry, class-conscious Pete Townshend and his windmill guitar theatrics and cockney-accented Roger Daltrey; the Rolling Stones had a lock on the bad-boy blues thing. The Beatles had John and his acerbic, deadpan, dead-on wit—hell, the Beatles had everything, they were the Beatles. But the Kinks were willfully ambivalent and ambiguous about their sexuality and allegiance to God, country, family, and especially, other bands. The only institution they remained true to was rock and roll itself. Although the lineup would change over 30-plus years, the Kinks had two constants: a truly genius songsmith with attitude and an eye for detail, and a guitarist whose work enhanced even the tiniest nuance in the singer's erratic delivery, no matter what the subject—from the new mod "Carnebetian army" in "Dedicated Follower of Fashion" to the sexual revolution/gay-friendly "See My Friends." But most notably, the Kinks dealt in England past and present, celebrating it in songs like "Waterloo Sunset" while devoting entire projects, like *The Kinks Are the Village Green Preservation Society* and *Arthur*, to the empire. Where do you think the term *Brit-pop* came from, anyway?

"The Brit-pop people—bands like Oasis and Blur, Menswear, and those sort of bands…they're all writing in the same vein as I write in," says Ray. "The sound, and writing about observations and things you see in England. Not so much trying to make it universal, like U2, who write a song and put a record out—they want to be targeted as being global so they can sell bucketloads of records everywhere. The good thing about Brit-pop, and why they've been received well in Britain by the British press and fans, is they've written songs about Britain and the things they see in the world that relate to people that go to see their shows. But also it travels to other parts of the world, like America. Particularly in Oasis' case," says Ray. "So 20 years later, suddenly it's the fashionable thing to do."

But another theme Ray would return to, again and again, was the intricacies of the star-making machinery—from its seedy business side to the personal, emotional, and psychological toll it takes on its victims. He had his reasons: there were the usual early, raw publishing deals; a lot of label hopping; and the three-year ban from touring in the U.S. imposed on the band in the '60s (purportedly some business with the Musicians Union, but the Kinks themselves claim no real knowledge as to why it happened).

Beginning with 1971's *Celluloid Heroes*, Ray foreshadowed our collective obsession with the cult of celebrity. It would seem he is singularly obsessed with uncoiling the mystery of his success or perceived lack of it—from *Lola vs. the Powerman and the Money-Go-Round, Part One*, right on through *Soap Opera*. Decades later, he covered the themes exhaustively in his late '90s science-fictionalized autobiography, *X-Ray*. After taking his songs and stories from *X-Ray* into the rock clubs, he refined it, and the show eventually landed in an off-Broadway theater, touring small theaters around the U.S. as *20th Century Man*. He debuted the format on VH-1, and they turned it into their series *Storytellers*, in which rock stars accompany their performances with stories, à la Ray (although no one in rock is quite like Ray).

"I was doing a lot of signings and readings, and I thought it would be good to actually put a few tunes in there. So I did a showcase at a club called Ronnie Scott's club—it's a famous jazz club in London—and it went really well. I did the try-out gigs in a little town called Maidstone in Kent in a 200-seater, and it worked really well there, so we gave it a shot. I took it to the Edinburgh festival and did two weeks there, and it was really well received. I think it evolved gradually. I still like to think it's evolving," he says. "I've changed a few things yesterday. I change things consciously, and things change naturally; it's a combination of both those things. Unlike, say, if it was a regular kind of theater piece, you wouldn't be able to fit those changes in quite as easily. I remember doing a musical before [*80 Days*] and we had about 20 people on the stage. We wanted to shift tunes around and put new things in, and it's difficult to do. But yesterday I went in and changed something, and it was just a quick rehearsal with the lighting person."

Ray, who lives part time in the U.S. and part time in the U.K., was in Chicago, performing a sizable chunk of his old material to packed houses. He says that all of his introspection and nightly performances of his work have led him to discover things about the 30-year-old songs that he didn't know were there when he wrote them. Through repeated performance, for example, he's come to recognize that the 1967 song "Two Sisters" from the album, *Something Else*, was probably written about him and Dave. "Last night before 'Two Sisters' I did 'I Go to Sleep.' You can tell, particularly with the response from the audience, they realize the connection it had with my life and why I wrote it. Things like that constantly come up," he says.

*20th Century Man, Raymond
Douglas Davies: The clever one*

Clearly, Ray's obsession with presenting musical theater runs deep, as he continually tried to launch projects like *The Kinks Are the Village Green Preservation Society* on the West End stage while simultaneously writing songs and leading a rock band. Not yet willing to bare all in a one-man show (although his band mates constantly feared he was priming himself to go solo) he was intent on making something click that merged rock and theatrics. He tried it one more time in 1975 with *Schoolboys in Disgrace,* although this time, instead of working with an alter ego, he tried someone else's story.

"The actual theme is based on my personal schoolboy experiences. I fell in love when I was 14 or 15, and she got pregnant, and it was a very big scandal at the time," says Dave. "We weren't allowed to see each other, and we were both thrown out of school. It was very autobiographical. Although it was Ray's observation," he chuckles, "it was based on *my* actual life!

"What was very different there is that we'd come through an experimental stage and I felt more confident musically. I wanted to get out and play live, since that's the greatest place to be, in front of people. I'd come through a difficult emotional patch anyway and I had a lot of emotional contact with the content."

The band waged a successful tour for the record, in costume, of course. On the record Dave's guitar has a lyrical quality that matches the nostalgic tone of the record. He'd graduated from an angry, razor-slashed amplified sound to a more emotional lyricism. Although he remained a riff monster, often copping his own for tracks like "The Hard Way" and "I'm in Disgrace," the tone of Dave's guitar lines complemented Ray's rage/desire/melancholy on "No More Looking Back," a summation of what's gone on in the story until that point and the starting point for the next phase. It's one of *Schoolboys'* most evocative numbers.

"I regard that as a great compliment," Dave says. "That's really what I've always tried to do; rather than dominate the music, I've always tried to use the guitar to enhance and color and add light and shade and be powerful and gentle and sensitive when necessary. That's always how I've seen my role as a musician, apart from anything else. *Schoolboys* was a very poignant and important record for us as a band. It worked on different levels. It's very emotional; everyone can relate—anyone who has strong feelings and emotions about their adolescence. Musically we needed to move on; we had the soap operas where the left hand didn't know what the right hand was doing, and it was time to reestablish ourselves. There was a kind of cohesion with the band that was very good, very healthy and creative as well.

"We decided to concentrate on America, because we'd had that ban and felt cheated. We thought, 'We've got to put that right, because we're good.' Besides, Britain in the '70s was piss-poor. That's why when the so-called new wave came along in 1977, it released a new energy in me," Ray told Jon Savage in his 1984 official biography, *The Kinks*.

Little brother, Dave Davies:
The spiritual one

Newly signed to Arista, Ray and Dave had officially survived the career draught when 350,000 American teenagers (myself among them), discovering the Kinks for the first time, bought *Sleepwalker* right out of the box. The Kinks were back on track; it was their highest-charting record since 1964's *Kinda Kinks*.

The album starts with "Life on the Road," a showbizzy anthem with the same kind of "C'mon kids, let's make a show!" spirit as their old theatrical pieces. But *Sleepwalker* wasn't a concept album; it sounds very American, perhaps because Ray had taken an apartment in New York the previous year. Lyrically, he was still singularly obsessed with the machinations of industry—touring, sleepless nights, evil, and band infrastructures. On "Mr. Big Man," Ray takes on a guy whose ego is no longer his amigo; a slow creeper of a number, Dave plays lead guitar with so many flourishes it's almost annoying in its Brian May-ness. Although not widely considered a jewel in the Kinks' crown, *Sleepwalker* was an overdue and much-needed commercial breakthrough.

"I have a great fondness for *Sleepwalker*," says Dave. "I think *Sleepwalker* was a very pivotal record for us. It did pretty well, we were getting back doing bigger gigs, it was fun again, and we were able to do a more rock-orientated show, which I preferred anyway. It was a time we signed with a new record company that really got and understood what the Kinks represented musically. We've often suffered because of that lack of empathy with record companies."

Misfits followed in 1978. Dave's "Trust Your Heart" affirms a burgeoning spirituality, while "Rock and Roll Fantasy" is one of those universal songs about the soul-restoring powers of music. Both brothers claim the song about a fan who "turns his stereo way up high" and the album reenergized them and reaffirmed their faith in themselves and their band.

"I think *Misfits* was a very curious record—another down period that a lot of positive energy came out of," says Dave. Bassist John Dalton had left before *Sleepwalker* and during the making of *Misfits*; his replacement, Andy Pyle, along with keyboardist John Gosling, walked. "It was virtually me and Ray making a record. I wrote a song called 'Trust Your Heart.' The two songs that made that album possible, 'Trust Your Heart' and 'Rock and Roll Fantasy'—although they were coming from two different places—were on the same page. One was an emotional, spiritual energy, the other was a reflective song about how music means so much to people." It also probably didn't hurt that by then punk rock had been swirling around, and the Kinks found acceptance among the new order—they were cool again. England's natty Jam experienced success with an old Kinks tune, "David Watts"; the Pretenders covered "Stop Your Sobbing"; and a new metal band, Van Halen, resurrected "You Really Got Me." Ray, with his skinny pants and skinny ties, made a perfect elder statesman for the new wave of rockers—neurotic, nervous, angry, a little punk-rock.

The Kinks continued to find success at home and abroad throughout the '80s and '90s, America once again a stronghold for them. The remainder of the later Kinks catalog was reissued by Velvel, including 1979's *Low Budget* (with its attempt at disco," [Wish I Could Fly Like] Superman") and 1983's *State of Confusion,* which revived the Kinks yet again when "Come Dancing," another nostalgic Davies family story, placed the Kinks at the top of the pops all over again in the early '80s. Although the remainder of their late-period albums were not always hits and didn't always rate very high on the critical barometer, music lovers know a good song when they hear one, and each Kink offering held at least one or two exceptional pieces of work. *Word of Mouth* is well worth having around, if only for the back-against-the-wall anthem, "Do It Again." The band also benefitted from the advent of video, which introduced a new generation to Ray's theatrical bent.

The brothers haven't spoken for some time, but Ray has finally found that comfortable niche for himself in theater. Yet unlike his British Invasion rock peers—Mick, Keith, Paul, George, Pete, Roger—after nearly 40 years in the business, Ray has never stepped out with a solo debut; he promises it's coming, and has been working some of the new songs into his show. "A couple of the songs will make it onto the solo record. But I kind of want to go back to this musical theater business…"

Although he says he hasn't spoken to his brother for more than a year, Dave is moving forward, too. In addition to his own autobiography, he released a collection of solo work, *Unfinished Business.*

"I would've loved my song 'Unfinished Business' to have been a Kinks single," Dave finishes, "but it wasn't to be. I think that the unfinished business idea applies to the Kinks as much as it applies to my own personal sense of a lack of feeling fulfilled or whatever. I'm a great believer in karma and stuff, and I think if we find ourselves in a bit of a sticky situation with a relationship, the whole lesson is that we've got to try and work it out somehow. The fact that there's conflict—it's an opportunity to deal with it, rather than running away, because we'll really have to come back and deal with it some other way or in another life. It's very difficult for all of us to learn. Sometimes the situations that hurt the most are the ones we need to deal with the quickest, in the most sure fashion. That's a big thing with me. I've still got this feeling that there's still something that we've got to do. It's not over till it's over, you know?"

Recommended Recordings

The Kinks Are the Village Green Preservation Society (Reprise, 1968)
> A lamentation on the obsolescence of the British Empire, Kinks classics like the title song meet the pop of "Picture Book" and the ambitiousness of "Big Sky."

Arthur (Reprise, 1969)
> Based on the true story of the Davies brother-in-law who packed it in and moved to Australia after World War II, before *Tommy* there was *Arthur.* The familiar ("Victoria"), the overlooked (the antiwar "Some Mother's Son), and the epic ("Shangrila") as heard in context, are part of one stunning whole.

The Kinks Kronikles (Reprise, 1972)
> Their greatest hits, from the early '60s like "You Really Got Me" to the '70s "Lola" and "Apeman."

School Boys in Disgrace (Arista, 1975; Konk/Velvel, 1998)
> The sound of the '70s, *Schoolboys* in part recounts Dave's dizzying school days. A fairly hard-rocking album, it includes the riff-heavy "The Hard Way," "I'm in Disgrace" and the poignant "No More Looking Back."

To the Bone (Konk, 1994)
> Live and unbelievably fresh takes on reworked classics from "All Day and All of the Night" and "Waterloo Sunset" to cultier favorites like "Autumn Almanac" and "Muswell Hillbillies," recorded at their own Konk studios.

SPARKS

> "[Nick] Hornby calls Sparks 'slightly annoy-
> ing.' I've always felt that we were extremely
> annoying." —*Ron Mael*

ow did the idea to cover your own songs on Plagiarism *come together?*
Russell: We had an album called *Gratuitous Sax and Senseless Violins* and "When Do I Get to Sing My Way" was a really big hit in Europe. To a lot of people's shock, they found out that Sparks was an active band with a long career and a bit of a history. We tried to figure out a way to introduce those people to us in a way that wasn't a compilation. And we thought if the versions were radically different, it would be interesting to our fans and to ourselves, because it's not our favorite thing to do, to be looking back.

Ron: The artists we collaborated with come from such different areas, and it speaks to a diversity in our music that artists that different would want to collaborate with us. The difference between Jimmy Somerville and Faith No More is pretty extreme.

They're not easy to pigeonhole, like yourselves. Do you think that has hurt or helped your career?

Ron: In a long-term sort of way, it's helped us, because we've been able to fly under the radar, not to be stamped as one particular thing. We pride ourselves on not being able to be pigeonholed, but obviously the danger of that, particularly now, is that it's important for everything to have its niche, and we don't fit into any particular area. But we don't have a choice. This is what we do.

Did you ever feel part of a scene or have any kindred spirits among your peers in what we used to call "art rock?"

Ron [*cracks up at reference to the arcane genre*]: No, we never did. In some quarters we became art rock. We thought that was pretty funny, because we always had screaming girls at our concerts in England, so we kind of gave up trying to make sense of it. It's not a conscious attempt to avoid anything like that, it just never worked out to be interesting hanging out with other musicians.

You were associated with L.A. bands in the '80s though.... Did Jane Wiedlin from the Go-Go's first approach you to collaborate as a fan?

Russell: [At one time] she had her own Sparks fan club running apart from the official fan club that existed. Apart from our physical beauty of course, one wonders what the original attraction was. We've had other musicians—musicians you might not think of because of the music that they're doing—who are interested in the music we're doing. At that time, we were playing with a band and within a certain L.A. scene, and we got typecast in that way.

Ron: The '80s were a more dangerous period for us, because we were starting to be known as an "L.A. band" when we had actually lived in Europe during a period in the '70s.

Russell: In the '80s anything that was quirky could easily be classified as new wave, but we've outlived about 75 other movements. Sparks is still one of the world's best-kept secrets but has a certain appeal to musicians because we haven't broken through in this mass kind of way or lost our ideals.

Before there was techno, there was you and Giorgio Moroder—that's nearly 20 years ago!

Russell: Techno is still lurking around, and we've always felt on the side of that whole movement. With Giorgio, we were in a period in our careers where we'd been working in a traditional band format up till then. Ron's songs and my singing are the basic given of the band, but we are always trying to figure a way to put what Sparks does in a different format as far as instrumentation, and to present something fresh. We liked Giorgio's "I Feel Love" [for Donna Summer] and thought if we could combine elements of that and put the Sparks stamp on it, it could be a real interesting marriage.

Ron: He wanted to do it too, because he wanted to work with a band. There were a lot of interesting factors that went into that album, *Number*

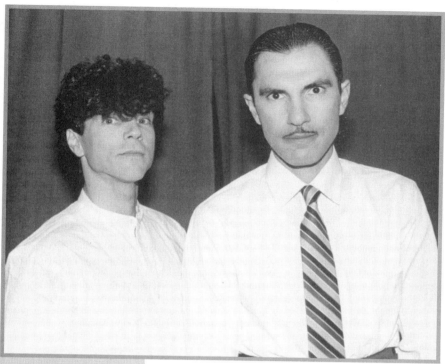

*The brothers Mael,
before they "went disco"*

One in Heaven. Since then, the rules have all changed, but people used to wonder how we could be a band with only two people.

Russell: People criticized us because they thought we "went disco." We just thought it was another Sparks album with a lot of electronics on it. Critically, people couldn't understand it, but the irony was that it had three hit singles in Europe. That album really paved the way for a lot of people in other bands—you didn't have to be a traditional band with five people working in it. To us, the whole thing with "guitars, verse, chorus, here comes the bridge" just isn't fresh anymore. We really like making use of computers—with an asterisk—there's good and there's bad.

Ron: That kind of impersonality is more interesting than badly done personal revelation in songs. If there's a choice between the two, I'd rather hear something that's impersonal, where you can't tell who the artist is, as opposed to someone who's revealing themselves in an inane way.

You mean in terms of emotional content in the lyrics?

Russell: He has no emotional content. He's heartless.

Ron: I wear that lack of personality with pride. There's an emotional content, but it's not on the surface, as it might be. I hate to give specifics, because it sounds defensive, but songs like "When Do I Get to Sing My Way" have an emotional element that's not obvious. ["When do I get to sing 'My Way'? When do I get to feel like Frank Sinatra felt" is pretty obvious!] Over time, a personal vision of what Sparks does developed, and that's in its own way revealing of personality, and if part of that is lack of emotion, well, then it's hard to defend.

Are there songwriters that you admired for that detached quality?

Ron: Very early on we liked Pete Townshend, before things got a little serious. We liked pop music. The early Who was a good statement of that—exciting and flashy—and the songs were different than folk music, which was serious and deep, but they were still suggestive of real things too, till in my mind, it got a little bit pompous. Serge Gainsbourg is somebody who stayed raw and worked in a variety of musical styles, and I admired him both for his songs and for kind of staying with it. And for having affairs with four of the top French actresses, too! We got to see him live once—and it's hard to be impressed when you've been impressed by so many things—but he was really impressive.

Russell: I wrote the afterward to his only novel, which is supposedly coming out here. It's parable of a guy who's got a serious farting problem. I know it sounds ludicrous, but it's one of the most well-written books I've ever read. It's really serious in tone because this guy has this malady and uses it to create art. It's not for the faint of heart.

How did you get involved in the Jean-Claude Van Damme action picture, Knock Out*?*

Ron: We'd written a musical called *Mai, the Psychic Girl,* and had approached the Hong Kong director Tsui Hark about doing it, and though it didn't move ahead, he approached us to do the music for this big movie. To be as diplomatic as possible, we're not used to other people being our boss, and if your boss has a lot more conservative musical taste than you do…it's just that we wish the music could've been more extreme than it turned out to be.

Russell: It was a coincidence that we had recorded two albums in Brussels and have some really good Belgian friends.

Ron: That's why when Van Damme goes on television and the hosts make lame jokes about waffles and French fries, we kind of cringe, because Belgium gets a bad rap for being an inferior version of France or Holland. It's not all that bad, really.

Have you heard of any desperate attempts by fans to find your out-of-print albums?

Russell: A Dutch fan sent us a 22-page list of records he has by Sparks, 17 albums, plus every single.

Time Line

1970	Brothers Russell and Ron Mael form Halfnelson, renamed Sparks, in Los Angeles
1971–97	Sparks release 17 albums, which are for the most part critically and commercially ignored, but which gain them a strong cult of fans, especially throughout Europe
1971	Debut album, *Halfnelson*, produced by Todd Rundgren, released
1974	The album *Kimono My House* is a U.K. hit, featuring the singles "This Town Ain't Big Enough for the Both of Us" and "Amateur Hour"
1975	Sparks collaborate with producer Tony Visconti and form a longstanding alliance on their record *Indiscreet*
1979	*Number One in Heaven*, produced by synthesizer wizard Giorgio Moroder, released, later becomes recognized as a watershed "roots of techno" record
1983	*Sparks in Outer Space* released, with the hit song "Cool Places," a duet with Go-Go Jane Wiedlin
1997	Sparks resurface in the U.S. with a tribute to their own music, *Plagiarism*
2000	Sparks release their 18th studio album the self-produced *Balls*, with drummer Tammy Glover

Ron: Bootlegs as well. He befriended our manager a few years ago, and so he got sent a few of our demos, and we noticed on his complete Sparks discography, in Holland, there is a CD of Sparks demos on his label!

After all these years, has working as siblings been all good?

Ron: I wouldn't put it that way. If we hadn't been brothers, the two of us wouldn't be working together for this long. Obviously there have been disagreements, but we're fortunate enough to have a common view about what our music should be. Generally it works out, though specifically it doesn't always work out.

Russell, do you have a sense of what to do with Ron's songs?

Russell: He instructs me about notes when I cheat and don't sing that one note.

Ron: Our songs are pretty strict, so they aren't open…

Russell: No interpretation…

Ron: No scat singing at the end or anything. It's pretty rigid.

Russell: He'll get pretty pissed off if I swerve off that note and show any kind of individuality.

Ron: That is to be frowned upon.

Russell: He wrote it, and that's how it's to be sung.

Ron: The next note is not always the logical note, so that throws a little wrench in the works. Generally, I know what his singing does to the song, so it isn't like having to babysit. It's only the little things…like notes!

Russell: There was no thought of [us] ever getting involved seriously in music. We weren't prepared at all. The opposite, I think. Ronnie had taken piano and I'd taken no lessons in anything and we were UCLA students. We were enamored when we saw bands from England, and that's what got us excited about pursuing music. We weren't from a showbiz family, didn't have connections. We had no prep whatsoever for this. It was all a totally naive approach to the thing. I think it's still reflected in what we're doing now.

I'm glad you're back, even though you technically never went away.

Russell: I'm glad you said that, because from the American standpoint—and we understand why—some people want to know why we reformed.

*The millennial-era Sparks
still juggling balls*

We've been really active all along, it's just more visible in Europe than it has been here. When we started playing again more, live in Europe, we decided we really have to play more in America again, no matter what the result. For various reasons, it hasn't gotten together, but with *Plagiarism*, it seems like the right time. The complete unit is Ron and myself and a drummer, Tammy Glover, and we're there and ready. We're one song away from finishing a brand-new album. We always try to make things appealing to our own set of standards.

And you still look the same!

Russell: People are kinda surprised that we look kinda like we do…that we haven't gotten overly pathetic. That was part of why we did this album, and why the new fans assumed we were a new band, because we didn't look overly horrible.

How do you do it?

Russell: ...a lot of spinning classes.

Recommended Recordings

Profile: The Ultimate Sparks Collection (Rhino, 1988)

In lieu of tracking down all of Sparks' fabulous '70s and '80s output, the highlights are collected here, and are probably all of Sparks the uninitiated, as well as anyone who hasn't listened in a while, will ever need.

Plagiarism (Oglio, 1998)

State-of-the-art Sparks; their old classics as reinterpreted by themselves, and with the assistance of friends like Jimmy Somerville and Faith No More.

CHARLIE AND IRA LOUVIN

THE LOUVIN BROTHERS

"Elvis really should've hit my brother...
but he didn't" —*Charlie Louvin*

e lvis Presley was one of their biggest fans. But according to Charlie Louvin, the surviving member of the legendary vocal duo the Louvin Brothers, Presley never recorded one of their tunes because the King and his brother Ira Louvin didn't exactly hit it off.

"We was on the road. We were doing about a 100-date tour with Presley in his early years," explains Louvin, now in his 70s. The Louvins, being the better known act at the time, were headlining.

"Elvis had just done a show, and there was a 30-minute pause before the second show started. He came back into the dressing room and sat down at an old piano back there. He could play just enough piano to sing songs like 'Amazing Grace.' He set down and started to play, and he said, 'Now this is the kind of music I like.' My brother called him a 'white nigger' and said, 'If that's what you like, then why do you do that trash out on the stage?' Elvis said, 'When I'm out there I do what they want to hear. When I'm back here, I do what I like.'

"Elvis was just a kid. In those days he wasn't a fighter. He really should have hit my brother, but he didn't. But there ain't no way to estimate how much that cost the Louvin Brothers song catalog. If he'd have recorded but two songs…but it didn't happen. Presley had put in writing that the Louvin Brothers were his favorite singers—because his mother was a big Louvin Brothers fan. But after that, Nashville was changing; Colonel Parker came along."

Although the story could end right there in tragedy, giving Louvin a reason to be bitter, it doesn't and he isn't. Louvin tells the tale like he writes and sings his songs—with a little bit of light and a little bit of dark, the very basis for his brand of traditional music. Any doubt about where the Louvins were coming from is spelled out in one of their most famous albums and its title, *Tragic Songs of Life*. Among some of the Louvins' bittersweet hits are: "When I Stop Dreaming," "I Don't Believe You've Met My Baby," "You're Running Wild," and "I Don't Love You Anymore." And then there's the album *Satan Is Real*—just in case there's any doubt as to where they stood on the idea of darkness.

"I had real good luck with 'See the Big Man Cry, Mama,' 'Will You Visit Me on Sundays,' and 'Think I'll Go Somewhere and Cry Myself to Sleep,'" says Louvin of some of his more famous "dark night of the soul" compositions. Most recently, neo-bluegrass artist Allison Krause recorded "I Don't Believe You've Met My Baby" as a duet with Jerry Douglas. "BR5-49 did some; Mark Knopfler from the Dire Straits band did a Louvin Brothers song; Nicolette Larson—when she was basically doing rock music—she did a Louvin brothers gospel song. It's been real healthy for the music catalog. I appreciate 'em all, regardless of what field of music they're in," says Louvin.

"I'll be sprinkling some of those in with 'Knoxville Girl' and 'Mary of the Wild Moors' or 'I'll Be All Smiles Tonight,' which are old folk festival songs that came to this country from England," he explains of plans for his rare Bay Area appearances. "I've been to California a dozen times in my 55 years in the music business. There's really no point in us driving 3,000 miles to go to California when Nashville is within 800 miles of 50 million people—the Northeast, Midwest, Southwest, and Deep South.

"We played a lot of shows from Seattle all the way down to San Diego. We just never did make a whole lot of money in California, because too many days would be canceled. Half of your 14 days would be canceled, and you just sit in the motel paying out money to feed the band and motel bills. Two days off out of five eats your profit up. So I just never did try to come out to California. But I always thought California was absolutely loaded with great talent."

It was on one of his early treks west with brother Ira that Louvin first met Guy Clark, with whom he toured in 1997. "I met Guy when my brother and I were doing a television show for some Dodge dealer in California," he remembers. And Louvin has links with other California singers, most notably Harris and Parsons.

Charlie Louvin in the '90s:
"I'm not a hot picker."

"I know Emmylou, but I never met Gram," he says. Before his death, Parsons cut "Cash on the Barrelhead" for his *Grievous Angel* album; more importantly, he sung the praises of the Louvins' music to a generation of fans who were yet to discover them, including Harris. "He was the one that introduced Emmylou to the Louvin Brothers," Charlie relates. "She was the first viable artist that reached back and got an old Louvin Brothers song and made a hit on it: 'If I Could Only Win Your Love.' The next four or five years she cut six or eight others and put them all on an album. There are qualities in her voice that are perfect for our kind of music. Some of her greatest successes was scored with simple, down-to-earth songs." But, he adds, "I think she's changed the last four or five years. I have problems understanding her. I listen to her records and I can't understand what she says. I don't know if that's intentional or just the kind of songs she's singing."

What Louvin does understand is the difference between what he knows as country music—the kind purveyed by the Grand Ole Opry (of which he's been a member for 43 years)—and the kind they play nowadays down in Nashville.

"I don't hardly know what to call it. Every time a new act comes on it's called 'classic,' 'pure,' or 'traditional.' They've got an artist on the Opry now that is *not* country. So it's changed. Slowly. Some people tell me Elvis was on the Opry, but I was there and I never heard of it. I've been 45 years in Nashville. Been on the Opry 43. Started in '55. It'll last me out."

Louvin and his brother worked their way toward their post on Nashville's Opry, from being boyhood music enthusiasts at home in Henegar, Alabama, and later in Georgia. "The good part was, we was raised by the same parents, so we thought alike. We loved the Delmore Brothers, cowboys, and we listened to the Opry. And we were raised in the part of the country where they have sacred harp music—five harmonies in their songs, but they don't use instruments at all." Contrary to popular belief, he says, "We never sang in the church choir."

Charlie was born Charles Loudermilk in 1927; he was just three years younger than Ira. "Louvin is just a made up name," he says. "It mighta been a French name, but I haven't heard the name—no one else has got it." Inspired by the other brother acts of the era—the Delmores, the Blue Sky Boys, and the Monroe Brothers, the pair plied a close, tight harmony style, Ira taking care of the highs and Charlie on the melody below.

"When we were very young, Roy Acuff came to within three miles of our house to do a show. Of course we loved Roy. We didn't have the money to see the show, but we wanted to go in. So we went and stood in the yard, as did two or three hundred other people. It was warm and the windows was open, and we could see him. The admission price was a dime, a quarter for adults, so we imagined that they got rich that night. And we knew that's what we wanted to do."

Working as field hands, they worked their way up to amateur musicians. "We sang everywhere they'd let us sing, and finally we got in an amateur contest in Chattanooga and we won, three Saturday nights straight. The prize was a 15-minute radio show on a 250-watt radio station at 4:30 in the morning, so we held our day jobs. We started getting some show dates, and when we could finally make a living at it, we quit our day jobs and put all of our efforts toward music." The brothers recorded their first album, *Nearer My God to Thee*, in 1952.

"When we came to the Opry we were still playing all gospel. The sponsor didn't want but one gospel song by each person, so when we could be on, we could only sing one song, and everybody else could sing two secular songs." Louvin says that's when the brothers knew they'd be forced to record secular music.

"We had a horrible time convincing our A&R man to do this, because gospel artists weren't accepted with the gospel audience once they started singing secular songs. We got a little flak from the hardcore Christian people, but we couldn't make a living just playing gospel. We'd go 300 miles to sing, and we wouldn't have the gas money to go home. That's exactly what they paid us, the gas money."

Time Line

1924 Lonnie Ira born in Henegar, Alabama

1927 Charlie Elzer born in Henegar, Alabama

1943 Amateur hour contest leads to radio program

1946 Recordings for Apollo

1952 Signed to Capitol Records

1955 First secular recording, "When I Stop Dreaming"
Louvins join the Grand Ole Opry, where Charlie remains

1956 "I Don't Believe You've Met My Baby" a hit

1963 Louvin Brothers break up
Both brothers pursue solo careers—Charlie goes on to record with Melba Moore, Roy Acuff, and Emmylou Harris

1965 Ira Louvin dies in car crash

1974 Gram Parsons helps introduce the Louvins' songs to a new generation of fans with his recording of "Cash on the Barrelhead"

1975 Emmylou Harris records "If I Could Only Win Your Love"

1992 Uncle Tupelo records the Louvin Brothers' "The Great Atomic Power"

1997 Charlie Louvin still touring and operating the Louvin Brothers Museum
Releases *The Long Ride*

Ira and Charlie Louvin in Grand Ole Style

Ultimately, the sacred merged with the secular when the Louvins recorded "When I Stop Dreaming" in 1955; the result was the legacy of Louvin Brothers gospel-inspired and country songs still performed by Louvin and other artists around the world today. But the success and career of the Brothers themselves was relatively short-lived, limited to a good run in the late '50s to the early '60s. Brother Ira's extremes in behavior proved hard on the two men.

"It's what broke the Louvin Brothers up, his drinkin'. I didn't then and I still don't know how to handle it when a drunk gets in my face. I just want to grab him by the shoulders and shake him. I didn't know how to handle it. Finally it got extremely bad and cost us work," says Louvin. "We broke the duo up in '63 and he got killed in '65." Ira and his wife, singer Anne Young, were killed in a head-on collision.

"I've been doin' a lot of the Louvin Brothers songs since, but I do them in trio form. My role hasn't changed. That old boy I've got singin' tenor's pretty good, but he's no Ira Louvin," he says, referring to one of the members of his traveling band. Louvin employs a pick-up band (a common practice among musicians of his generation) as he moves from town to town. He chips in a little on guitar. "I hold it as an accessory," he jokes. "I'm what they call a second. I'm not a hot picker."

In 1997, Louvin's mother, who was 96, passed away. "I lost a brother, a sister, and a daddy, but it wasn't as bad as this one. I knew it would be the big one. I've had all kinds of love, I suppose. But mothers are my favorite people." His mother's side of the family is still active in the lost art of sacred-harp singing. "My mother's people were part of a [singing] reunion—they've been going for 102 years. People sing for about two or three hours, and then the ladies will go out and spread about 100 tables and break and eat and talk about who didn't make it this year, who passed away, old times. And then they go back inside for about two-and-a-half hours and call it a day. They still do that. But there are fewer young people getting interested in doing it, so I think it's a dying style of music that I hate to see go."

But Louvin still has his own career. He continues to tour, and in 1996, he released *The Longest Train*, a collection of his and others' songs recorded with a group of young, traditional musicians. He also leads a peaceful life with his wife, and together, the pair operate the Louvin Brothers museum in Bell Buckle, Tennessee.

"My wife's saved everything that was printed on the Louvin Brothers. We got a world of pictures, reading material, musical instruments, clothing, memorabilia. We're only open three days a week. If you ever get down here, we sure hope you'll take the time out to see us."

Recommended Recordings

Close Harmony (Bear Family, 1992)
> This is an eight-CD box set retrospective by the assiduous German label Bear Family; it's all the Louvins you'll ever need—over 200 song titles.

Tragic Songs of Life (Capitol, 1956/1996)

Satan Is Real (Capitol, 1959/1996)

Among the titles reissued by Capitol in recent years, you could do worse than to pick one of these classics. *Tragic Songs* is a mostly acoustic record dabbling with the theme of life's tragedy and features "Knoxville Girl"; *Satan Is Real* is known not only for "The Christian Life," later popularized by the Byrds, but for its outrageous cover art depicting the Louvins in hell.

> "You know I'm a super girl
> Yes, I'm a punky girl
> I never say die
> No one can stop me."
> —Naoko Yamano

SHONEN KNIFE

three Japanese women named after a brand of penknife seem the unlikely embodiment of punk rock, yet Shonen Knife may be among the genre's last rebels. The power trio makes a pop-punk noise comparable to the Ramones, and count Sonic Youth, Redd Kross, and the former members of Nirvana among their fans.

But after six albums, 50 singles, and more than ten years together, in 1995, the band headed stateside in search of a record deal, having cut all management and U.S. label ties.

"We didn't have enough control, so we quit," explains guitarist, songwriter, and de facto group leader, Naoko Yamano, at home in Osaka, Japan. She was due on the West Coast in a few days, where she intended to test the waters and play a couple of dates with Shonen Knife. "We have about 20 new songs, and we've demoed all of them. Our shows in America are going to be our showcase show to play our new songs and find a record company."

In her excitement, Naoko reels off the new titles: "'E.S.P.,' about people who have extra power, 'Explosion!' about anger, 'Buddah's Face,' and how he looks at you as if you've gone too far this time."

The band's last American album prior to the split with Virgin Records, *Rock Animals*, with its metal-lite sound and hellbent for leather meets *Spinal Tap* parody graphics, may have given the wrong impression that Shonen Knife had given up on punk.

"I love hard rock and punk rock. Hard rock has the spirit of punk. But I think our managers may have pushed things in the wrong direction," says Naoko. Aside from the album's opening song, "Quavers," a riff-heavy strutter, the album was filled with the type of songs that have become the Knife's trademark: fanciful tunes about animals, boys, and food with titles like "Catnip Dream," "Johnny, Johnny, Johnny," and "Brown Mushrooms." In 1986, Naoko described Shonen Knife's influences to author Richie Unterberger as "'60s pops, psychedelic music, before and after '80s punk, Southeast Asian pops, reggae, Motown sounds, rock and roll, and more…" Shonen Knife are all that; sometimes the riffs haven't changed, but they attack their songs with a playful, rebel spirit, and whether a song is in English, Japanese, or both, the result is singularly "of the Knife."

At the end of 1981 Naoko asked a former college classmate, Michie Nakatani, to join what she called her "project."

"She had no experience, so I picked out a bass for her, because bass guitar has four strings and is easier to learn than guitar." Naoko asked her younger sister, Atsuko, to sit in on drums. Together, they began writing songs with simple chord progressions and melodies to match the three-chord power-punk of the Ramones and Buzzcocks, and Shonen Knife was born.

"We had a very boring time growing up listening to daytime rock stations. Then we heard punk rock and we wanted to be like that," says Naoko. How old were the young women at the time? "We are 75 years old now." Perhaps I phrased the question incorrectly, or Naoko is cagily avoiding the answer, so I'll venture an educated guess: in their early 20s or younger.

Less than a year after their formation, they were discovered playing live and were picked up by Zero Records in Japan. Not long after, Calvin Johnson of Olympia Washington's K Records traveled to Japan and brought home a copy of the band's *Burning Farm* EP. He released it as a cassette with bonus songs, and it helped introduce Shonen Knife to American audiences, although it hardly shook the world. However, influential fellow musicians took to the band, and the Knife found fast friends in the punk scene, among them Redd Kross, Fugazi, Sonic Youth, and Nirvana, with whom they toured in 1991.

Every Band Has a Shonen Knife Who Loves Them was a testament to their superstar status among the rock and roll cognoscenti. The 1989, 23-song tribute by various punk bands was partly conceived by Jeff McDonald of Redd Kross. The L.A. band and the Knife had a mutual admiration society going: Shonen Knife recorded a song called "Redd Kross" while Redd Kross

Hard rock animals Shonen Knife, left to right, Michie, Naoko, and Atsuko

cut the song, "Shonen Knife." For the tribute record, Sonic Youth gave "Burning Farm" its creepy "Land of a Thousand Dances" treatment; the East Bay's Mr. T. Experience did a boy-punk version of "Flying Jelly Attack," and the now-defunct Big Dipper worked up a straightforward version of the Knife classic, "Bear Up Bison."

With a fuzzbox mimicking a revving motorcycle, a drum and guitar sound that belongs backing the Ramones, and a guitar lead that could be from a science fiction soundtrack, "Bear Up Bison" has a truly unique theme: a message of love and strength to an endangered animal. Part of its lyric is

68

borrowed from XTC's pop song, "Making Plans for Nigel"; the other part is uniquely Shonen Knife: "*We're only making plans for da-da-dirty dirty bison/He's on his way to extinction/We only want what's best for him.*"

"We went to the zoo in Tokyo, and there was panda's cage and bison's cage, very close together," says Naoko of the song's beginnings. "And there were so many people in front of panda's cage. Then we went to bison's cage, and there were no people in front of bison's cage. Bison was cared for very badly. His hair was very dirty. We felt very sorry for him. So I wanted to present a song to bison.

"I want to write a song about panda someday," she continues, admitting she's been obsessed with the animal "ever since the day with bison." "Because panda is two colors, black and white. It shows both sides: cute panda and evil panda."

On the ensuing American dates, the band would be dressed as bears, in "very cute panda costumes" designed by Atsuko, who's not only a Shonen Knife member but also the band's chief clothing designer, responsible for

Time Line

1981	Band forms in Osaka, Japan
1985	*Burning Farm* EP reaches U.S. via K Records cassette
1989	*Every Band Has a Shonen Knife Who Loves Them*, a compilation of American bands playing the songs of Shonen Knife, brings them to wider attention
1991	Tour U.K., opening for Nirvana
1993	Record *Rock Animals* for Virgin U.S.
1995	Seek new record label
1997	U.S. independent label Big Deal releases *Brand New Knife*
1999	Founding member Michie Nakatani leaves band
2000	Atsuko and Naoko Yamano continue to work as Shonen Knife and release *Strawberry Sound* in Japan only

all of their matching outfits, including their old Mondrian-style shift dresses (Atsuko also performs a mean version of Ringo's Beatle number, "Boys").

Shonen Knife are true fans of rock, and quite simply aren't afraid to let it shine through in a primitive, innocent way; through the years, like natural musicians, they developed technically. Augmented by cheesy effects, the melody to "Devil House" could be any song by the Ramones (OK—"Beat on the Brat"), but after hearing the women sing, "Time warp, time trip!" you'd have to be a real sourpuss to hold their borrowing against them. So endearing are their originals and cover versions that their cover of the Carpenters' song "Top of the World" has been used in no less than three feature films, as well as a computer advertisement. Admittedly, there's nothing very punk about that, but no one said punks shouldn't be allowed to make a living. All things considered, Shonen Knife appear to be living their dream as they sing: *"I don't want to get up early in the morning, I want to sleep all day/ I don't want to work a boring job, I want to play all day."*

Shonen Knife simply share their experience. One of the early songs that stirred some controversy was "Twist Barbie." It starts off sounding like an advertising jingle for the all-American dress-up doll, but turns into a backward anthem—not exactly a rant—about what girls who buy into the beauty myth are forced to deal with from the earliest age: the pressure to look like something they're not. Naoko explains how as a child she preferred the blue-eyed, blond-haired Barbie over the Japanese version, Rica.

"Rica had the body of a child. Barbie had the shape of a woman, and I wanted to be like her," she says. Writing and singing about what they know and dressing the way they want is a big part of Shonen Knife's engaging purity of vision. When a group of men or boys dress in clown makeup or masks and sky-high platform boots, no one questions their right to rock or their mode of dress while doing it. Yet the Knife have been teased mercilessly, often by otherwise intelligent male critics, because they "can't play"; critics wrongly attribute their mystery appeal to the "cute factor" and on their "funny" accents when they attempt their second language, English. It's hardly fair to mock the achievements of a band that has stayed together for nearly 20 years, whose members came of age at a time when forming a rock band was a serious transgression for girls within Japanese society. Shonen Knife are not anyone's girl-group puppets, nor anything to sneer at; they've wrested control of their band back, and no one tells them what to do.

Image-wise, the women are not fashion followers; rather, they are typically modern and stylish Japanese women—and a tad more. In the early '90s, American women and girls in alternative rock sub-circles carried stuffed animal purses and Hello Kitty accessories and wore baby barrettes in their hair (some still do). Back then, the look was a partly politicized statement, an emblem among young women looking to reclaim the childhood that was robbed them as a result of abuse, incest, and rape; for others, it was just a fashion. The Shonen Knives, who'd been dressing that way for years, had been doing it for fun, to celebrate the innocent pleasure of childhood dress-up; it complemented their songs about silly things like candy. And it wasn't so radically different from when the street punk–looking Ramones sang about the pleasures of sniffing glue. Yet detractors went as far as to say that Shonen Knife's pose was antifeminist. On the surface, it's easy to see why the band's Bizarro vision and rebel, free-to-be-you-and-me spirit was mistaken for naiveté and entirely misunderstood. But Naoko says that to perceive the band as political is to miss the point; Shonen Knife have their own reasons for being themselves. For your sake and mine, they are strictly for entertainment, and that's by design.

With the shift in Japanese and global culture, Shonen Knife may be welcomed with open arms upon their reentry into the U.S., instead of ghettoized in the novelty, girl band, or Japanese sections of stores. Film and literary giants like Akira Kurosawa and Yoshio Mishima, among others, are embedded in our culture. Throughout the '90s and beyond, Americans embraced Japanese authors Haruki Murakami and Banana Yoshimoto, filmmaker and actor Takeshi Kitano, lounge act Pizzicato Five, children's collectibles like Hello Kitty and Pokémon, "and the animation" adds Naoko. Without Shonen Knife, Japan's latest girl group sensation Puffy certainly wouldn't have been possible.

"I like Murakami. I think he is very popular to Japanese people, too; that's the idea when things are from Tokyo. Shonen Knife rejects that. The members of Shonen Knife are living in Osaka, and we want to stay punk rockers."

Naoko expresses a gracious but seemingly true enthusiasm for the U.S. and its culture. She speaks of San Francisco—how much she and the band love it here—but she is more practical than ebullient as to why they will spend two vacation days in Northern California before returning to Japan.

*Naoko and Atsuko Yamano ponder
their next move on the Knife's edge.*

"We would rather stay in San Francisco than Los Angeles because we have no car," she says.

But given that the purpose of their mission to the States is to find a record company, wouldn't their time be better spent in the epicenter of the music universe?

"We will take our time and choose very carefully. I'm asking all the people we know in bands to tell us which record company would be best for Shonen Knife," she says. So for now, Naoko and Shonen Knife are in no hurry to get the next record out, to ride on the tidal wave of globalization, or to exploit their all-female status in the so-called hot climate for new and emerging "women in rock." They plan to be together for a long time.

"Shonen Knife is our life's work," Naoko says of a vow taken by the three women long ago. "It is equal to ourselves. So we will do it as long as we live."

Recommended Recordings

Pretty Little Baka Guy + Live in Japan (Rockville, 1986)
> *Pretty Little Baka Guy* contains the roaring classics "Bear Up Bison" and "Devil House," while the eight live tracks show off the band at work in 1982 and 1990—a must-have when overviewing the Knife's career, and an energizing listen for its own sake.

Brand New Knife (Big Deal, 1997)
> The band is at its short, sweet, and buzz-saw best on songs like "Explosion!" and "E.S.P."

Every Band Has a Shonen Knife Who Loves Them (Various Artists)
(Giant Records, 1989)
> Shonen Knife has won the hearts of alt-rock legends, from Sonic Youth to L7. They are covered here extensively by their friends and allies in indie rock.

love is the answer

Julie and Buddy Miller
Chuck Prophet and Stephanie Finch

Julie and Buddy Miller
Chuck Prophet and Stephanie Finch

everyone's heard of football, the Internet, or a passion for shopping coming between couples, but fewer may be familiar with the plight of the rock and roll widow or widower. He or she is the person who stays behind, keeping the home fires burning, caring for the children, and doing the things that couples ideally do together. Meanwhile, the musician in the partnership is required to make his or her living on the road, sometimes for the majority of the calendar year. It's an arrangement, as is any where one spouse must be away from home, that can have its advantages and disadvantages.

Some couples would probably kill each other if they spent every day together—we've all heard the dilemma of the stay-at-home partner whose spouse retires. But for those who like or need to spend a good bit of time alone, a half on/half off arrangement can be the perfect solution. Relationships that might otherwise be past their sell-by date can stay fresh longer—there's actually something to the old saw about absence and a fonder heart.

Of course separation by distance has its perils, as many couples will attest. Time differences and punishing itineraries have long been deterrents to good communication for separated couples (although cell phones and e-mail have solved that problem to a degree). Certainly infidelity can be a factor in the demise of long-distance relationships, although that's hardly a scenario exclusive to traveling musicians. But probably more than any other business, the entertainment industry has long had a reputation for wild and loose lifestyles, which in turn can lead to any number of indiscretions due to the real or imagined presence of copious amounts of drugs, free sex, and, of course, that damn rock music—long known to make people act just plain irrational. But really, those things are only excuses.

The road, as it's been romanticized by so many singers in so many songs, definitely has its cachet; for some artists it can be their lifeblood—as essential as air and water. However, except perhaps in the case of the mega-star, it is hardly a glamorous place to be. Anyone who has traveled across the country in a van, slept on floors, or had the pleasure of staying at Motel 6s and Holiday Inns for weeks on end will tell you so. Why would a person want to be alone in a strange bed, or, worse still, with a strange roomie, when he or she could be at safe at home, sharing their own bed with the partner of their choice? For some couples, it's an arrangement that simply will not do, and the solution is obvious. They travel together.

A number of couples have figured out how to make that proverbial sweet music together while avoiding lonely nights away from home: by working with each other, paralleling their marriage vows, they've committed to literally hitting their high notes and low notes together. Crafting songs, although it will remain a solo pursuit, can also be satisfying when done together. Performing those songs can also be a shared experience. Couples can eat those bad coffeeshop breakfasts together, and endure strained backs and sore butts from uncomfortably long rides together. If one of the partners is a group leader, the couple may agree not to take sides when the inevitable band conflicts arise. When disagreements arise between couples traveling with a band or as a duo, there is an implied agreement that at the end of the day, they'll be going to their room together, and that, one way or another, by the next day everything is going to be resolved—that is, if life on the road is to be anything resembling bearable.

So OK, there are some examples of romantic and musical liaisons that did not work: the twisted and intermingled love lives of members of groups like the Jefferson Airplane, Fleetwood Mac, and the Mamas & the Papas, and couples like Carly Simon and James Taylor, to name a few. In those cases, documented abuses of drugs and alcohol had something to do with the undoing of those partnerships.

Women also have to deal with stigmas and stereotypes attached to their presence around bands—still largely the domain of men and boys—and the perceived notion of how they mess up that whole dynamic. There are some who subscribe to the theory that Yoko Ono's presence in the studio at the Beatles recording sessions was the undoing of that band. But look at Bruce Springsteen. Long the leader of a boys-club band, he found his true heart when he hired backup singer Patti Scialfa. He promptly fell in love with her, and they married and had three children in quick succession. His E Street Band didn't have to break up because of it (but his first marriage certainly came undone in the process).

Some couples find love or keep it through business partnerships; they can also lose it. Billy Joel, Dolly Parton, and Michelle Shocked are a few performers who have had romantic liaisons with their managers. Curiously, nowhere have these team efforts thrived more than in the heavy metal arena, such as in the longterm management and creative agreements between Sharon and Ozzy Osbourne and Wendy and Ronnie James Dio.

Wanda Jackson, married to her manager, Wendell Goodman, for 40 years, says, "It's a long time—especially in this business." She explains that Goodman just couldn't stand the thought of men adoring her from afar, night after night, so he decided to join her on the road, and they've lived there together happily ever since. The genesis and endurance of their relationship is discussed further by Jackson in a chapter devoted to her later in this book.

As musicians and husband and wife, Johnny Cash and June Carter have lived, loved, and worked together on and off over a 30-year period; Kim Gordon and Thurston Moore of Sonic Youth have been happily ensconced in a band, a business, and a marital partnership for nearly 20 years; Chris Frantz and Tina Weymouth of Tom Tom Club and Talking Heads approach three decades of connubial and musical bliss; Pat Benatar and her husband, guitarist Neil Giraldo, have worked together for 20 years. Paul and Linda McCartney reportedly only spent two nights apart over the course of their 29-year marriage; John Lennon and Yoko Ono bravely endured scrutiny and epithets from the public from the day they hooked up through their well-publicized '70s split and reconciliation until Lennon's death, which was their ultimate parting.

Two often-maligned Beatle wives, Yoko Ono and Linda McCartney joined their husbands in their post-Beatle band incarnations. The women's musical talents were often criticized, although it would seem to me they did a perfectly fine, if not an exceptional, job of living in the public eye, raising their children, and continuing to do good works in the name of human rights while sharing their personal and creative lives with their partners, whose talents were roundly hailed as genius. When it came to their shortcomings, critics never failed to mention that collaborating with their spouses was a Beatle pursuit of questionable intent. Although Linda always claimed to have reluctantly entered the musical realm at the insistence of her husband, Yoko's musical innovation and pace-setting feminism through her art and actions cannot be dismissed so easily. Linda ultimately found her voice in animal rights activism, Yoko in business. While both possessed a wealth most of us can't even fathom, and while their music might have been a sideline pursued in vanity, neither flaunted their material possessions; in fact, they used their celebrity to advance global causes. When Linda passed away in 1998, I thought of Paul. And then I thought of Yoko. The two share a bond in having both lost their partners, the parents of their children, and the greatest loves of their lives far too soon. It fuels my compassion for husbands and wives trying to make it work—in music and in every walk of life—former Beatles or otherwise.

The two couples in this section both work quietly on the sidelines of the Americana genre, and have conducted semi-anonymous careers over the last couple of decades. In the case of Julie and Buddy Miller, their collaborative labors over a nearly 30-year period have finally brought them some long-awaited recognition. Beginning as bar singers in the '70s, by the late '90s, their compositions were being recorded by twangy superstars and prestige roots artists from the Dixie Chicks to Emmylou Harris. Also, their solo recordings—Julie's *Broken Things* and Buddy's *Cruel Moon*, on which they both contribute equally—were among critics' most lauded albums of 1999.

The Millers' music, both as individuals and together, is a mesmerizing blend of new and old; rock, country, and folk. To see them perform together is to witness two rare and extraordinary talents who were clearly meant to work in tandem. Theirs is an example of a working partnership seen all too infrequently in music, where the attendant media is quick to focus on the chinks in the relationships of couples who have found success together.

Chuck Prophet and his wife, Stephanie Finch, have been players on the San Francisco scene since the late '80s, and have seen their share of good times and bad. Prophet's career as a professional musician dates back to when he was the guitarist for the prototypical Americana band Green on Red. It was at that time that Finch set her sights on becoming his collaborative partner. So while Prophet was winding down with Green on Red, he embarked on a solo career with Finch at his side as multi-instrumentalist and vocalist. The couple married in 1998, and continue to work together in Prophet's band. When I spoke to Prophet in 1997, around the time of the release of his fourth album, *Homemade Blood,* he said that someday, he hoped to record Stephanie's songs. Later that year, the couple got around to it when Finch debuted with her own band, Go-Go Market, in which Prophet plays guitar and contributes some songwriting and as a solo artist. Meanwhile, Prophet's band, with Finch, released a fifth album, *The Hurting Business.* Merging new technology with old and incorporating a turntablist, the record booms with the clankity-clank groove of a Tom Waits, Beck, or latter-day Los Lobos record. It's a sound Prophet believes best captures his aggressive, "sideways" spin on roots rock.

Prophet and Finch's story is largely about what they've learned during their years on the fringes of the music business. They've turned their experiences into an enduring creative and romantic partnership, and it's a story from which anyone who has a heart will derive inspiration. By all accounts, it would appear that Finch and Prophet are ready to receive the rewards that were similarly hard-won by the Millers—in both love and music.

Husbands and wives playing music together can be a rare blessing. In the case of the Millers and Prophet and Finch, their strength and harmony as couples is inspiring, their faith enviable. Their talents are worthy of far more recognition then either has currently enjoyed. But along with finding their true romantic and musical partners for life, these couples are also enjoying one of the more overlooked benefits of constant togetherness: minimum long-distance charges on the monthly phone bill.

JULIE AND BUDDY MILLER

> **"For where your treasure is,
> there your heart will be also."**
> —*Matthew 6:21*

"**h**ey Julie, I'm on that interview we have, and I'll buzz you up for your portion in a minute, 'cause that's what I'm doin','" says guitarist and singer-songwriter Buddy Miller to his wife, Julie Miller, singer-songwriter and occasional guitarist. "We have an intercom," he explains. "I'm in the studio room, which is really just underneath where I'm talking to Julie, but I'm tired of running up and down the stairs," he says.

Although Julie and Buddy Miller are a two-musician household, they maintain individual recording careers and very different styles. Julie's jangle-roots-folk rock album, *Broken Things,* and Buddy's twangy *Cruel Moon*, both released in 1999, ended up on critics' year-end lists and charted only two places apart on the annual *Village Voice* Pazz and Jop Poll (slots 51 and 49, respectively); Julie sang on Buddy's album and Buddy played and sang on Julie's. While Julie writes all of her own songs and some of Buddy's too, Buddy also collaborates with friends like Jim Lauderdale and Steve Earle. Between them, they've worked with such artists as Earle, Emmylou Harris, and Victoria Williams. Their songs have been covered by country stars like the Dixie Chicks and Brooks & Dunn, as well as jazz vocalist Jimmy Scott. But few, except for a handful of diehard No Depression and new-country devotees, know the Millers by sight or by name. Maybe it has something to do with their low-key, live/work aesthetic.

"We're just like leaves in the wind," says Julie, the ethereal one, in her characteristic gentle and poetic style. While Julie's speaking and singing voice is childlike, she steers clear of adolescent lyrical fantasies or naive musical devices on her records. Instead she favors universal themes and classic roots-rock sounds, shying away from traditional country melody. Buddy, on the other hand, is forthright and all about hard country; that's how he came to the attention of Earle, who signed him up as a touring guitarist and with whom he now trades songs. Yet when the Millers collaborate, instead of the oil and water-ish combination one might expect, the pair wind up with the perfect proportions of yin and yang.

"I go, 'Look, I won't sing punk rock on your record, and don't sing like, so hicked-out on mine,'" says native Texan Julie. Oddly, it's her Ohio-bred husband who embraces everything countrified. "Isn't it the craziest thing? It is all completely bonkers. Nothing adds up. It's the funniest thing in the world." Julie laughs easily and right now, she's busting a gut.

Julie's songs are generally serious in nature. Although she embraces rock's structures, she sidesteps its usual adolescent themes in her lyrics, coloring them instead with images and feelings that could only come from an adult life of experience. "I don't really consciously think about what I'm

Julie and Buddy 2000, together, on stage, at last...

doing. I just think, yup, this is Buddy's, when it comes out," she says. "There are two places I can write from, and both of them I enjoy; I can put myself in the place of someone else—have empathy with them. Or I can write from that place from my own heart and express my own situation. Usually, there's a guy's perspective in the stuff I do for Buddy, and I really enjoy going from expressing my own feelings to putting myself in a guy's place. I do have roots in a lot of different kinds of music.

"I grew up with country. My father would always play it, but I have to admit when I was about 15 years old, I'd say, 'If you don't turn that off, I'm literally going to throw up.' And then the Burrito Brothers, and Gram Parsons and Emmylou and some early Linda Ronstadt stuff had me come into it from another angle. I have this country part of me I can really get into, but I don't think my voice can carry doing a totally country thing. But Buddy is as great a country singer as it gets. So I can be this songwriter for this incredible singer who will sing the song, so it's inspiring."

Of those songs Buddy says, "For me, it's the only thing for me that feels comfortable. Julie just kind of writes what's in there—what comes out. Even though I'm coming from a different place, being more country than her, she knows what feels right for me—it's stuff that feels natural to sing about to me."

And what does Buddy contribute to Julie's pieces? "To tell you the truth, just being around and available, to play when inspiration strikes," he says. "I think she likes me to do that. I don't think she needs me for that much—she knows what she wants musically. She knows what she wants the songs to sound like before they're even finished. She'll talk about it in a way she doesn't know what it is, but we've hung out for so long, I'll know what she's talking about. On the other end, left to my own devices, I can tend to be a lot more country than she likes. She'll tell me to stop, and direct things in that way," he says.

"I was thinking…" says Julie, "I've had some people ask me about country music and how it's not really country music these days, it's pop music and all that. I don't really care what music is as long as it's not phony or contrived—if it has a ring of 'I'm doing this so I look good' as opposed to 'I'm doing this because it's in me and I want to get it out.' So I think I could be a fan of most types of music when it comes from that true place inside and its not jivey and show-offy and contrived and fake."

In between stops on a U.S. coheadlining tour, the Millers have a couple of days off at home in Nashville. "Who would think, 'I'm so excited to clean the house!'" says Julie. They're about to begin work on their first collaborative album. "We're probably going to start on it this evening," she says, with the kind of ease one associates with cracking open a bottle of Coca-Cola on a hot Southern night. Although all of their solo recordings are collaborative and made at home, a Buddy and Julie album proper—like a Tammy Wynette and George Jones album once was—is a highly anticipated affair in new-country circles. At first the album was going to be a duets project, but for now that idea seems to have been scrapped. The couple isn't quite sure what's going to end up on it, but Julie's having some fun working up prospective titles: "*Julie, Come Downstairs Where Buddy Is!*" she jokes. "*Julie and Buddy: Together at Last.*"

"We do most of our writing at home," says Buddy. "I don't know that Julie writes too much out on the road, but we can write some music when I'm out there. You don't get a real big block of time when you're out—it's kind of taxing and it's hard. I'm not one of those guys who is very disciplined, spending two hours a day writing. I just want to make it a little looser than that. We just like to have fun with it and hope it always kind of stays that way."

For a couple who operate outside the boundaries of the Nashville scene and spend most of their time on the road, their decision to set up a home studio in Country Music City was, like everything else in their lives, a happy accident. "We always joked about Nashville, but we don't plan things or really figure things out," says Julie. "We were eating spaghetti and Buddy goes, 'You know, if we ever move to Nashville, we could buy a house.' And I took a bite, and he took a bite, and I said, 'OK, well, let's move to Nashville.' I saw the front of one of the Nashville papers and I saw that Emmylou was queen of the Christmas parade, and I was like, 'We'll go be with Emmylou!' We'd met her maybe a year before and she talked all about Nashville, and we thought, 'If Emmylou Harris is there, how bad can it be?!'"

The couple had grown restless with their jobs singing in bars from coast to coast; they'd done stints in Seattle, New York, and L.A., among other stops. For three years in the mid- to late '80s, the pair were living in San Francisco, but weren't playing much music, save the occasional gig at Sacred Grounds, a small cafe that at the time hosted rare folk nights with

love is the answer

players like Guy Clark, Townes Van Zandt, Peter Case, Victoria Williams, and then-local J.C. Hopkins.

"J.C. was sort of an inspiration—what he was doing, just going out and working really hard," says Buddy of Hopkins, a folksinger-cum-Victoria Williams sideman, producer, and contemporary musical theater composer who's since relocated to New York. "And he was supportive. He came over and I recorded some demos for him and eased back in that way. We played at Sacred Grounds—and that's where Julie met Victoria." The Millers have rolled with Williams' Rolling Creek Dippers, a loose group that also includes Jim Lauderdale and Williams' husband, Mark Olson. Williams and Julie Miller, with their naive and quirky mannerisms, unique voices, and shared faith, could be sisters; when they sing together, some of their bits evoke the sibling Southern Gothic of the Louvin Brothers.

The Millers also forged another connection during their stay in San Francisco. "There's a fellow, Joe Goldmark, a pedal steel player, and his wife Kathi,"

Time Line

1952	Buddy born in Fairburn, Ohio
1956	Julie born in Dallas, Texas
mid-1970s	Julie and Buddy meet in Austin, Texas
1983	Julie and Buddy marry
1993	Millers settle in Nashville
1995	Buddy's solo debut, *Your Love and Other Lies*; Steve Earle calls it "the country record of the decade"
1997	Julie makes her secular music debut, *Blue Pony* Buddy releases *Poison Love*
1997–98	Millers open shows for Emmylou Harris and Steve Earle
1999	Julie's *Broken Things* and Buddy's *Cruel Moon* end the year on the *Village Voice*'s annual Pazz and Jop critics poll at numbers 51 and 49, respectively

says Buddy. "When I first got back into playing, I played bass in Kathi's band. I hadn't been playing for years, and that got me back into playing."

Kathi Kamen Goldmark and her husband Joe continue to quietly foster a San Francisco country music underground with their various bands and side projects, unwittingly inspiring musicians like the Millers in the process. They are genuinely complimented and surprised to hear about the role they played in the Millers' career. "He's the best musician I've ever played with," says Kathi.

Her band at the time, Four Shy Guys, had placed a "Bass Player Wanted for Country-Rock Band" ad, and Buddy replied. "He could play every instrument better than anyone in the band," she remembers.

There would be a few more years scraping around before the couple got a break. "I always did want [to make a record], and by the time it came around, I didn't think it would even be happening," says Buddy, who was 43 at the time. "I got sidetracked with a lot of other things, and I was doing whatever I needed to do to pay rent, which a lot of time was playing some real funky gigs. I know how to do a lot of other things that are related to music, so I was always working with something. When the phone rang for me to do a record for Hightone, at that point, I kind of had resigned myself to not doing a record. I don't know what went wrong with their release schedule…maybe somebody fell out, but they needed a record and they asked me if I wanted to do it."

"That sounds like Buddy," laughs Larry Sloven, managing partner of Oakland's Hightone label, who doesn't remember the details of Miller's signing but remembers first coming upon his songs. "Jim Lauderdale said this guitar player friend of his was a great musician, and we thought, sure…" But the label was happy with Buddy's songs and used them for a sampler called *Points West: New Horizons in Country Music*, released in 1990. For whatever reasons, it took five more years for another callback. Buddy debuted with *Your Love and Other Lies* in 1995; the legend surrounding the recording today is that every song on the album has either been covered or is awaiting release by a major country artist. It's also the album that brought him to the attention of fellow artist Steve Earle; the country music outlaw was telling anyone who'd listen he thought it was the best record of that year.

Buddy followed with *Poison Love* and *Cruel Moon*. He continued to tour as a lead guitarist and vocalist with Emmylou Harris' Spyboy Band, and eventually did the same on Steve Earle's *El Corazon* tour. He also co-produced Harris' Spyboy Band album as well as others including Jimmie Dale Gilmore's album *One Endless Night*, and continued to tour as a guitarist with the Emmylou Harris/Linda Ronstadt band.

Meanwhile, Julie had been busy writing and recording her own songs as a Christian artist. On the strength of her contributions to Buddy's debut, she was invited to join the Hightone roster as a solo artist; she made her secular debut with 1997's *Blue Pony* and followed with *Broken Things* in '99. She and Buddy followed with tours opening shows for Earle and Harris. In the late spring of 2000, the pair returned to San Francisco to appear for the first time ever as headliners at Slim's. It was a powerful performance as Buddy showed off his pro but never too slick stuff, while Julie looked visibly, but charmingly, uncomfortable on stage.

"I'm never pleased with my performance—I certainly couldn't bear to watch myself on TV," she says. The Millers had recently finished a taping of a segment for the prestigious public television series, *Austin City Limits*, which Julie had no intention of watching. "I'm so inside myself—if I see myself, it's disconcerting."

Yet the introvert pressed on. "[This] was really always what was in my heart to do," she says. "And the Christian thing was something that I didn't ever really see myself doing. I think I do have things that I could put into song to express my feelings about God to other believers, so I went ahead and did that, but really, I felt it was something just for that period of time. This is what I always intended to do," she says. Although there were roadblocks along the way, Julie kept plugging. "I became a believer in Jesus in 1980, and before that I'd sung in bars for several years, and that's when I started writing songs. I think because I suddenly felt that God loved me whatever I did—like a little kid who draws a picture for his parents—it doesn't matter if it's good or not, the parents love him anyway. And so it set me free to be able to just feel what was in my heart creatively and spiritually. But I always felt God wanted me to be where I had been. That it didn't happen nearly as quickly as I had expected it to, as is the case so often in life…I don't know if you are familiar with the story of Abraham and Sarah

The perfect blend of yin and yang: studio pro Buddy and relaxed Julie

in the Old Testament, but Sarah had this baby when she was 80, and I thought, that's about right, God! I'm 40 years old, and it's time to have this rock and roll baby! That's what I love about God. His timing and his ways are *waaaay* off from what we're picturing."

Married since 1983, Julie credits the success of her and Buddy's creative and romantic partnership to their shared faith. "Not to sound overly religious or dogmatic, but the truth is, we kinda had a relationship before we came to know Jesus, but it was completely explosive and completely nuts and just as crazy and stupid as it gets. Tumultuous. It really is God, because we get our ultimate security and deepest fulfillment from Him, so that we don't have to get all of our deepest fulfillment from one another—we get it from God. He gives you guidelines on how to just be patient with one another and put the other one first. Buddy is the easiest to get along with— he's unselfish and patient and kind just by nature and I'm the opposite. So, if it wasn't for God, oh God, he might be doing OK, but I definitely would not be. We've gone through all kinds of experiences and troubles, but when we made our commitment and abandoned ourselves to God, it's like when we made that commitment to each other...we'll never break it. Unless somebody runs over us and kills us, there's just no way! It's just not even a consideration to break it," she says.

It's also not a consideration for Buddy to don a big hat while Julie stands by her man in hopes of becoming a part of the bigger, flashier Nashville scene. "Maybe a long, long time ago," says Buddy. "At this point, I'm too old to fit in. When I made my first record, I really thought I was making a regular country record. I thought it was along the lines of what was being done in Nashville. I was aware of Steve [Earle] but I didn't know about the No Depression scene—I don't know if it was around then. People were talking about stuff—I didn't know there was a magazine [*No Depression*] yet. I met Steve as a result of my first record and I was a big fan of his, but I didn't think much would come of doing a record. I really didn't think there was a chance of me breaking into Nashville country music. Things have worked out so much better than I imagined they would."

That country music hitmakers are decidedly interested in what the Millers are doing—"Don't Tell Me" and "Does My Ring Burn Your Finger" were recorded by Lee Ann Womack, Brooks & Dunn recorded their "My Love Will Follow You," George Ducas does "I'm Pretending," and Buddy and Lauderdale wrote "Hole in My Head," recorded by the Dixie Chicks— doesn't mean the couple fit in or that there are any "hey y'alls" offered up at the local grocery or coffeeshop. Nor does Julie have any idea how a jazz vocalist, Jimmy Scott, came to record her song, "All My Tears."

"I only saw a documentary on him. I didn't even know who he was," she says. "He's a very unique person. I'm still not exactly sure how he got a hold of the song. I think it somehow came from him hearing Emmylou do it—a producer of Emmylou's or a friend of a producer. I never have heard exactly how that happened. I would really like to know and I'd sure love to meet him. Buddy and I have had people cover our songs we haven't even met," she says. "It's really weird. When I started out in music, I'd see all the names and I imagined all the people being best of friends and knowing everything about each other; maybe it did used to be that way, but it's not like that. It's so strange."

Recommended Recordings

Cruel Moon (Hightone, 1999)

Honky tonkin' is the name of the game for Miller when Julie, Emmylou Harris, and buddy Jim Lauderdale gang up on his third album, featuring the twangy Miller family number "Does My Ring Burn Your Finger," the Earle-penned "I'm Not Getting Any Better at Goodbye," and the Barry Mann and Cynthia Weil standard, "I'm Gonna Be Strong."

Broken Things (Hightone, 1999)

Patti Griffin sits in on the ballad "I Still Cry," Julie's pal Victoria Williams joins her for the folk dirge "Orphan Train," Steve Earle twangles throughout "Strange Lover," and Christmas queen Emmylou duets on the title song. Of course Buddy is also on board for Julie's stunning second secular album.

CHUCK PROPHET AND STEPHANIE FINCH

> "I absolutely had this idea I wanted to be in a band with Chuck Prophet. It took a couple of years. . ."
> —*Stephanie Finch*

Chuck Prophet literally lives large, so we arrange to meet for coffee with one caveat: "It's got to be the right place, because I take up a lot of space," he says. That's OK. He has plenty to shout about.

His fourth solo album, *Homemade Blood*, shows off his stunning songwriting, guitar playing, and vocals—a traditional, rootsy, raw, and heartfelt stew that digs for the source but comes out "sideways." He has a new label, Cooking Vinyl, and he's been to Europe twice since the first of the year; he's off again for the summer for four European festivals and a U.S. tour with his mighty band—Max Butler, guitars; Anders Rundblad, bass; Paul Revelli, drums; and Stephanie Finch, keyboards and vocals. He just saw the release of a live collaboration with buddy and Memphis music legend Jim Dickinson and he remains happily ensconced in his San Francisco digs with his band mate and sweetheart, Finch.

It was Finch who originally had the bright idea nearly ten years ago that the pair play some songs together. Prophet was winding down his commitment with the L.A. Paisley Underground cum roots-rock outfit, Green on Red. The band had devolved into Prophet and founder Dan Stuart making records and tirelessly touring the European markets from which they'd grown a healthy cult audience, and it just so happened that Prophet was looking to spice up the grind. So along with a handful of other players, including Patrick Winningham and Steve Yerkey, Prophet and Finch picked up their guitars and started putting on shows in the back room of the Albion, a sketchy watering hole on 16th Street in San Francisco. And it wouldn't be long before they recorded the loose *Brother Aldo* with a few friends and neighbors—like Chris Isaak's bassist, Roly Salley, and Memphis-soul keyboardist, Spooner Oldham. They followed with the more calculated, backwoodsy *Balinese Dancer*, and *Feast of Hearts*, a record that Prophet believes has some worthy cuts on it, although he wasn't happy with the end result. But with *Homemade Blood*, Prophet is finally pleased with the recorded output.

His song "You've Been Gone," from *Homemade Blood*, perfectly explains his lost-weekend lifetime of experience: "*You've been gone, you've been gone/ clouds make rain and days make years/I think you'll find some changes here.*"

"The line, *Sweet Lorraine's on SSI/her mind walked off before she said goodbye* made me think of all my drinking buddies at the Albion. All of those guys were on SSI. I swear it's gotta be more work than working, but I wouldn't know," Prophet says. Ain't it funny how time slips away?

Eleven years is a long time for anybody to sustain the kind of musical career Prophet has (without ever holding a day job), particularly because his music supersedes trends. His lyrics fuse the honesty and artfulness of Bob Dylan with the tunefulness of, say, Tom Petty. For more contemporary references, you could compare him with the Jayhawks and Wilco (Americana/No Depression), but that would be doing Prophet a big disservice—he belongs in a class by himself. And although his past struggles with drug addiction could make a case for the contrary, Prophet appears to finally be comfortable in his own skin. He looks like rock and roll personified—tall and thin, hair that looks like it's never been washed, a cigarette dangling from his lips— the kind of musician they don't make too many of these days. He was simply born at the wrong time.

Had he been born earlier, his keen sense of rock history and his continual search for "the source" probably would've earned him the accolades of an Eric Clapton or Keith Richards. Had he been born later, he would be as lauded and adept at deconstructing rock as Beck. But Prophet belongs to the middle generation who live in the shadow of Boomer musicians and fans and precede X-ers—a generation that for the most part, doesn't care much about the source.

"I feel like Rip Van Winkle. I got way too many miles on me, man," he says. "I wish I had a generation. I would've made a great slacker, but I'm just a little bit old and I wanted to do things."

So what he does, ever since his days as young guitarist in L.A.'s no-frills Green on Red, is present his songs in a down-home style with none of the artifice that is currently fashionable (think of the lamest band on the charts that uses mandolin and accordion). Yet commercial enthusiasm for Prophet's brand of real songwriting has never reached critical mass, but as someone who's weathered a number of temperature changes within his business, Prophet is no longer one to get worked up over it. Today, he possesses a certain wisdom well beyond someone of his 30-some-odd years.

"Part of being real is what you learn from good literature, like Raymond Carver poems. They're really plain, and the way people talk is really plain, and it's so plain it hurts, because it's not glamorous. If you get real you get closer to the truth, and if you get closer to the truth you get closer to God, and that's art. If there's a just God, those people who are pretending are going to get busted anyway," he jokes.

Funny that a man who looks to rock's poet laureate, Dylan, as king songwriter would be espousing the pleasures of plain. "Most of Dylan's greatest songs are painfully plain," Prophet asserts. "Even though 'In the Garden' has got the most complicated chord structure I can think of, it's really a straightforward song, as is 'Knockin' on Heaven's Door.' You know what he's talking about. Anybody can tie a bunch of lines together, but if you know where you're going with it, then it's a lot harder.

"I could've dressed up the songs on the album in all kinds of gothic shit, and I didn't. People don't need to come to me for that," he states matter-of-factly. "You can't find a source for this music. It comes from some guy strumming a fence on barbed wire. The Stones took traditional music and turned it sideways, and that's what I'm trying to do," he explains.

Prophet's own version of plain songs for his fourth solo album were inspired by a detox break he took in 1996 at his parents' suburban East Bay home, where he went to wean himself "from sucking the glass dick." More commonly known as the crack pipe, he's since kicked it for real.

"I went back home and I realized it was the last place I'd been before I was kind of fucked up, and I could smell everything, and it was weird and brand-new and kind of spooky. That's where I wrote 'K-Mart Family Portrait.' I know exactly what happened. It has a Linda Ronstadt melody from her album, *Mad Love,* that my sister used to have. I got kind of inspired because I got kind of creeped out. I don't really get that when I walk up and

Prophet and Finch in the Mission District years

down 16th Street anymore. I've strip-mined the Mission. There's nothing there," he explains. "And all the rural stuff has been strip-mined, too."

Consequently, the album's deepest vein is that of suburban angst, right down to the artwork, inspired by Bill Owens' influential fine-art photographs of suburbia from the late '60s and early '70s.

"I started having dreams about being a kid," said Prophet. "I'm not precious enough to write my dreams down and think I'm going to turn them into songs, but there was a lot floating around. It was new subject matter to stick into songs—I wanted to stay off the known roads.

"My favorite Raymond Carver poem is the one where he's sitting in his driveway in his station wagon drinking a six-pack, and he can't go inside because his family's in there," Prophet says, no doubt explaining the car parked in front of the pick-a-suburb home on *Homemade Blood*'s cover. When he finished writing, Prophet took his band into the studio to cut the songs live, to give the record the kind of freewheeling feel that the group has developed as a consistent live act.

"Everything was a reaction to spending too much time in the control room on the last record. I wanted to have some fun with the songs and break out of the singer/songwriter mold," he says.

Having kept the lineup intact for some time allowed the band to roll with the free-form and immediate recording process. "I wouldn't have done it like this if I didn't have a band. Stephanie can sing around me, which isn't easy to do, but I never had a guitar player till I found Max. If it gets too comfortable, it's not good, but when we're on the road, we have these telepathic workouts. He knows when I bend over it means to do this—we don't have to talk about it."

As for living with a band mate, "It's weird. You don't really want to show anybody a song till it's done. I got up one night to go to the bathroom, and I went and picked up my guitar and Stephanie was yelling, 'What are ya doin' in there?' and I was whispering a song into a tape recorder. I yelled back, 'I'm writin' a song.' When I'm just pulling things out of the air, I don't want anyone around."

"Credit" is one of those fantastic songs that came out of the air while Prophet and one of his repeat collaborators, Kurt Lipschutz (credited as klipschutz), were working together. "It's one of those character songs and a play on words. A song like 'My Generation' doesn't look very good on paper, but when he stutters it means so much more. Or like 'Unsatisfied," by Paul Westerberg, when he screams—it means so much. When my friend Kurt and I printed it out and it didn't look that good, we thought, 'We're really on to something now,'" he laughs. "And I get to scream in it," he says, "I want some CREDIT."

Prophet has more credits on his resume than your average musician most people haven't heard of. He doesn't really look for outside projects, but he says they often find him. He played guitar on little-known singer/songwriter Calvin Russell's album. "He used to walk about ten steps behind Townes Van Zandt," he explains. It was produced by Dickinson and features the legendary Muscle Shoals rhythm section. "It's a Top 30 album in France, as we speak. And I got to record in Memphis with Dickinson, and that was great." Last year, he recorded with another songwriter's sidekick, Dylan's pal, Bob Neuwirth. Prophet spoke of the thrill of recording with yet another legend.

"There were eight guitar players in the room...Steven Soles, Billy Swan, Neuwirth, Rosie Flores...we did a rundown of the song, and I wasn't sure who was going to play guitar, and Swan said, 'you take the lead,' and I got to play my Telecaster with Billy Swan playing rhythm guitar. He played rhythm guitar for Kristofferson, you know?"

He also recorded with beat poet Herbert Hunke. "He's dead now, so no one else is going to get to do that. I'm not the biggest Chuck Prophet fan, so I don't have 50 side projects where I think everything I touch should be released. I do a lot of things and most of them are invisible, and they probably just should be.

"I'd still like to do a record with Stephanie, but we move at our own tempo," he says.

Although he may have profited more had been born alongside his spiritual mentors—Dylan, Petty, Springsteen, Young, Dickinson, Van Zandt, Kristofferson, Neuwirth, Chilton, and the like, Prophet won't back down. Plus, he's already made a couple of marks on the pages of rock history. "I survived the Paisley Underground—now that was dumb. Some journalist was trying to get me to dis the No Depression movement—I wouldn't, as long as we understand they didn't invent it. I actually think Uncle Tupelo were pretty good, and I like Wilco," he says breezily.

"I'm not nostalgic and I don't think things used to be better. I think these are the good old days."

Three years later, I spoke to Prophet and Finch upon their return home to San Francisco from their first-ever American tour, preparing to leave for the second leg.

"We were playing this gig in Tampa, and there were all these people there and they knew the words to the songs…the old albums!" says Prophet. The Iguanas were there, Alejandro Escovedo was there, the Waco Brothers were there, and it was amazing. Everyone had really great shows. People amazed me at these radio stations, the nonprofits; they know all this stuff about music and they're incredibly supportive. The guy in the Iguanas said, 'If every city had a station like this, we'd be rock stars.' I told him, 'I learned a long time ago, fair isn't fair.'"

In Randy Newman's song, "It's Money That Matters," he sings how the real heroes of society are the people who work for free at public radio stations and for minimum wage in bookstores.

"Yeah, yeah, yeah," says Prophet. "'*All those people are so much brighter than I am/In a fair system, they would flourish and thrive,*'" Prophet quotes,

"'*But they barely/get by/they eke out a living/they got babies in knapsacks on their backs …*' I totally agree! For me, rock and roll, when it all comes together, is high art, it's divine, it's closer to God than anything else. But it is such a paltry ambition, to play rock and roll. It's pretty pathetic. And sometimes I don't even feel like I'm in the music business."

Homemade Blood turned out to have a less than visible profile on these shores (although it was named the top record of 1997 by critics in *Rolling Stone* in Germany and was described as "essential listening," by English popular music bible *MOJO*). But since then, Prophet and Finch have returned to doing what they do best and went back to work. They made *The Hurting Business*, a stylistic departure: between the cut-and-paste grooves, which feature the work of a turntablist, Prophet says, "It's super-traditional. I'm completely a slave to traditional structure. The challenge now is how we can bend that beyond recognition."

He's had to add more pages to the old resume as offers for collaborations and work for hire continue to find him. He played guitar for alternative group Cake and country's Kim Ritchey, and he wrote for alternative country artist Kelly Willis. In between, he made regular trips to Nashville looking for a hit.

Time Line

1985–92	Prophet joins L.A. Paisley Underground cum roots-rock band, Green on Red
1990	Prophet and band (with Stephanie Finch) release solo debut album, *Brother Aldo*
1993	*Balinese Dancer*
1995	*Feast of Hearts*
1997	*Homemade Blood*
1998	Chuck Prophet and Stephanie Finch marry
1999	Stephanie Finch forms pop band, Go-Go Market, with Chuck Prophet
2000	*The Hurting Business* released
	First U.S. tour for Chuck Prophet Band

In 1998, Prophet and Finch got married. Following a traditional church wedding, the couple threw a rock and roll reception at a local nightclub and scene of many of their local live triumphs. And as promised, they got to record Finch's songs when she struck up her own band, Go-Go Market. All is well at home and abroad.

"I said to Chuck, we should have done a tour seven years ago. But there are certain things that are lined up more around this record," says Finch. "We were on labels that didn't even have phones, from what I could tell," says Prophet. "All that planetary alignment crap—what do they call it now…synergy…at least three things going on at the same time, like a booking agent, a label, and an artist thinking along the same lines…those things never really came together," he says. "Probably through our own dysfunction and a random element. Whereas in Europe, we were dealing with small territories and small labels, and we'd return there and it wasn't rocket science to do it."

But far from being played-out like others who've been on the treadmill for awhile, Prophet feels like he's just beginning. He's nothing but grateful for his past and present circumstances. "I feel like I've had really good luck with all that stuff. All things considered. I'm always amazed. But you bum out. You see other people, and you think, 'Why?' I see people and I think there's holes here and you should patch that there, take that thing down, rotate the tires, and take care of it. Work on it. You never want to think of yourself as being that way," he admits.

"We had really high moments, like that radio station show, and then the festival that was going to pay for the whole tour fell through, and we had to send the band home, and Chuck and I stayed in a Motel 6 and the people below us were going in and out to score crack all night, and I thought, 'Well, I hope this was worth it,'" says Finch. In the end it was, because this time, something about their album captured a pocket of attention in the heartland and the southland.

"I think the most fun we had was when we first started playing and never made a record," says Prophet. "When we made the record, it was one of those rare things where nobody gave a shit, no one was looking. You may not have known this," he says to Finch, "but I'd already been chewed up by the machine and I wasn't really thinking I was gonna get a second big go-around, because Green on Red already had nine lives. So when we made *Brother Aldo* we just put it out there and thought if people respond, maybe we'll make another one. And then somebody said, why don't you come make a record for us? It was always kind of like that. We didn't start out thinking that grand. It was enough to just do it."

"Back then I had such a naive approach to everything," says Finch. "My aspirations weren't big. Everything that I wanted to happen was happening. I thought, 'I'd like to be in a band with Chuck Prophet.'" So, she moved from Southern California to San Francisco. "And then I thought, I'd like to play at the Great American Music Hall, and we did that. And then I thought, I'd like to make a record, and we did that."

"That was one of my favorite periods of time ever," says Prophet. "And I told everybody when they started getting cranky, 'This is gonna be as good as it gets. You'll look back on this and think, "Man, it was really happening."' I knew when everything started to get professional, it was gonna be a drag."

Prophet and Finch only had five or six songs in 1989, yet they'd find themselves in support slots at the Fillmore, like one time when they opened for Nanci Griffith. "Stephanie had just started playing guitar, and had just like a handful of cowboy chords," remembers Prophet.

"Or else I would put cardboard under the strings and play like it was a rhythm thing," says Finch. "I was having a really good time! In hindsight, it was really bad. It was endearing, I guess, but I could never figure out why Chuck was so miserable after the show. Now I know!" "That's the funny thing. I wouldn't have done it if you hadn't had that spirit," he says. "I've always been a collaborator. That's one thing that hasn't changed at all. Later things got harder, and we had to start listening to what the song needed instead of what our needs were, and that's when we had to kind of…get better. Initially, we were just doin' it. But a lot of times there were tears. And a lot of times we worked with producers who may not have been enamored with our thing as much as we were, so we were forced to step back and look at it and reevaluate it. But our relationship probably survived because it was never show business."

"That's not to say that after that there weren't a lot of disappointments," says Finch. "And the way the music went—it was getting louder and louder. I had to keep up all the time. I started out on accordion and eventually ended up on Farfisa just to cut through all the sound."

In many ways, Finch is the perfect opposite of her husband. Whereas Prophet is a loud and commanding presence, opinionated and often con-

*Prophet and Finch shift into
mid-career, world stage-mode*

tradictory, Finch is quiet, bordering on shy, although she has a point of view
and isn't timid about asserting it. And although Prophet will be the first to
admit that he's hardly everybody's best friend, I've never met anyone who
didn't like Finch. Fashionistas would describe her as gamine; compared to
Prophet's rock and roll good ol' boy, she is positively genteel. In every way,

they are each other's better halves—in the best sense of that outmoded expression.

Even before they toured extensively behind *Homemade Blood* in '97–'98, Finch was getting the itch to step into the spotlight and had had the seedlings of an idea for her own recordings. "I was cowriting the songs for Go-Go Market with a mutual friend while Chuck was out of town, and he came home and he sorta pushed his way in. Which is how I was hoping it would happen, that I wouldn't have to seduce him into it or say, 'Now that I've done this for you for so long, will you…' I didn't have to."

"When you're lucky enough to find good people to work with, everything's a collaborative process," explains Prophet. "Some people will bring a lot of experience to it and some people will bring a certain sensibility, some people will bring craft, but you want people to bring love to it—that's the thing." He simply wasn't going to let an opportunity to pitch in for his wife pass him by. "I never thought that anyone was going to care more than I did…there's just no way."

The Finch-led Go-Go Market is a swingin' amalgam of Dusty Springfield strength, Mantovani string and horn tracks, and funky, back-porch soul music. "The songs themselves, just me on the guitar, could've gone [a folk] way," she explains. "But then we started to write songs that were more conducive to the band members we had at the time. And the more we started writing the songs, it developed into its own thing."

"If you trust the process and you trust everyone involved and you let 'em go, they'll inevitably bring more to it then you could ever imagine," explains Prophet. "Instead of saying, 'I'm hearing this horn part and it goes like this,' if you chill out and keep your ears open, then they'll bring something maybe beyond. I've heard people talk that way about actors—just letting them do their thing. We were trying to cut real understated, stoic stealth tracks, as if we were the American House Band—that was kind of my fantasy. I really thought we were doing something that people should hear." And so before Go-Go Market had even released a CD, the roots rock band Vagabond Lovers picked up on their song "Him," and released it on theirs.

"We feel like we actually did our job!" says Prophet. "To have somebody cut it was gratifying. It lends this kind of credibility to a song, because other people can sing it. Stephie wasn't so excited about it, though," he says.

"When the CD was mailed to us and I actually *heard* it, I got kind of excited," she counters. Aside from the unexpected cover the first time out, there was another bonus in starting a new band; the pair could play live gigs again without a lot of fanfare. It was a practice Prophet had given up a long time ago—at least locally—that pesky professionalism to which he referred to as having taken the fun out of playing his own music.

"We got to the point where we were making records, and the machine itself, the band, it's like you're on this steamship and you want to pull a U turn, and it takes like a day. This is like, not fun," he explains. "This isn't like the Albion, where we could write a song on Thursday, play it on Friday, work on it, and do it again on Saturday. I'm always gravitating towards what's more fun—what's more instantly exciting, because I'm a spaz. It's just the way I am."

As they prepared to leave for tour again, revisiting some of their new friends in the U.S. and expanding their North American territories further, the band was up against one such dilemma: Prophet band member Max Butler was sidelined by commitments to another band, effectively turning the Prophet band into a four-piece with new bassist "Teenage" Rob Douglas and new drummer Winston Watson (known primarily for working with Bob Dylan).

"We've been doing gigs as a four-piece—this is a huge argument we just had earlier tonight. I mean a huge argument. I want to play more gigs as a five-piece, and Stephie likes it better as a four-piece. What are ya gonna do?"

"Hear my logic," says Finch. "We can't afford to go on the road with a five-piece." The couple continues to work out a resolution to the four-piece/five-piece dilemma while they attempt to explain their varying logics. For tonight, there appears to be no answer.

"Couples fight about money—that's what I've heard," says Prophet. "We don't really fight about money. There's been years where it's just been horrible. There's been times where it was like, 'What happened to the PG&E bill?' 'I got my speaker re-coned, man, and it sounds *goood!*' It's just irrational and it's not practical," he says by way of copping to his missteps. "Strangely enough, as bad as things get, as much as a strain as it is on our relationship, when we go out on the road, which is completely dehumanizing and grueling, the gigs are generally great, and when the music's good—it's brought us closer together. And it's amazing how when you're playing, it just goes away.

Things could be as hopeless and dismal and dark as you could possibly imagine in the relationship, but when we're playing it just goes away. I can be in a tizzy on stage and I can see everybody getting tense, and she's just laughing, she's not scared of me."

Prophet is never one to underestimate his circumstances as a working musician with a life partner who shares his persistence in this business of making music together. The way he sees it, at this point it's no longer optional to think of anything else. "There's a body of work and we get to do all this stuff. We don't really get to choose what we want to do. It's too bad, but we don't," he says.

"Yeah, I guess it's just…" Finch begins.

"We're in," Prophet finishes.

"Yeah, we're in," Finch says.

Recommended Recordings

Homemade Blood (Cooking Vinyl, 1998)

Prophet and band are captured live in the studio. Inspired by a series of semiautobiographical stories, the singer-songwriter and fiery guitarist gives his sideways spin to traditional sounds and comes up with a compelling group of downbeat but hopeful songs.

The Hurting Business (Hightone, 2000)

Stretching out in a stylistic departure incorporating a turntablist, found sound, and Farfisa organ, Prophet brings his songs into the present with the same ease and panache he brought to roots rock. The title song features Finch on wacky vocals; "God's Arms" goes Eastern, and "Lucky" is all mood and beat treatment with a great chorus.

psycho killers, qu'est-ce que c'est?

Elvis Costello
Talking Heads
Tom Verlaine
Elvis Costello
Talking Heads

the new wave

Tom Verlaine
Elvis Costello
Talking Heads

i have to admit, I would not count the 1977 debut albums by the Talking Heads, Elvis Costello, or Television among my top 10 or even top 20 recordings of all time. But if I were asked to name the artists whose work most contributed to the shaping of the music that immediately followed theirs (the college and alternative rock of the early '80s) and the so-called alternative music on today's charts, then I would have to say that those artists and their albums—along with the Sex Pistols' and the Ramones' debuts—are in the top five, without question. So what do the terribly influential punk-era artists Talking Heads, Elvis Costello, and Television have to do with breaking the rules of rock and roll? Well, just about everything.

For those who've forgotten, here's a quick recap: punk was the great noise that shook rock music to its core about 20 years after its inception, at the height of what was known as '70s corporate or dinosaur rock. The rebellion began in the late '60s with the sonic boom of the MC5, Velvet Underground, and the Stooges; it spread a little further with the loud and snotty glam of the New York Dolls and the naive/bad attitude of Jonathan Richman; it blasted like a rocket out of New York in 1974–75 with the birth of the Ramones. Down in the Bowery, the bands formed in clubs like CBGBs and Max's Kansas City: Patti Smith, Television, the Heartbreakers, the Dead Boys, Blondie, Talking Heads.

Punk made its way to England via the Ramones and into the international headlines with the Sex Pistols. The summer of '76 saw the overseas emergence of the Clash, the Damned, the Buzzcocks; then came the Stranglers, X-Ray Spex, Costello, and many more. Or so the legend goes.

Since most of my cues on how to live as a teenager came from music and musicians from a distance, the art school snobs and bratty, angry individuals who populated the new wave and punk rock scene felt like my people. As an adult, my preconceived ideas about the Talking Heads, Elvis Costello, and Tom Verlaine as artists and musicians were so deeply ingrained and hard to shake, I tended toward writing about them as if I knew them, or worse, as if I was conducting a therapy session. It's only now that I see that these interviews could easily be interpreted as psychoanalytical portraits of the artists. Ugh. My only defense is that the music of my subjects had its greatest impact on my life as an adolescent—an age when most of us are impressionable and think we know everything. It's a time to shape ideas about who we will be and what we will stand for as young adults. Obviously, my feelings about the Talking Heads, Tom Verlaine, and Elvis Costello are tied to my adolescence, a period to which I've long been attached (a phenomenon, for better or worse, not uncommon to those of us whose lives are intrinsically linked to rock and roll). I believe I have better ideas and stronger insights into all this now, in part thanks to these interviews, which happened in the late '90s, exactly 20 years after the music had had its initial impact on people like me.

One of the conditions of interviewing ex-Television songwriter, guitarist, and vocalist Tom Verlaine was that there be "no discussion of the old days," and I understood where the line between old and new would be drawn. Old meant no discussion of his two recordings with Television circa 1977–78. As a journalist, I think there is nothing worse than being given direction at the top of an interview—it tends to bring out a bad punk-rock attitude in me. So it must be acknowledged then that the Wild West, gonzo and freewheeling, drug-taking, "I'm with the band" days for journalists as depicted in films like *Almost Famous* and insider documentaries like Robert Frank's *Cocksucker Blues* or D.A. Pennebaker's *Don't Look Back*, are a thing of the past (with a few rare exceptions).

That said, it was to my great surprise that the extraordinary guitarist Verlaine was a ordinary, nice guy to interview who didn't seem to mind when the subject neared the old days. After over 20 years in the business, and as a founder and reluctant spokesperson for New York punk rock, it's understandable that he'd be worn out talking about it. The low-key Verlaine's reason for talking at all was that he was about to appear at the 1999 San Francisco International Film Festival with his musical partner, Jimmy Rip, to play a live accompaniment to a series of five short silent films. Verlaine has recorded plenty of instrumental music and music for film, which, while not so much a departure from the downtown New York milieu with which he has long been associated, is definitely not rock and roll.

Although he doesn't paint himself to be a spokesperson for any one group, as one of punk's heritage artists, Verlaine has found himself (like many others of his generation who've shifted their musical focus) without a record deal and thus no easy way to get his current recordings heard. He discussed how the major and indie label system had failed him, how the Internet might help him, and how artists like him might prepare themselves for their artistic and financial futures—without any bitterness or remorse associated with those subjects.

I'd expected notorious curmudgeon Elvis Costello to fire a few shots at me, but maybe that's because I wanted to fire some at him. By the time I interviewed him in 1996, I'd long stopped listening to Costello's music for pleasure; in fact, the idea of it caused me pain. Even as I write this, I wince; some of the records in his catalog really disagree with me. Inspired by the old Costello and his infamous rancor, I even began a review of one of his late '90s concert appearances with these rather impulsive assertions:

"Elvis Costello hasn't made a decent record since 1986. This is a widely held belief among critics and fans who've followed his career closely since 1977, and they are largely the people who stayed away from his sold-out show Thursday night at the Warfield in San Francisco. Instead, the seats were filled with misguided souls who wrest meaning out of Costello's more recent work…"

I wish I could take it back. But I include the review in its entirety here for some cheap laughs as well as to illustrate the depths of passion and contempt music can inspire. Only truly great music can do that; bad music isn't worth thinking about that hard.

In 1996, Costello's song "God Give Me Strength," a gut-wrenching tale of love lost penned with Burt Bacharach for the Allison Anders movie *Grace of My Heart*, had actually restored my faith in his songcraft. Whatever I think or thought of Costello's "less interesting period"—the collaborations with string quartets, the oratorios, and outside songwriting for hire—ceased to be relevant, because his music had once again touched me. I felt something I hadn't since 1986's *King of America;* what ensued was one of those joyous rediscovery periods when everything I'd ever loved about his music came rushing back to me—those basic qualities like smart lyrics and Beatles-caliber melodies. All the quirks and ticks and mannerisms that annoyed me, in particular during his performances, faded away.

So the interview with Costello was admittedly loaded, if only in my mind. When we spoke, Costello was tentative. He explained he'd been put in the difficult position of having to defend his album, *All This Useless Beauty,* which had been largely dismissed by critics. And so, although I'd expected an acerbic, snappish, and intimidating figure with an arch wit—in other words, a caricature of Costello or a character from one of his bile-filled songs—instead I got a person who dared to admit that his work being slammed was hurtful to him. EC had gotten older, and changed the way he chose to communicate—both through music and publicly; honestly, instead of angrily. As a fan, I'd perceived him to have taken musical missteps and cast judgment on him; as a critic I'd maligned him. As his fan again, I wanted to forgive him, and it felt good to be back on his side.

The concept of forgiveness is not something that seems to have permeated the Talking Heads camp, although it was officially dubbed a '90s trend by the media. Twenty-plus years after forming, its members are still at odds with each other, although that doesn't take away the Talking Heads' collective contribution to rock music.

"We kind of spearheaded two things—the new wave alternative approach," says Tina Weymouth, former bassist for the group, "while at the same time we espoused complete integration of funk into the performance." She's right. The Talking Heads were not only among the first bands among the downtown New York punk set to converge on CBGB's and Max's Kansas City in the mid-'70s, but by their second album, 1979's *More Songs About Buildings and Food* (their first of three with producer Brian Eno, who helped them to make two more watershed recordings, *Fear of Music* and *Remain in Light*), they began to incorporate funk, and later, world beats—specifically African rhythms—into their art-school sound. As the Talking Heads, vocalist and lyricist David Byrne; drummer Chris Frantz; bassist Weymouth and multi-instrumentalist Jerry Harrison had an official tenure that spanned 20 years, although throughout there were stops and starts, side projects, and family business to tend to. From 1984–94, their last ten years as a band, they didn't perform live at all. Yet in their absence, their legacy as musical pioneers began to crystallize; their stature as part of new wave's first wave is unquestionable, and the increasing integration of world music into rock was in no small part due to the band's interest in it. Their unique spin on performance, rock and roll, and world music was captured on celluloid for all time by director Jonathan Demme in his 1984 film *Stop Making Sense*, which documented the band at the apotheosis of its career. It was on the occasion of the film's 15th anniversary in 1999, when a new, digitally remastered print of the film opened at the San Francisco International Film Festival, that the four members of the Talking Heads reunited for the first time since their break up in 1994. And what a time it was, as you will read…

Whether you still play their records at home or never did, the Talking Heads, Elvis Costello, and Tom Verlaine belong in the pantheon of rule-breaking rock greats; their punk-era status is important, although not necessarily what singles them out as rulebreakers. They are great because as they moved beyond the messy, rebellious three-chord genre, they matured into respected artists whose work embraced multiple forms of music. They are great because they expressed themselves in new and daring ways at a time when conformity was the order of the day. They are great because their example allowed others to do the same, whether it was in music, film, visual art, or life. They are great because they played loud. Great because they were arrogant and snotty and then had the humility to temper themselves as they got older. Great because they continue to blow all expectations of what is expected of them. Great because back then, they wore their short hair and clothes with an insouciance that helped to define the next 20 years of hipster fashion, and they still keep it sharp. Great because their music has meant so much to so many, especially other musicians. Great because collectively, they've contributed songs like "Marquee Moon," "Psycho Killer," "Alison," "See No Evil," "Pump It Up," "Radio, Radio," "For Artists Only," "Red Shoes," "Glory," "Accidents Will Happen," "Once in a Lifetime" and (insert your favorite here), to the eternal rock and roll songbook. Anyone who recognized the spark in them was on to something. By adopting the spirit of rebellion and the musical standards of excellence brought forth by the Talking Heads, Elvis Costello, and Tom Verlaine, any musicians and visual artists who followed in their wake cultivated and nurtured values born in the punk-rock tradition—most significantly, a dedication to upsetting the status quo. And whether that's in our own worlds or in the world at large, I think it's a great idea. "Thank you for sending me an angel."

TOM VERLAINE

> "Time is expressed in the heart of an instrument
> something that stops in the heart of a man..."
> —*Patti Smith*

I ask Tom Verlaine if he's been busy in the studio today and he laughs. "Not really." With three finished albums yet to see release and a program of silent films he's accompanying at the upcoming San Francisco International Film Festival, he's feeling pretty relaxed, so we start talking pictures instead of music.

"I don't think there's a whole pile of great films that have been made in the last ten years, and I think everyone else kind of agrees—kind of really bad billion-dollar films," he says. "I think it partially has to do with the writers and films being made by committee. Classically, a production committee doesn't turn out a good film; rather, it should be a collaboration between a writer and a director. But they didn't collaborate in the old days, either— the writers always complained about the directors and the directors complained about this and that..."

"On the other hand, there's a lot of indie films that seem to exploit something that those films don't. Some of those aren't very good either. A silent is in a way easier than working with a talkie, because you don't have to work with dialogue."

Or a living director.

"That's right. And I've always written a lot more instrumental music than I have songs, so there's a lot of stuff I have around—some of which worked with the films—so that was kinda fun, too."

Verlaine, along with guitarist Jimmy Rip is to accompany five silent shorts at the festival: *Emak Bakia* by Man Ray, *Ballet Mécanique* by Fernand Leger,

Fall of the House of Usher by Dr. James Sibley Watson, *Brumes D'Automne (Autumn Mist)*, by Dimitri Kirsanoff, and *De Naede Faergen (They Caught the Ferry)* by Carl Theodor Dreyer.

"It's particularly fun because in the shorter films, some of them might have slower sections, but it's not like sitting through an hour-and-a-half film where you have to develop all kinds of things or watch out for dialogue. You just sort of figure out the mood, watch it a million times, play along, figure out what you like and don't like, and figure out how to interpret the director, even although you may be totally off," he chuckles. "It's hard to think what these directors might think of it," he chuckles again, "they might think it's really bizarre."

"I'd seen a couple a really long time ago—maybe at a museum show in the '70s—like the Man Ray films and the *Ballet Mécanique*," he continues. "The *Ballet Mécanique* had a score written by a composer with percussion instruments—I remember it was kinda fun."

So how do his scores compare to the originals?

"Two electric guitars with a lot of effects going, it's a little more *modern*, I guess is the word. There's improvisation, but it is structured to scenes, so it's very much a film with live music rather than a live music concert with a film behind it on the wall. I'm very much hoping we can sit in the orchestra pit or front row, because there's nothing to watch except the film. It's totally eye-on-the-screen playing."

Doing the work, which was cocommissioned by the Wexner Center for the Arts in Columbus, Ohio, and Tim Lanza of the Douris Corporation (through a grant from the Ohio Arts Council), was a gradual process. "I was sent things on video over the period of a year. The first ones were longish and someone came up with the idea of a program of shorter films by different directors, which I really liked because of the variety involved. I saw a bunch of those and basically we agreed on six or seven."

Verlaine and Rip have committed the silent film scores to tape and hope to release them. "We should've finished it last year, before we started, because people have been saying if we were selling it in the lobby, people would be grabbing it up. Because it not only commemorates an event, it's really listenable."

In addition, Verlaine has a completed instrumental record and a vocal record that just needs a little finishing. "I have three records laying around. That's why I haven't had anything out in so long," he says. "I tend to be really lazy or unambitious about it all. It's just a matter of how to get it out there. I think the one with Jimmy will be the first one, because it's done. But whether we're going to do it through a Web site or through a store or through a distributor…I don't know. It's easier nowadays to do it yourself, but on the other hand, there are lots of details. Like, a distributor wants to sell it on his own Web site, and we have to come to agreements on what the price is going to be on their Web site, and what this is going to be and that's going to be, so there's some talking to do."

That accounts for the last couple of years in the life of Tom Verlaine, but he has a long history prior to updating silent film scores. His people (well, actually just one guy) say we are not to speak of those times, so here's the backstory, as it's commonly known:

Verlaine was the cofounder, along with Richard Hell, of one of the first American punk bands, Television. As early as 1971, the pair (formerly known as Tom Miller and Richard Meyers) were playing as the Neon Boys with drummer Billy Ficca. It took until 1973 and the addition of Richard Lloyd on guitar to become Television. Aside from the so-called pre-punk New York Dolls and the developing Patti Smith/Lenny Kaye duo, it's arguable that Television were the first New York punk band to play live (although the Patti Smith Group beat them with a 45 rpm single).

Television's recording debut came with the summer of '75 single, "Little Johnny Jewel." Nearly two years later, *Marquee Moon* was released; it's considered to be among the all-time greatest punk records (although it wasn't particularly punk), if not one of the all-time greatest records period, in no small part due to Verlaine's edgy guitar with vocals to match. It was an atypical punk album; the songs were long—the title song, at nearly ten minutes, was an outrage—as were the guitar workouts, which were not exactly de rigueur, yet they became Verlaine's stock in trade. The sleeve notes, also very uncharacteristic for the era, were careful to point out who played which *solos* (the note on "Marquee Moon" reads, "Richard after the second chorus, Tom after the third"). Meandering guitar notwithstanding, the stripped-down sound and whiny vocal approach sounded different enough alongside the corporate rock that had saturated the mid-'70s to make Television stand out as new. Verlaine stood head and shoulders above his peers not only because he had a more complex vibe to his playing, but because he's also really...tall. But Television pulled the plug shortly after the release of their second album, *Adventure*. Although they'd sufficiently impressed critics and earned what can only be called a cult following, according to most accounts there was one major problem: The band mates never really got along.

But Television's guitar rock, provided by the distinct sound of Verlaine's Fender Jazztone, would later become one of the prime motivators behind the second wave of American guitar bands that flourished in the early '80s. In particular, R.E.M. pointed to them as an early influence and at one time covered their "See No Evil." It was right around that time that Verlaine graduated to releasing a series of moody, guitar-based solo records, one after the other: his self-titled debut was followed quickly by *Dreamtime* and *Words from the Front*, and all were critically well received. And then he started to slow down; while he'd surface every couple of years, after the '89 album *The Wonder*, Verlaine began moving farther and farther away from the rock realm. His most recent release, 1992's *Warm and Cool*, was instrumental. That same year, he also re-formed Television for an album and a tour. So he's spent the last eight years or more in a different mode, working on his instrumentals, scoring the independent film *Love and a .45*, working with Rip on the shorts, and sitting in (or rather, sitting down—he had an injured lower limb) on tour with Patti Smith. I ask Verlaine if he's through with rock music.

"I wouldn't say that. The way it is now is incredibly complicated and expensive. It's also really hard to deal with, because the people who used to be at music companies I think, even in the '50s, may've been crooked or this or that, but they were music lovers. Now they're kind of like, 'I'm only going to be here a year because I want to do video promotion,' you know? There's no way to establish anything with people in companies. It's not completely true, but it tends to be true. There's trouble with indie companies, too. Some of them tend to be great, honest, music-loving people but...it's something I have to look at again."

For the time being, the lower-profile, specialized work suits him. He may

Head and shoulders above the rest,
Television-era Tom Verlaine

even work up a program of different silent films for museum and festival presentation in 2002. He prefers the logistics of working with film over the contemporary music business. "This is a whole lot better, because the film foundation sends out what they have, what's available, and the price. So I literally don't have to do anything except sign a contract, which is great for me. Record contracts, the record business now, is so vastly different than when

Time Line

1949	Tom Verlaine born in New Jersey
1971	Tom Miller and Richard Meyers (Richard Hell) form the Neon Boys
1973	Tom Verlaine, Fred Smith, Richard Lloyd, and Billy Ficca debut as Television
1975	"Little Johnny Jewel" single
1977	*Marquee Moon*
1978	*Adventure*
	Television disband
1979	Solo debut, *Tom Verlaine*
1981	*Dreamtime*
1982	*Words from the Front*
1984	*Cover*
1986	*Flashlight*
1989	*The Wonder*
1991	Television re-forms
1992	*Warm and Cool* solo album
	Television reunion album, *Television*
1993	*Love and a .45* (soundtrack)
	Television disbands again
1999	*Original Music for Silent Film* debuts with co-guitarist Jimmy Rip

I was involved in it, I don't mind not being involved in it. Particularly the way things have changed toward marketing certain things now instead of developing things."

He has no plans to reprise his performances with Patti Smith as she continues to tour. "I think she wanted something extra for her comeback tour," he says of his involvement with his co-New York punk-pioneer and one-time girlfriend. "After her husband passed away, she asked if I would do something on the record or on the tour and I said yeah, I could do that."

Just a few hours prior to speaking to Verlaine, I'd read news that he had auctioned his famous Fender Jazzmaster guitar, the one he used to record *Marquee Moon*, on eBay. It was reported as having sold for over $30,000. He's taken aback that reports of the sale of his guitar are already making the rounds of online chatrooms and mailing lists.

He explains, "Yes, a dealer sold it. But it was all a big bunch of baloney. It was a phony bidder with a phony e-mail and a phony phone number. So everybody said, 'Jeez, Tom you're rich,' but I said, 'seeing is believing.' The dealer started tracing it, and it was all complete bunk. To tell you the truth, I hadn't played that guitar for a couple of years. The guitar itself is a really great old Fender, as they say, but I always play this other stuff I have around my house, so I thought maybe I'll just sell this. Apparently if you put up [for auction] a record or a book or something simple, you don't have troubles, but once you put up stuff upwards of a couple of thousand, you get idiots having their fun there."

I tell him I'm sorry it wasn't the gold mine his friends had anticipated for him. "I'm not living in poverty," he says, "but I'm not wealthy…it was just really an experiment."

I never doubted (nor even considered, really) Verlaine's financial status, but as we consider the Jazzmaster's fate, we tread dangerously close to the *verboten* territory known as the "old days." It seems like a natural time to close, but it's a shame. I hadn't yet had the chance to tell him that throughout 1977, I listened to side one of *Marquee Moon* every day after school.

Recommended Recording

Marquee Moon (Elektra, 1977)

An epic punk rock–era record, *Marquee Moon* is atypical. Television dabbled in urban noir like other punks, but they didn't throw the baby out with the bathwater; instead, they incorporated long, interweaving guitar passages into their sound, and came up with something wholly unique. The intensity between guitar players Tom Verlaine and Richard Lloyd and their edgy influence is as timeless as it is electrifying, over 20 years later.

10

ELVIS COSTELLO

> **"I'm not angry anymore."**
> —*Elvis Costello*

e lvis Costello, that former angry young man of rock, is neither young nor particularly angry anymore. But resist the obvious temptation to perceive him as a mellow, middle-aged man. At 46, Costello is middle-aged all right, but he's definitely not mellow.

Ten years after abandoning his band the Attractions to pursue a solo career, Costello has filled out his artistic resume with work in film, theater, and classical music. He's collaborated with an impressive roll call of musicians, either composing for them or having his songs covered by them. In 1996, he hired the indefatigable Attractions again to record and tour for his *All This Useless Beauty* tour.

"All of the projects give me more links to draw from," says Costello, explaining his return to rock. "You go through a door here, a door there; it doesn't necessarily mean you don't want to go back," he says. This time, he simply used a different door.

The grown-up, gentle sounds of *All This Useless Beauty* would seem to be an outgrowth of his many years away from the band. Although they had reconvened in 1994 for the recording of *Brutal Youth*, Costello began branching out as early as 1986, when he called in legendary jazz bassist Ray Brown and guitarist James Burton (the other Elvis' guitarist) for the recording of his fifth album, the rootsy *King of America*. At the time he told journalist Bill Flanagan, "I've lost interest in pop music. Most of it bores the pants off me… I've lost my love for the neurosis of the pop process."

Presumably, when pop maestro Paul McCartney contacted Costello in 1987 looking to collaborate, Costello, a lifelong Beatles fan, let his interest in

115

pop music resurface. For the listener, sadly, the pairing was more exciting in theory than in reality. The fruits of the songwriting duo first showed up on a B-side, followed by tracks on Costello's albums *Spike* (the sparkly pop "Veronica" and the throwaway "Pads, Paws and Claws") and *Mighty Like a Rose* (the triumphant "So Like Candy" and the lesser "Playboy to a Man"), and McCartney's 1989 album, *Flowers in the Dirt* (the Top 40 "My Brave Face").

By 1992, Costello had made a foray into classical music, composing chamber pop for the Brodsky Quartet on *The Juliet Letters*, and later composing music for the London Philharmonic and the viol group Fretwork, among others. As a fan of the Brodsky string quartet, he came up with the idea to compose a song cycle for them, *The Juliet Letters*, based on a newspaper item. Apparently each year in Verona, Italy, the postal service receives a quantity of letters addressed to Juliet Montague from lovesick people around the world.

"With classical musicians like the Brodsky Quartet, it's a whole other challenge for me to write music for them. In a funny sort of way it's more punky than anything else. It's just that it's not high-speed and high-volume," he says.

"The entire piece is about people communicating, or failing to, which is a universal experience. Far from being an elitist or pretentious thing, it's incredibly down to earth," Costello explains in Brian Hinton's biography of the artist, *Let Them All Talk, the Music of Elvis Costello*.

It would seem that for bandleader Costello, communicating with the Attractions has never been much of a problem (his feud with bassist Bruce Thomas having now been forgotten). They have a telepathic feel for his music; their work outside of the foursome has rarely equaled anything they've done with Costello.

"With the Attractions, we have some relationship to the sound we started with, which was a fairly uncompromising sound, to say the least," Costello says. "Certainly we've made records over the years where we get to play with just as much delicacy and touch as any of the other players I've ever played with—and I've played with a lot of different people. But I think maybe people who aren't so familiar with the range of other music we've played perhaps aren't aware they can play that way, particularly Steve [Nieve, pianist]. He can be very thrilling when he's playing full-out, on the big pop sound, but he can

The Attraction-less Elvis

play with the lightest touch—as you can hear on this record,—that is equal to anyone else in the world."

Costello was keen to put the versatile Attractions to work on *All This Useless Beauty,* his 18th original recording, knowing without a doubt they were the best men for the job. "I thought, this is the way these songs go—there isn't a lot of point in adding a lot of stuff to them," he says. Although the record has been criticized for containing material previously recorded by other artists, the songs belong to Costello—a kind of inverse covers and collaborations record. Songs he'd composed with Aimee Mann (whose work he'd admired

Time Line—Covers and Collaborations

1954   Born Declan MacManus in London, England

1976   Begins his career as Elvis Costello

1977   Debuts with *My Aim Is True*

1978   *This Year's Model* begins a long and successful tenure with the Attractions: Pete Thomas, drums; Bruce Thomas, bass; Steve Nieve, piano

1981   Makes first blatant stylistic departure with the collection of country covers, *Almost Blue*

1986   Changes name back to MacManus for the recording of the Costello Show's *King of America*, an American folk and roots-orientated album featuring Ray Brown and James Burton

1987   *Out of Our Idiot*, a rarities collection filled with covers and duets with friends like T-Bone Burnette, Nick Lowe, and Jimmy Cliff

1989   Songwriting sessions with Paul McCartney yield two selections on *Spike*: "Veronica" and "Pads, Paws and Claws"; later their cowritten "My Brave Face" appears on McCartney's *Flowers in the Dirt*

1993   Collaborates with the classical string group Brodsky Quartet for *The Juliet Letters*

1994   Reconvenes with the Attractions to record and tour for *Brutal Youth*

1995   *Kojack Variety*, a collection of cover songs

1996   Tours with the Attractions in support of *All This Useless Beauty*, an album that includes a few of Costello's own versions of his songs recorded by other artists

       Writes and records "God Give Me Strength" with Burt Bacharach for the Allison Anders film, *Grace of My Heart*

       Collaborates with Burt Bacharach on the album *Painted from Memory*

from her days with 'Til Tuesday), and vehicles for English pop star wannabe Wendy James and former Byrd Roger McGuinn all ended up on the set.

"I haven't given a lot of thought about what this record means in comparison to my others. I know it's distinctly different. My sadness about it is that people tended to exaggerate the importance that the songs had been recorded by other people. I think it rather diminishes people's curiosity as to the content and virtues of it. There's quite a different approach vocally and lyrically, and certainly in terms of the musical opposition and arrangements. Something that should have been a footnote ended up being the main story," he says. "We're only talking about four songs! I feel it's been a bit of a coward's way out."

Critics assailed him, suggesting he'd run out of material—obviously the worst-case scenario for any songwriter. Having just released his own collection of cover songs, *Kojack Variety*, it was a plausible assumption, yet Costello's attraction to a good song was nothing new. He freely admits to having used old standards as blueprints for his own work as the ultimate homage; it's a not so unusual practice for prolific songwriters like himself. In addition to consistently squeezing out other people's songs as a tip of the hat to his favorites in concert, he's played around with novelty recordings for years; he'd even recorded an entire album of old country favorites, *Almost Blue,* in Nashville with producer Billy Sherrill in 1981. But he wasn't happy with the result of that collaboration, nor was he happy through the years with the versions of his work others had laid down. So what was so terribly wrong with the cover versions?

"It's a little bit demeaning to the people that did the songs…" he says tentatively. But since when has that ever stopped him from elaborating? He goes ahead and admits, in at least one case, to attempting to right a wrong. "For instance, 'You Bow Down' was written in 3/4 time, which Roger McGuinn's producer perhaps prevailed upon him to straighten into 4/4, which seemed a bit defeating to the imagination of the piece. But in every other respect, I like Roger's version," Costello says.

His latest collaborative attempt appears in the film *Grace of My Heart*, a fictionalized story of songwriters working in the Brill Building in the early '60s, written and directed by Allison Anders. It was the director who paired Costello with Burt Bacharach in much the same way the fictionalized sub-

costello's material clutters his act

Singer filled show with crowd-pleasing numbers,
but one has to wonder if fans aren't misguided

by Denise Sullivan, *Times* correspondent

elvis Costello hasn't made a decent record since 1986. This is a widely held belief among critics and fans who've followed his career closely since 1977, the same people who stayed away from his sold-out show Thursday night at the Warfield in San Francisco. Instead, the seats were filled with misguided souls who wrest meaning out of Costello's more recent work—and there are plenty of them, judging by the response to his '90s repertoire.

This breed of Elvis fan giggles when he makes a gesture, laughs uproariously when he tosses off a funny line, as if it's filled with hidden meaning (it isn't) and as if they haven't heard it a zillion times on disc. Worst of all, they sing along on cue, as they did to "God's Comic," a song from 1989's *Spike*—the very record on which a lot of old fans fell off the bandwagon but a few more got on.

These neoconverts tended to roll their eyes and sit it out during more classic numbers like "Red Shoes," rarities like "Talking in the Dark" and "Motel Matches" and "Temptation" (the last two from my personal favorite, *Get Happy!*). This was best evidenced when they missed the cue to sing along on "(I Don't Want to Go to) Chelsea" from *This Year's Model*.

Who knew there was a whole culture of people out there just waiting to hear selections from *Brutal Youth* and *All This Useless Beauty*? This was a scary revelation to me—as if to say, "Hey, we've chosen the inferior over the superior, thank you very much."

Roughly a third of the songs Costello played with keyboardist Steve Nieve were from his questionable Warner Brothers era, the rest from his more fertile '70s and '80s Columbia Records reign—a time during which he recorded very few clinkers. Yet, the crowd—comprised largely of people in their mid-30s to 40s—treat Costello, who just turned 44, as if he were our own generation's Bob Dylan or a one-man John Lennon and Paul McCartney.

All this is not to say that there were not things to enjoy during Costello's performance. His voice was in extraordinarily fine shape—something which one could not say about Costello in the '80s, when he frequently suffered from vocal strain. And even in the theater's notorious black hole (stage right, back wall—don't ever sit there), he was, for the most part, clear and strong, with enough dynamics to keep even the most banal selection ("All This Useless Beauty") interesting.

"Little Triggers," which made an early appearance, is one song from Costello's now ancient catalog that most resembles the best of his later period with its calculated and dramatic arrangement and lyrical gyrations; it's the bittersweet love song (mostly bitter) in which he specialized for 20 years, though clearly, he mastered the form long ago. It stood out among the 31 songs, as did the very recent Costello/Burt Bacharach song, "God Give Me Strength," toward the end of the set. His reading of this one was imbued with so much emotion it was stirring.

When Costello merged others' songs, as he did with Van Morrison's "Jackie Wilson Said" during "Radio Sweetheart" and the standard "Fever" during "Inch by Inch," we got a taste of the lighter-hearted Elvis of yore.

But lest you think I am in favor of a pure nostalgia, *au contraire, mon cherie.* Not all of the old songs are keepers. For exactly 22 years, Costello has been performing an extended version of "Watching the Detectives" as if people want to hear it. Why, why why?

After all this time, surprisingly, Costello's skills on guitar haven't improved much, but with Nieve on keyboards that's hardly a problem—he more than makes up for Costello's lack by keeping himself and the audience entertained with his crazy jams.

A brand-new song, "45," about old records and growing old, was simply wonderful. But to encore with "Everyday I Write the Book"? It was pulled from the very first bona-fide dreadful Costello album, *Punch the Clock.* He made up for it with a bile-soaked "I Want You."

Having been born into the home of a working musician, Costello has made performing his birthright by writing music for his rock band the Attractions and others, and collaborating with string quartets and songwriting legends McCartney and Bacharach. He takes putting on a show very seriously. So it's ironic that in "God's Comic" he should poke fun at the excesses of musical theater giant Andrew Lloyd Webber, when his shows have become as cluttered with pat gestures, facial expressions, crowd-pleasing war horses, overly fussy melodies, and undiscerning fans as a matinee of Webber's long-running Broadway musical, *Cats.*

Costello delivers the goods to a new generation of Elvis fans.

jects of her film were thrown together at the infamous New York hit factory; she had a scene for the songwriters in mind, suggesting to them it reflect the main character's predicament. So Costello and Bacharach wrote the song "God Give Me Strength" by phone, never having met each other. "It was the 6/8, 12/8 thing I used to write in, that I hadn't done in years," Costello says. In the film's pivotal sequence, the main character, a struggling singer-song-writer, achieves a personal and creative breakthrough as she sings an incredibly heartbreaking but hopeful song. Kristen Vigard is the singing voice for Ileana Douglas' character in the film. In the Bacharach/Costello version, a melancholy horn melody leads into the verse, punctuated by Bacharach's piano and orchestral swells. Old-fashioned, yes; cheesy, no. The song has the intensity of emotion of "Walk on By" without its breeziness. Bacharach likened it to "Don't Make Me Over," and certainly in the darkest passage of the main bridge that's true, but "God Give Me Strength" holds its own. Costello's vocal performance is top of the line. As he shifts from character to character, neither voice loses its effectiveness; he is equally compelling and convincing in both parts—his voice nearly breaking from emotion.

At the time of this interview, Costello had no idea (or at least didn't let on) that by 1998, he would release an entire collaborative album with Bacharach, *Painted from Memory,* fulfilling what would seem to be a longtime ambition to work with a composer he rates right up there with Richard Rodgers.

"I've had that ambition to have certain songs done, sung by other people, but I was imagining something that was very unlikely to happen. George Jones, Dusty Springfield, Chet Baker; that's the highest possible achievement to actually have them choose my songs to record," he says. "There isn't a checklist of people I want to work with; the next project could just as easily be someone I haven't heard of yet, or I could just write on my own, or I could just not write for awhile. There's any number of things that could happen."

Recommended Recordings

Covers and Collaborations

Almost Blue (Columbia, Rykodisc 1981)
> Costello has gone on record on his dislike of this collection of country songs, recorded in Nashville with producer Billy Sherrill, but fans are partial to Costello and these pumped-up (Hank Williams' "Why Don't You Love Me Like You Used to Do"), syrupy and sugar-coated (Don Gibson's "Sweet Dreams"), and truly heartfelt (Gram Parsons' "How Much I Lied") versions.

Out of Our Idiot (Demon, 1987)
> Hardly a compilation without its flaws, as a way to showcase the depth and breadth of Costello's inspiration in cover material, it's not bad, as he goes from Yoko Ono's "Walking on Thin Ice" to Richard Thompson's "Withered and Died." He collaborates with friends Nick Lowe ("Baby It's You") and T-Bone Burnette and Jimmy Cliff on the originals "The People's Limousine" and "Seven Day Weekend."

TALKING HEADS

> "And you may ask yourself—well...
> how did I get here?" —*David Byrne*

dolby Laboratories' state-of-the-art screening room in San Francisco is housed in an austere brick building in the exact sort of warehouse district you'd expect. Following a showing of their self-produced concert film, *Stop Making Sense*, for the 1999 San Francisco International Film Festival, former Talking Heads members David Byrne, Chris Frantz, Jerry Harrison, and Tina Weymouth milled in the building's solemn lobby. An enthusiastic press corps and some old friends who'd been invited to the private viewing waited patiently while drummer Frantz and bassist Weymouth, the band's husband-and-wife rhythm section, signed autographs as a team. While they struggled over a young man's bulky limited edition of *Speaking in Tongues*, its sleeve designed by abstract expressionist Robert Rauschenberg, keyboardist Jerry Harrison, a Marin County resident, chatted amiably with a group of local female journalists his own age. But the big cheese, David Byrne, stood alone: giving his ex-band mates a wide berth, he played the role of the art-rock celebrity so well that I remarked to a friend, "I think he looks a little *too* perfect." But slowly, amid the press-fleshing and picture taking, he began to relax as friends and fans approached to congratulate him on his performance.

All four ex-members of the Talking Heads were a bit edgy, since they were about to hold a press conference that required them all to be in the same room at the same time—a rare occurrence since the band's breakup between five and eight years prior (depending on which member's recollection you subscribe to). Given their illustrious and industrious career, the circumstances of their breakup could only be described as anticlimactic. But no one,

Talking Heads, '77

not a friend, journalist, or loud mouth in the crowd that day, broached the subject, nor did anyone ask what was on everyone's mind: had the fence been mended? Had they come to announce a reunion? Was this a public way of apologizing to each other? The answers would eventually be revealed to be no, no, and no. Things were far from resolved among the former group's members, contrary to the line from the song "Making Flippy Floppy" we'd heard in the film a few moments earlier: "*Nothing can come between us/nothing gets you down.*"

It was almost 30 years ago that David Byrne and Chris Frantz met in Providence as underclassmen at the Rhode Island School of Design. Within a couple of years they would relinquish dorm life, along with their friend, Martina Weymouth, and move to New York City to share an apartment and start a band. The Talking Heads don't talk much about those days. They've been so well documented, mythologized and revised that we accept what we know as fact, although later Weymouth will tell me that everything we know is wrong. But there are some unalienable truths: a three-piece Talking Heads made its debut at CBGB's opening for the Ramones in mid-1975, just six months after they began practicing together. By the next year they would be courted by major record labels, and by the following year, they would be signed to Sire Records and have released a single ("Love—Building on Fire"/"New Feeling"). Before recording its debut album, *Talking Heads '77*, the band added keyboardist Jerry Harrison, a former member of Jonathan Richman's Modern Lovers, to the fold. Although mixed-gender bands were becoming the norm among the new wave crowd, very few women were actually playing bass at the time; tiny Martina, now Tina, was among only a handful of women who held down the bottom end in bands. "There was another girl [who played bass]...Gail Advert, from the Adverts," she remembers.

Talking Heads '77 earned the band the tags "quirky," "arty," and "neurotic," thanks to the combination of Byrne's stage persona, the jerky rhythms of the music, and songs like "Psycho Killer" (ubiquitous during the summer of '77, it helped the album crack the *Billboard* Hot 100). Alongside their peers and friends in Blondie and Television, Talking Heads were one of the top bands that year.

The follow-up album, *More Songs About Buildings and Food*, produced by art-rock musician and ambient music composer Brian Eno, included the old Al Green spiritual "Take Me to the River." The unusually soulful version by the upper-crust, white, new wave band lifted them into the upper reaches of the charts. Perhaps they made the song more immediately accessible, or maybe, after years of rock and roll bombast, the nation's collective ears had become attuned to the new wave of sound. It's hard to say why it clicked, but there was an element on *More Songs* that hadn't yet been fully developed on '77, and that was *groove*. Ultimately, the band would incorporate that funk more completely into its sound, but that album marked the beginning of a new phase. Collaborating with Eno again on *Fear of Music* and *Remain in Light* (the latter arguably the band's finest recorded achievement) would be where the funk met the punk. Their "new wave" tag would be shed for something far greater: Talking Heads would become a rock band for the ages.

For both their tours and subsequent albums, Talking Heads would employ outside musicians, former members of bands they liked, to augment their sound: Parliament and Funkadelic, the Brothers Johnson, and Labelle. With what the band called its "big bands" in tow, a Talking Heads show was no longer a nightclub gig or a rock concert, but an *event*. In 1984, following the release of another watershed album, *Speaking in Tongues* (which charted higher than any of their other records, thanks to a hit single, a dance floor remix, and a killer video for "Burning Down the House"), the band embarked on its final concert tour.

Stop Making Sense, a film by Jonathan Demme, was the result of that tour. Conceived and staged by Byrne, it's not so much a concert film as it is a concept. The band performed over two nights at the Pantages Theater in Los Angeles for the filming. The four Talking Heads played characters (or more accurately *caricatures*) of themselves: Chris was the happy one, Jerry the serious one, Tina the shy one, and David the confused one. Although it was followed by another film, *True Stories* (directed by Byrne and not as successful), three more studio albums (*True Stories, Little Creatures,* and *Naked*), and various solo, side, and compilation projects, a protracted hiatus would follow *Naked*, resulting in the dissolution of the band. They would never record as a unit again, although Frantz, Weymouth, and Harrison would continue to work together as the Heads and pursue other interests such as solo work and producing. Byrne, meanwhile, would release several solo records and become involved in projects ranging from running a record label to hosting a television show.

Since they all helped produce *Stop Making Sense* ("the band put up the money," says Frantz), all four still have a vested interest in promoting its rerelease—a limited theatrical run followed by commercial DVD and video. Yet there seem to be some other things the four ex-band mates are looking to get off their chests as the reunion of sorts takes on the air of a therapy session. The only thing lacking is a facilitator, but, it seems, that's where I come in…

"I wouldn't disagree that *Remain in Light* had the most influence on other musicians," says Harrison. "I think the things we were doing in that middle period have resonated in other people's music. To tell you the truth, the guitar part in 'Cities' is very similar to what the Edge developed—this very fast strumming with delays. And Living Color covered 'Memories Can't Wait.'"

"We just got a record by an artist, Wasis Diop, which was produced by Wally Badarou, who's a friend of ours," chimes in Frantz. He does a cover of 'Once in a Lifetime' which is in Senegalese…it's really cool."

Weymouth reports hearing tapes of Phish performing *Remain in Light* in its entirety. "David thought it was going to be impossible for us to do *Remain in Light* because it'd been done piecemeal—Brian Eno would play one bass note on the one and then David Byrne would play one bass note on the three and they thought it was going to take all these different people to play the stuff when in fact, the band Phish did a perfect replication of that record with what, six people?"

"Nevertheless, to do a song like 'Crosseyed and Painless,' there are like three guitar parts, and it's just impossible to do them all at the same time," says Harrison flatly.

"If you listen to Phish, they actually did it," says Frantz. "I don't know how they did it. I wasn't at the show, I just have a tape of it, but I was surprised because I thought, like you, they can't do it. It's weird. Just really good guitarists, I guess."

Weymouth isn't completely in agreement with Harrison on her former band's legacy just yet: "Time will tell. It's impossible to see it till the end. The blues comes out of Africa and so does jazz, and what Talking Heads always did too—even before Brian Eno wrote this whole bibliography of these books that we read. As Chris pointed out, he *was* the drummer on those albums, and nobody told him he was playing African rhythms! We all had a good laugh at that."

"I thought I was playing James Brown," Frantz confesses with a laugh.

"We always did that right from the start. We mixed it up," says Weymouth. "Part of our American heritage are African roots—we cherish it. And we mixed it with the European tradition." Weymouth has a contrary streak that is oddly charming, although one can see how it continually put her at odds with Byrne. But there's one point on which Byrne and Weymouth both agree.

"There seems to be in the history of a lot of things in this country a kind of splitting apart and then coming together of the races and the black culture and white culture, and then there are creative cross-fertilizations. And it seemed to be one of those times," explained Byrne during a separate interview held earlier in the day.

Although the Talking Heads and Byrne in particular would simultaneously get skewered by critics as having imperialist leanings as opposed to a purer integrationist intent, Frantz notes that the Talking Heads were the least guilty of those who would later make the appropriation of world music their stock in trade.

"[*Stop Making Sense*] has a whole lot to do with what Peter Gabriel came out with, the moment we stopped touring," notes Frantz with his perpetual smile.

During that same period in the Talking Heads' evolution, Frantz and Weymouth were conducting their own experiments in hip-hop, yielding the Tom Tom Club hit, "Genius of Love." Inarguably, the era was an incredibly fertile period for all the members of the Talking Heads.

"['Genius of Love' is] one of the most sampled songs of all time," quips Tom Tom Club's number-one fan, Harrison, "besides the 'Funky Drummer.'"

"We didn't do a oneupmanship on Talking Heads," explains Weymouth. "We just did a sidestep and went into the hip-hop vein. That was early hip-hop. We knew that we were pioneering something, but we didn't know it would have the influence it did…and had it not been for collaborators like our manager, Gary Kurfirst…we would be in one of those books, *Most Influential Bands You Never Heard Of.*"

"'Genius of Love' was highly influenced by the band Zapp," continues Frantz, "'More Bounce to the Ounce,' to be specific." Oddly, just two days prior to our meeting, Zapp founder Roger Troutman (more recently known as the vocoder-voiced singer on Tupac and Dr. Dre's hit "California Love") was found dead in Dayton, Ohio, allegedly murdered by his brother. I hadn't yet heard the news, and maybe Frantz hadn't either, because we didn't discuss it.

"There were other groups before us who were doing it," Weymouth enthuses, referring to the cross-genre fertilization in which the Talking Heads and Tom Tom Club specialized. "Like the group Can from Germany. I wish I'd heard that stuff then. We never owned a Can record. We had Kraftwerk and we had Manu Dibango from 1970. And pop too. We still love pop."

So from Dusseldorf to Senegal and all ports in between, the distinctly American Talking Heads embraced music from every possible country and genre. But there is one country that has yet to embrace the Talking Heads: the U.K. The Talking Heads' essence was never quite captured there the way that its members might have liked. Frantz says, "When I buy these English magazines today…where they have the 100 Most Influential Singles or the 100 Most Influential Bands of the '80s, I never see Tom Tom Club in there. I don't even see Talking Heads in there."

"They get Massive Attack until it's coming out of their ears!" he says, noting that the Bristol band that fuses dub, R&B, techno, and sampling put genre-crossing music on the map a full 15 years *after* the Heads virtually invented it.

Time Line

1949 Jerry Harrison born in Milwaukee, WI

1950 Tina Weymouth born in Coronado, CA

1951 Chris Frantz born in Ft. Campbell, KY

1952 David Byrne born in Dumbarton, Scotland

1970 Byrne and Frantz meet as freshmen at RISD and form a five-piece band, the Artistics/Autistics

Friend Weymouth helps Frantz and Byrne write "Psycho Killer"

1974 Byrne, Frantz, and Weymouth relocate to New York

1975 Begin practicing as a three-piece; band changes its name to the Talking Heads

First gig, opening for the Ramones at CBGB's

1977 First single, "Love—Building on Fire"/"New Feeling"

Jerry Harrison joins group

Talking Heads '77 released along with single "Uh-Oh Love Comes to Town" "Psycho Killer"

1978 *More Songs About Buildings and Food*

1979 *Fear of Music*

1980 *Remain in Light*

1981 David Byrne's collaboration with Brian Eno, *My Life in the Bush of Ghosts,* Chris Frantz and Tina Weymouth, *Tom Tom Club*

Jerry Harrison, *The Red and the Black*

1982 *The Name of This Band Is Talking Heads* a double live album of material from '77–'81

Byrne produces *Mesopotamia* EP for B-52's

1983 *Close to the Bone,* Tom Tom Club

Speaking in Tongues becomes the band's highest-charting (#15) album

Tour captured in *Stop Making Sense,* directed by Jonathan Demme; Talking Heads' last live tour

1984 *Stop Making Sense* spends two years on the charts

1985 David Byrne writes music for playwright Robert Wilson's *The Knee Plays*

Little Creatures released

1986 Byrne directs *True Stories*

Time names Byrne Rock's Renaissance Man

1988 *Naked*

Jerry Harrison *Casual Gods*

Byrne collaborates with Riyuichi Sakamoto on *The Last Emperor* soundtrack; earns an Oscar for Best Score

Chris Frantz and Tina Weymouth produce *Conscious Party* for Ziggy Marley and the Melody Makers, yielding the hit "Tomorrow People"

Byrne forms Luaka Bop label to release Brazilian, Cuban, Asian artists

1989 Tom Tom Club, *Boom Boom Chi Boom Boom*

David Byrne solo debut, *Rei Momo,* on Luaka Bop

1990 Jerry Harrison *Walk on Water*

Escape from New York Tour with Tom Tom Club, the Ramones, and Deborah Harry

1992 Byrne's *Uh-oh*

Popular Favorites 1974–1992: Sand in the Vaseline, includes four new and final tracks from Talking Heads

Tom Tom Club, *Dark Sneak Love Action*

1994 Talking Heads officially breaks up

David Byrne released

1999 15-year anniversary and rerelease of *Stop Making Sense*

"Psycho Killer" included on soundtrack to Spike Lee's *Summer of Sam*

2000 Chris Frantz and Tina Weymouth release *The Good the Bad and the Funky*, the first Tom Tom Club record in eight years

*David Byrne and the
notorious big white suit*

"When we first went there, we opened for the Ramones, and one girl wrote in *Melody Maker* or *NME*, 'These people must have been locked away in a closet with their Sam and Dave albums,'" says Weymouth. But maybe the journalist—the notorious Julie Burchill ("Oh, she's so bovine," Weymouth remarks)—wasn't that far off the mark...

"Even from our very first record, it reflected what we were listening to," says Byrne. "It wasn't picked up on right away. The European press heard it—they go, 'These people are listening to soul music, but they're also listenin' to Velvet Underground and Roxy Music and whatever else, but they're playin' it funky.' Here, it was mainly that we were a bunch of nerds or college students or whatever—the whole excitement was over the CBGB's thing. The fact that we were bringing in R&B elements and eventually African things and whatever else into white pop music got picked up on later," he says.

The pigeonhole of New York new wave was difficult to bust out of, and the Talking Heads were the personification of both. The idea that they should bring on da funk was not within every listener's grasp at the time. Byrne attempts to explain the evolution of the band's "middle period."

"You could be a 'new wave band' or a whatever. But we were having a good time. It felt great to bring in some of the people whose records you were listening to, whether it was Bernie [Worrell] or Nona [Hendryx] or Alex Weir, who played with Brothers Johnson. You didn't have to just copy what they were doing, but you could actually collaborate with these people. The first time we played with the big band live in Toronto, we took this incredible risk—playing a lot of new material with a new band in front of a huge audience—and we pulled it off. It was a lot of fun. When you take a risk and the risk pays off, you get the instant reward, and it all felt great for everyone.

"But it was also really difficult for us. For instance, *Remain in Light* killed us commercially. Although it gets played now, it wouldn't get played then. That record died at radio," he says.

I'm jarred by Byrne's use of the music business jargon "died at radio"; because, after all, he is an artist, an auteur. In 1986, *Time* magazine called him a "Renaissance Man." Prior to our meeting, I'd always perceived him as a little boring, even pretentious, but at that moment he seemed completely vulnerable and human—not the automaton I had come to know from his image. I was wondering why he set himself apart from his former bandmates. Maybe he was just preoccupied with his next project, a compilation release by Brazilian psychedelic band Os Mutantes for his label Luaka Bop, or the upcoming taping of the TV series he hosts, *Sessions at West 54th*, but it seemed as if every word was a strain for him—that he'd prefer to be in a studio or on a stage or anywhere other than in a room talking to a stranger. Did he feel awkward that the people with whom he'd spent almost 20 years of his adult life with, in the band that helped to make his name, were shuttered away in another room?

"Jerry from the band I see once in awhile. And Chris and Tina I communicate with by fax, and it's a very tense and uncomfortable relationship." He refers to the awkwardness of the day prior. "A press conference is a weird, artificial relationship to begin with. That said, we're all extremely proud of that tour and this movie, and so we were kind of all happy to shut up about our differences."

All interviews with Byrne must be cleared through separate management, while his three band mates hold roundtable discussions together, freely recalling the halcyon days. I hadn't requested an interview with Byrne for that reason—if I need "clearance," it will be a controlled exercise. But for reasons unknown to me (a hole in the schedule? Byrne having second thoughts about his inaccessibility? luck?) I was shuttled, unprepared, into an interview with the artist formerly known as the head Head.

I suggested we wing it, so he asked me how I thought the rerelease of *Stop Making Sense* would be received, and then expounded, "Well, then, what's gonna happen…when an audience who's maybe heard some Talking Heads stuff on classic rock radio or whatever, maybe seen a couple of the old videos on MTV, and that's about it….When this came out the first time, for that audience it was like going to another show. They figured, the band's doing something else at the moment, but we can go to this and treat it as if it's a show on the tour. Now the different audience—I'm assuming, a younger audience—won't know the songs as well. I'll be interested to see what happens. That'll be the test, to see whether people see it and go, 'That's a great show, those are good songs,' and it's a film that draws them in."

I tell him I think that film buffs will be drawn to the early Demme work, art students may enjoy the staging, but I think hip young people will go because of a burgeoning '80s nostalgia craze. He's vaguely amused and lets out a titter.

"You have to ask me something now," he says. Right. It struck me at the beginning of the film that the band looked so happy playing together; I wondered to myself how it could've gone so wrong. Did it really break down on that tour?

"Yeah, there were some backstage problems," he says, again chuckling, seemingly to himself. "It's hard to tell what's real and what's not. When you get onstage, you can have backstage or personal problems with somebody, but when you get onstage, the music and the audience, etc., kind of carries you away. You just forget it. So you're there in that moment and not thinking about, 'Oh that person, what an asshole.' For those couple of hours, those problems don't exist. For the most part. On a good night. When they do, it can be pretty bumpy. When I look at that," he laughs again, "I don't see myself as a happy person, but someone who desperately wants to be happy and finally achieves it by the end."

David Byrne, or his character?

"Yeah."

 I tell the threesome that I just finished talking to Byrne about the tour, and they all start talking on top of each other.

"It was actually the tour before the tour," says Harrison, in case I'd mistaken the film version as the first "big band" tour.

"His memory…" tsks Weymouth, motioning to the room where he-who-shall-not-be-named sits. "That was a huge band. Every person in this room was duplicated," she explains.

"Some of the people took up a lot of space," says Frantz, smiling sardonically. "Especially on the bus," says Harrison, also smiling.

Clearly, these musketeers love each other's company, but the tension is palpable, their fearless former leader within spitting distance.

"I'll have to ask David about that communicating by fax," says Frantz. "It was him who faxed us in the first place about this type of thing. It gives you the impression that we wouldn't take a phone call from him, which is absolutely false."

Weymouth adds, "It's the other way around. He's completely turned it around."

"Don't make a big deal about it," Frantz says to me. "It's just one of those things, and you try to be a good person and you try to be fair to people—"

"—and they're stabbing you in the back the whole time—" Weymouth says, shaking her head.

"—And it just doesn't work out," Frantz finishes, chuckling again.

The publicist steps in, and I suggest we wrap it up, but Weymouth encourages me to continue. How exciting to have been collaborating and making music with the very people they had once listened to on record and admired from afar, I say, changing the subject.

"You mean P-Funk?" says Weymouth, lighting up. "It was through our manager."

"No, it was me," says Harrison.

"Gary Kurfirst introduced us to Busta[Jones]," insists Weymouth.

"But I was hanging out with Busta, and that's when I met Bernie [Worrell]," says Harrison. "Bernie had heard about Steve [Scales] and Busta knew Dolette [MacDonald] and I called Adrian [Belew]. It was amazing because it all happened in about two hours. Part of it was because we said we were going to do this thing for two weeks."

"It probably saved the band, too," says Weymouth, then digresses. "Because Christmas 1979, we were being interviewed by this Czechoslovakian guy in Germany who had escaped. And remember [to Harrison] you got that embolism in your arm in the elevator?" Harrison gives her a sideways, if-you-say-so look, and nods.

Weymouth continues, "We were sitting there being interviewed, and he said, 'How do you feel that David is leaving the group?' And we said, 'This is news to us.' And he said, 'What did he tell you?' 'Well, he told us he is going to make a solo record with Brian Eno.'"

She continues, "We had just been in Berlin in Connie Plank's studio with Holger Czukay from Can. Holger Czukay said, 'This is my secret project, but because I love Brian Eno and you're his friends, I'm going to play it for you and tell you about it.' He sat us down and played us all these really cool, funky grooves that he'd put together with—get this—radio and found voiceovers. He's still bitter about it to this day."

Weymouth is referring to Byrne and Eno's high-profile 1981 record of funky grooves and found sound, *My Life in the Bush of Ghosts*, which eclipsed Czukay's recorded experiments.

"Have you seen him since?" Harrison asks her, and Weymouth says that a mutual friend told her Czukay is "very pissed off." "Consider it on the record that Holger Czukay came up with that idea," says Weymouth, adding, "And people credit those guys. There was an article in the *Village Voice* not three weeks ago that said, 'Yes, if you look at all of sampling today, you can trace it back to Eno/Byrne, and it's no accident that "Genius of Love" also came out of this time, because Chris and Tina knew David Byrne, so it must be that he gave them the idea how to do that!'

"What happened was, we were to make our third record with Eno, *Remain in Light,* and he didn't even want to make it with us because he'd just been working with David on *My Life in the Bush of Ghosts,* and they'd had a falling out. But we didn't know that. And he didn't tell us. Chris and I, who had always loved Brian Eno, asked him once more to come in and jam with us," she explains.

"But because we'd hired Rhett Davies..." Harrison interjects.

"Uh, yeah, that's part of it too," Weymouth agrees. "So we went down to the Bahamas, we wrote all this stuff all together, and we made an agreement between us, enough of this nonsense that [David Byrne] wrote everything, because we all sit down and we jam. It's even documented in [an] interview, 'We all sit down and we all play our instruments, and before I know it, I've written a song,'" says Weymouth, quoting Byrne.

"So we did this record and we agreed it would say 'words by David Byrne and Brian Eno, music by...' and five names. That was the album cover. OK?" Weymouth pauses to catch her breath, then continues: "David went to the printer; the day it went to the printing—"

"This has nothing to do with Eno!" says Harrison, losing patience with Weymouth's round-about way of storytelling.

"Yes it does!" she counters. "They took our names off."

The picture is becoming more clear. The infighting, the Byrne vs. the rest of them and the final dissolution of the band, was all about the only thing it's ever about—money and egos. But according to the sleeve of *Remain in Light,* "All songs by David Byrne, Brian Eno, Talking Heads" looks like an improvement over *More Songs'* "All selections written by David Byrne except as noted" and *Fear of Music'*s "All songs written by David Byrne except..."

"On that album," says Harrison, whom I surmise is speaking of *Remain in Light,* "We did this thing where all five of us wrote on a piece of paper what proportion we thought the other people had done for the record, and then I added it all up and basically averaged it. So unlike on the other albums, where we have a fixed percentage, it's a mutating amount. In a certain way, it balanced itself out," he says.

"It was not so much about money as 'can we have the ability to live?'" protests Weymouth as to why shortly after, conditions within the band soured. "If we do something and then he cuts us off, how are we supposed to go and get another record deal and live again? And if he kicks and screams and has a temper tantrum at the record company…" Again, she has taken to referring to Byrne as he-who-shall-not-be-named, and imitates him, "'I don't even want them on the same label as me, because it's diverting attention from me!' Then you get into this trouble where you can't even feed your kids!" she says, pissed. "Jerry, who is a great performer and musician, is never on-stage anymore. He's locked up with these baby bands, half of whom can't even play!"

Chris Frantz, leaning back in his chair, with his hands folded across his middle, lets out a large belly laugh.

"To me, it's a crime," says Weymouth, clearly still disgusted by the whole mess.

Stop Making Sense, its accompanying double live album (which spent over two years on the charts) and the follow-up, *Speaking in Tongues*, was, if not a career high, then a commercial apex for the Talking Heads. Whether it was due to the period being caught on film, the injection of additional musicians, or something in the air, in 1984, the band could do no wrong. But it wouldn't be long before the Talking Heads would be vanquished. *True Stories* was a misguided experiment; *Little Creatures* was pleasant enough but too much about age and responsibility, parenting and other "non-rock" topics to bring the next generation along; *Naked* was terrible. The long hiatus and dissolution of the whole in favor of outside interests didn't help matters either. But the band defends its middle period and concert film as territorially as a pack of pit bulls. Even having to confront their nemesis in Byrne and vice-versa couldn't dissuade the Frantz/Weymouth clan from attending the quorum at the San Francisco International Film Festival, although I bet if you'd asked any of the musicians' intimates, all bets would be off on a united foursome. How did it happen?

"We love this film and we love Jonathan Demme," explains Weymouth.

"It's a representation of something we did together," says Harrison.

"And it doesn't hurt to let people know you are alive and well," adds Frantz. "We knew were were good live because, especially with that show,

The good, the bad and the funky:
Chris and Tina Tom Tom, 2000

we were blowing away every other live show that was happening at the time. When we would go to a festival, nobody wanted to follow that show…not even Der Stingle—Sting and the Police." He is positively gleeful at the memory. This isn't the first time Frantz has ridiculed the Police chief. Is it because of the singer's habit of appropriating the music of third world countries?

"He has a *lot* of problems," says Frantz. "Who knows, he might be a wonderful guy, I just don't think so."

"He's not as bad as Paul Simon," says Weymouth, rolling her eyes.

"A lot of hubris," says Harrison, and they all laugh again.

"What would happen was, we would open for them, and the Sting, I mean the Police, would book these giant stadiums, and they wouldn't sell enough tickets, and then they'd add us to the bill and it would sell out. And then they would have us go on before them," says Frantz.

"But then they would only let us use half the speakers," adds Weymouth.

"And then the next day the papers would say, 'Talking Heads Shoot Police' and stuff like that," Frantz howls.

"We were connecting with each other on stage," continues Weymouth. "You felt like you were part of something and each person was contributing to the whole, and it created something very special and very warm." She credits the big band for making it work. "Those people taught us how to be. When we had been on stage before, my whole experience was just being David's whipping boy."

Frantz and Harrison's eyes widen at this one.

"I mean, frankly," states Weymouth. "And then it switched to Jerry."

"You were *Jerry's* whipping boy?" Frantz inquires.

The trio erupts with laughter again. They are unstoppable. Even Harrison, who's spent most of the morning trying to make up for Frantz and Weymouth's Frick and Frack routine, has given up and given in.

I wondered if this is what it was like for them in the good old days, when they were young and in a band together, a tightly knit rock family unit. Weymouth takes a sober tone as she spells out precisely what this journey through the past has been all about for the three remaining Heads.

"When *Time* magazine came out," she says, referring to that story more than a decade ago in which Byrne was declared rock's renaissance man, "David said, 'Then I thought to do this and then I thought to do that,' and there was no credit given. Fifteen years later, they still haven't figured it out!" She points over yonder, "'And then I did this and then I did that, and weren't we funky'? And I want to say, '[Weren't] Bernie Worrel and Steve Scales funky?!' I just want to make sure that our crew, who worked their tail off, would get some satisfaction, because the only satisfaction they get when they see the stars go up there and receive awards is that they were part of the team."

Stop Making Sense was the story of a band falling apart—the confused man in the middle desperately wanted out. Can a person assume that the big white suit Byrne wore in the film was a symbol for his unhappiness within the band?

"Yeah, they could, they could," Byrne agrees. "I've noticed that it's not unusual that I've written a song or performed something or whatever, and I've realized that it's a prediction of what I'm gonna do and it happens the next year or very shortly afterward and I think, 'I predicted I was going to do this in a song I wrote.' In the song, I could put down my feelings that I wasn't able to acknowledge to myself, and sometimes it would take a year or a couple of years before I would act on those feelings, before they become manifest. It's interesting. I'd better be careful what I write."

Though Byrne had written confusion into the script before there was a breakup; before the factions and before the band members started parenting, producing, directing, and pushing 50, there was a vital band that helped to change the face of rock and roll as we knew it. The name of that band was Talking Heads.

"This is where history really messed up," announces Weymouth. "Our singer was supposed to be Debbie Harry—we asked her to be our singer. Think of what a group it would've been then. David was just supposed to be like the rest of us."

Ultimately, the Byrne-less band the Heads ended up working with Deborah Harry during their Escape from New York Tour in 1990 with the Ramones—what Weymouth refers to as a precursor to Lollapalooza. The three Talking Heads minus Byrne supplied the music while a rotating cast of vocalists stepped in to fill the void.

"We were ahead of our time. It was very unfortunate, because they called us 'aging rockers,' and I think we were all like 39 years old. We weren't even in our 40s," says Weymouth. "The press gave it this whole nostalgia angle," says Frantz dryly.

But if ever there was a time for a Talking Heads resurgence, surely the time is now, at the beginning of a new century, when everything old is new again, and new generations are discovering rock from the '50s through the '80s for the first time. There is an entire industry built on rock nostalgia. What about "Talking Heads: Behind the Music"?

"Don't count on it," Harrison quips.

"There's been so much revisionism," says Weymouth, exasperated. "For instance, some people date our breakup to December 1991. We never broke up! One person left the group, and that actually took place in May of 1994."

"However, we stopped touring in 1984. And our last studio album was 1988," Harrison clarifies.

"David told us he was on sabbatical and to wait for him," says Weymouth. Harrison asks her, "What did you say I said at the time?"

"This is typical Jerry understatement," she notes, quoting: 'I do believe this hiatus has gone on a bit beyond what could be considered sensible.' We called up his offices and they said, 'That is correct, the band is broken up.' And we said, 'But we *are* the band!'"

Back to playing diplomat, Harrison jumps in, "It was pretty obvious we weren't doing anything. We had deliberately decided not to say we'd broken up, although I think we were all pretty aware that we weren't doing anything."

"I think we hoped at some point we would continue," says Frantz, and unusually, he isn't laughing when he says it.

"I suppose we were in denial—we couldn't see that we were being stabbed in the back," Weymouth says.

The Weymouth/Frantz family have a home studio in rural Connecticut. Frantz explains how this saves them the trouble of having to go to the record company "hat in hand"—they can record at any time—which they do with Tom Tom Club and friends. Additionally, the duo bring in musicians from around the globe: projects through the years have included recordings by Shirley Manson of Garbage's first band, Angelfish, to remixes for Bette Midler and Ofra Haza, among other eclectic artists.

For Harrison, the post-Talking Heads action takes place in a Northern California studio, a stone's throw from his new home, which he shares with his wife and their children. He's headed back to work on those "baby bands" to which Weymouth referred, two of which he had a hand in helping to break: Live and Kenny Wayne Shepherd. He speaks glowingly of his own children aged 7, 9, and 12, and tells a story only a parent could love about his youngest, Dylan, "assisting" at a Sheppard session.

"They actually looked at a house down the road from us in Connecticut," says Weymouth about Harrison and his wife Carol. "We thought about that, because we really do enjoy each other and we're godparents to Jerry's firstborn, and we love that family so it seemed a logical thing, but now we're on two separate coasts," she mourns.

 Anticipation is building among the band mates for the evening's public screening of *Stop Making Sense*.

"I want my kids to see it," says Harrison. "I've never watched it with them. I think that it will teach them something about me."

Weymouth and Frantz also have children, two boys aged 16 and 12. "The older boy is really into scratching," says Frantz. "He's a turntablist." Mom brags that her boy is competitive on the wheels of steel, much like her old pal, Grandmaster Flash. "He dragged us to a battle last summer that was so exciting we wrote a whole song about it called 'Who Feels It Loves It,'" she says.

The couple is leaving the next morning, just in time to make it home for a Tom Tom Club gig in New York the following night. The new group has six members, including Steve Scales, the percussionist who toured with the Talking Heads during the *Stop Making Sense* tour.

"In fact Steve, Chris, and I, with this band, we have that same feeling. I think I'd be crying and really nostalgic about this *Stop Making Sense* thing if it weren't for the fact that we have this wonderful band now. No money, but the same feeling we had as musicians" (they released *The Good, the Bad and the Funky* in the fall of 2000).

These three Heads appear to operate as a family—supportive of each other as individuals and as a unit and with a great affection for each other. But I leave our meeting feeling queasy. Four strangers had just doled out 20 years' worth of sadness, anger, disappointment, and—mercifully—a few jokes, and I wasn't looking forward to the task of sifting through what it all meant. Save for straight-shooter Weymouth, I felt a little like they'd been speaking in tongues.

Recommended Recordings

Remain in Light (Sire, 1980)

The Brian Eno-produced Talking Heads perfect the experiments begun on *Fear of Music*. Fusing rock and roll and world music, it stands as a classic and a leader in its genre, and features the Heads standard, "Once in a Lifetime."

Stop Making Sense (Sire, 1984/Palm Pictures DVD)

An unusually good live album, it both sounds and looks great while it conveniently captures the Heads at their career apotheosis. Thank Jonathan Demme for having the foresight to shoot the band when he did—they were never better than this.

Popular Favorites 1976–1992: Sand in the Vaseline (Sire, 1992)

This is an overview of the Talking Heads' career, pulling from each of their albums up until 1992. Greatest hits collections are rarely recommended as must-own recordings, but short of buying all of the band's studio albums, you could do worse than begin with this one

the chords
of love **and pain**

rock   &   folk   troubadours

U. Utah Phillips
Ramblin' Jack Elliott
Peter Case
U. Utah Phillips
Ramblin' Jack Elliott
Peter Case
U. Utah Phillips
Ramblin' Jack Elliott

t isn't easy to be a maverick in the folk idiom, a music often mired in its own dogma, but that's not to say there aren't a few performers in the genre who've dared to live by their own code. But the vanguard folk performers who've had a profound influence on rock and vice versa often find themselves filed in the nether world between the two genres, forced to chart their own way not only because they broke folk army rules, but because they made up their own as they went along. Such is the case with Ramblin' Jack Elliott, U. Utah Phillips, and Peter Case, who have each paid a price for their iconoclasm but whose contributions to popular music are peerless.

Folk acts can be broken down into several subgenres, such as solo acoustic artists, singer-songwriters, and rockers-turned-folkies. Some are more country than others, some are more pop. Some are fakes, but the trick to achieving authenticity, a quality that Elliott, Phillips, and Case all possess in spades, is a commitment to living life by ones's own lights. Their respective tones lack the stridency that many of the genre's '60s revivalists possessed, yet this works in their favor. Although reinvention is common among show people, it's a tricky business when your only armor is an acoustic guitar. Only a handful of artists in the years between Bob Dylan and Beck Hansen have done it successfully, having taken some tips from performers like

145

Elliott, Case, and Phillips, who've defied the traditions of a very traditional music. By using their abilities to trail-blaze, they introduced a new set of standards within the songwriting and performing tradition.

There are few who have reinvented themselves as thoroughly as Ramblin' Jack Elliott. In 1996, the hard-travelin' folk singer and one and only protegé of Woody Guthrie received the National Medal of the Arts for his achievements in keeping American traditional music alive after 40 years in the business. For 26 of those years, Elliott didn't even make a record—something unheard of among viable artists, but which remarkably managed to leave his legacy intact as he pursued other vistas. By turning his back on the recording industry and a traditional lifestyle, Elliott sacrificed his financial security and home life, but spawned more than one generation of folkie imitators.

Born Charles Elliott Adnopoz in Brooklyn, from the time he was a small child, Elliott viewed the world through a different looking glass. Interested in anything that would take him away from his environment—planes, boats, or horses—Elliott settled on the cowboy life when he ran away from home at 15 and discovered the rodeo. From then on, his life took him on one adventure after another. Sometimes he traveled beside his mentor and friend Guthrie, other times on his own, spreading American traditional songs throughout Europe and later throughout the plains, southern and mountain states of the U.S. Although Jack's most significant contribution to American song is as an interpreter, he's written his own handful of classics ("912 Greens," from his breakthrough album, *Young Brigham,* is a sprawling, 17-minute travelogue; before trucker anthems like "Willin'," "White Line Fever," and "Convoy," there was Jack's "Cup of Coffee"). Yet his greatest contribution to folk and rock is the idea that one can revise his own history, an idea so simple it's radical. Jack became the person he believed himself to be—a cowboy rogue—although his regional and class background belied the plausibility of that persona. But he made it work—in an unusual, discursive, and idiosyncratic style.

Jack was not from the West, the Mississippi Delta, or the Dust Bowl, but by thoroughly exploring those places and their music in a young life devoted to reading and exploring, the music and fiber of those regions became a part of him. Although he set himself up for all kinds of embarrassments by insisting he was a cowhand from Brooklyn, he wasn't dissuaded from learning the ways of the buckin' bronco, wearing his wide-brimmed hat and boots, pickin' and singing his cowboy songs on his guitar. Meeting political folk pioneer

Woody Guthrie took Jack into another sphere, but it wasn't Guthrie's activism that he would adopt as much as his mannerisms, which eventually came to be considered Jackisms. Without that kind of model, would young Robert Zimmerman from Minnesota have been able to take his act to the astonishing heights that he did as Bob Dylan? Certainly without Jack, there would be far fewer copycat Dylans and other folksingers affecting Okie accents, strumming beat-up guitars, and reaching into people's hearts and souls with distinctly American music. Bruce Springsteen is a perfect example of an artist who borrowed from the tradition of reinvention. Ever since his sparse acoustic album *Nebraska*, Springsteen has toyed with the idea of the nomadic folksinger model, inhabiting other worlds and essentially becoming the characters about whom he sings (though he's yet to settle on one).

Peter Case is the kind of songwriter that Bruce Springsteen could never be, given his rapid rise to acceptance, but Case's experience as a traveler for the last 30 years is enviable to anyone in search of a good song. Case has no shortage of them, and almost all are drawn from some element of his life and experience.

Case was the first new wave/punk-era musician to put down his electric guitar, and by doing so he helped to redefine and repopularize the singer-songwriter genre in the late '80s after its long sleep. He is perhaps one of Elliott's most direct descendants; like his heroes, Mississippi John Hurt, Lightnin' Hopkins, and Muddy Waters, Case keeps getting better as a picker and player as time rolls on. Inspired by the wealth of traditional music he was raised on and continues to explore, he crafts his songs in the Guthrie tradition while also drawing from the rock and roll well.

Also hailing from New York state, Case booked out of there as soon as he could as a teenager, working his way across the country by busking and playing coffeehouses, winging it as he went along, and ending up in San Francisco. He lived on a houseboat, in a junkyard, and on a street corner, his guitar at his side. Although he has experience with rock bands, any time he finds himself between groups or needing to regroup, he takes to the road, the place that has served both as a support and inspiration for him for over 25 years.

For those who remember the totally '80s cult movie *Valley Girl*, Case soul-shouted the Plimsouls' anthem, "A Million Miles Away," in his band's cameo. But for another set of fans, Case started a new movement in American singer-songwriter music and folk rock, beginning with his 1986 release *Peter Case* and its 1989 follow-up, the watershed new acoustic music album, *The Man with the Blue Postmodern Fragmented Neo-Traditionalist Guitar.*

Among the very first '80s performers to unplug, as they say, Case launched a new folk alternative; it could be argued that the No Depression movement's beginnings date back to Case's 1986 debut, wherein he opened up the acoustic genre to the generation weaned on '80s college radio. He also convincingly reinvented himself as he went from a peg-legged-trouser–wearing new wave bandleader to a baggy-suited, Depression-era–style singing hobo. Only a couple of so-called rock players had dared to pull back and perform in such a stripped-down style at the apex of '80s modern rock. What may have begun on a whim for Case turned into seven solo acoustic excursions, with a number of diversions along the way, including the re-formation of the Plimsouls in the late '90s. Establishing himself in the acoustic music world and then re-forming one of the most notoriously rocking and loose bands rock has ever known was a bold stroke. There isn't another performer out there who has managed to be the leader and frontperson of a bash and pop band while simultaneously having a career as an extraordinary solo acoustic performer and songwriter. Despite the time he has logged in the more success-driven rock arena, by going solo, Case has managed to give his career longevity, which is why he's still playing. Unlike Elliott, Case speaks little on stage when he performs, although like Elliott, his songs are indistinguishable from his life—his songs are his stories and his stories are his songs.

The same may be said of U. Utah Phillips, whose life has been intrinsically linked to the power of tall tales, truth, and songs. Known primarily as a storyteller and union activist, Phillips sheepishly plays guitar while wearing any number of hats, from radio show host to collaborator, fellow worker, politician, and performer. Another man with a history of running and rail riding, Bruce Phillips hopped his first freight train out of Utah at 15 and headed off to make a living with the National Parks Service. When that didn't pan out, he served in the Army, and upon his return signed himself up for a life of anarchy. As a card-carrying member of the Industrial Workers of the World (the Wobblies), Phillips has devoted his songs and stories to passing down the teachings of union organizers and pacifists like his mentor, Ammon Hennacy, who helped him recognize his gift. Heading west, Phillips settled in Northern California, where today he collects sounds and information for presentation on his weekly public radio broadcast, *Loafer's Glory.* He often travels to folk festivals, union rallies, and peace gatherings—either with his guitar or a friend in tow—where he's greeted with open hearts and keen ears by new generations of politically aware activists. Phillips is a master observer of our culture—both past and present—and as an archivist and historian, he's a national treasure. But even more inspirational is his belief in change through action and organization and the way he uses song to do that. It's a mission from which he rarely rests, although he steers clear of pedantics— after all, he's an anarchist. He moves with ease from collaborations with blue- grass artists and old school folkies to hanging out with peace punks. His latest incarnation is as friend, mentor, and collaborator to alternative music's do-it-yourself diva, Ani DiFranco.

Overall, the '90s were a good time for folk music. As acoustic sounds and word-driven songs with little or no embellishment returned to the radio, the genre's heritage artists lived to witness a revival of their music—their records were reissued, their songs were rerecorded, and they received long-overdue awards. A new generation picked up guitars for the first time. The coffee- house and festival circuit was reinvigorated in a way that hadn't been seen since the singer-songwriter explosion of the mid-'70s and prior to that, the early '60s folk revival. Time and devotion to craft finally won out; no one can take the years away from Elliott and Phillips, nor will they from Case—as he continues on the footpath.

By continually honing their skills or by creating new destinations for themselves, Ramblin' Jack Elliott, U. Utah Phillips, and Peter Case are among the most dedicated workers in the folk-inspired tradition, simply because they keep playing, breaking the barriers of ageism and genre-ism and con- tinually beating a deck that's been traditionally stacked against artistic truth seekers. By reaching just a little further, they've touched people beyond the middle-aged sandal-and-sock–wearing brigade known to favor folk music: Elliott by supporting Americana and living the songs he keeps alive; Phillips by crossing over with his stories and knowledge; Case by cutting through with his passionate melodies and words, which distill the redemptive power of song. They all embrace humor as a universal salve.

After years of running, riding, and searching 'round the globe, all three men have come to call the great state of California their home—an adver- tisement in itself for the wild western life that may have attracted them here in the first place. They've taken different paths down the main road. They've navigated their own ways, bringing their message, music, and stories to the people night after night, year after year—doing it any other way has never been a consideration. With no rulebook in hand, they continue to sing their way home.

12

PETER CASE

> "Everyone suddenly burst out singing
> And I was filled with such delight
> As prisoned birds must find in freedom."
> —Sigfried Sasoon

" **I** 'm starting to see that after 10 or 12 albums, there's a thread through all the things I do—the same temperatures run through all of it," says Peter Case, who's been singing and writing songs for more than 25 years.

"The first song on the first Plimsouls album, 'Lost Time,' was a song about the past, and I was only 22 or something. I've always used songs as a way to sing up the past. They could also be about singing up reality, singing me back home, or singing me out of here. Hitting a plane where songs exist, especially if you're in prison or in a situation where you're stuck in a room, and there's an avenue of freedom offered through a song—that's always really appealed to me.

"The secret to songwriting to me, the only one anyone can be let in on, is that you have to create your own whole world of songs, sing your own songs, and be completely dedicated to writing your songs—whether they are good or bad or commercial or people hate 'em.'"

Songwriting is the one thing that has been a constant in Peter Case's life. He busked on street corners before fronting a successful rock band; he recorded three solo albums for a major label, then rebounded with a self-released CD; he led a vagabond's life till he became a family man; he cut two more folk records in the midst of writing new songs for his now-defunct rock band. Each episode on the road helped to shape and define his songwriting, bringing Case back full circle to the kind of spare acoustic music he cut his teeth on in upstate New York as a teenager.

"It kind of worked out for me, because now I just have a regular life. I've written so many more songs since I got married and had kids than I used to, and they are so much more powerful,"says Case. "On the other hand, for years, when I first became a musician, all I did was play guitar. I lived in junkyards and on the street and played guitar. I didn't have anything to fall back on. I didn't have two cents. But I had a guitar, and that was my total identity at that point, so who am I to say how to do it?"

Case began writing and performing in coffeehouses as a teenager, but ironically, he first found success in the Los Angeles–based garage band the Plimsouls in the '80s. By the spring of 2000, Case had released seven solo folk-based albums (including one recording of covers) and a Plimsouls reunion disc, and was firmly entrenched in writing and recording music.

On each of his solo records, there's always a song or two harkening back to Case's power-pop past, although more often than not, the recordings are loaded with Case's distinct brand of song—one kind stars drifters caught on the outskirts of society, the others are love songs. Most are composed on guitar and played in the finger-picking style he adopted from listening as a kid to old records by Mississippi John Hurt. All, he claims are about finding a place and a way home.

"It's really tricky to talk about. Some are personal and some are made up. Others are a mixture of both—like 'Poor Old Tom' (from Case's second solo album, *Blue Guitar*). When I say, 'He never took a free breath,' it might be me talking about myself, I hate to say it.

"Some songwriters are like magpies, and they collect bits and pieces of thread all day long. And other people have visions. It's all valid. But if you have to ask what it's about, it's almost like the song wasn't good enough," he says. "Songs are very mysterious. What if you really loved a song and you found out it was about something really boring?" Like some songwriters, Case is reluctant to dissect his craft—as if by talking about his gift it will somehow be taken away.

"I talk about songwriting with songwriters sometimes…lately it seems like there's a million books on songwriting, and songwriting workshops, magazines, castles in Ireland you can go to, but there doesn't really seem like there are that many more great songs, does it?

"There are some weird songs going around, and you go, 'I love that song, what the hell is that about?' When I started writing songs, I wanted to have something that was really complete. I wanted my songs to be strong and clear enough that I could walk into any bar in America and sing them and the people there would feel it—they'd know what I was talking about. They might not agree with it, but they'd get it."

Growing up in Hamburg, New York, Case first picked up a stringed instrument at about age three—a Mickey Mouse ukulele; starting to play in earnest at age 11, he learned the acoustic guitar and some chords from *Sing Out* magazine, picking out favorites from rock song books, like the Kinks' "Well Respected Man." His family was musically inclined—an uncle played trombone, his sister plays piano, and his dad was a fan. "My dad and his brother Pete used to travel around and see Bennie Goodman and Cab Calloway. They used to hitchhike to gigs and follow bands."

Although like his peers he was profoundly affected by Elvis Presley and the Beatles, and was equally interested in the early rock and roll records his older sister kept, as a teenager Case also made time discovering the blues and folk of Mississippi John Hurt, Leadbelly, Muddy Waters, Lightnin' Hopkins, and Woody Guthrie. He also led a string of rock bands, while continuing to pursue the singer-songwriter's life of coffeehouse gigs and open-mic nights.

"I was awkward, and didn't really know how to relate to people outside of my music," he says. When he caught the first bus he could out of Buffalo, he found himself busking to survive, living on the streets of San Francisco. It was there he was discovered in 1975 by songwriter Jack Lee, who invited Case to join his power-pop combo, the Nerves.

"Jack said, 'How much do you make a night?' and I lied and said $50, and he lied and said, 'I'll double it if you play with my band.'" The meeting led to a move to L.A., the recording of a now rare EP, and the band's demise after two years, but not before they'd recorded a new wave classic as a three-piece (Paul Collins was the third). Lee's "Hanging on the Telephone" would later get covered by Blondie.

Following a between-bands stint as a house painter, Case formed the Plimsouls in 1980. The ramshackle, maximum R&B outfit pulled tunes from British Invasion bands and wrote their own, like "Hush, Hush" and "How Long Will It Take?" in a similar boy-meets-girl vein; they earned a reputation for their party-all-night live shows. In 1980 they recorded the EP *Zero Hour*, and followed with a self-titled debut in '81. But after four years of playing and touring, and even after finding a measure of success with the single "A Million Miles Away" from the '83 album *Everywhere at Once*, Case felt the pull of folk music.

"After shows we would sit around in hotel rooms…we had a jug band with the roadies," says Case of the time when he began to rediscover the music of his youth. "The after-gig sessions started to become more important to me than the Plimsouls shows. I was picking up some things I'd left behind—music that was important to me."

Amidst the Plimsouls breaking up in 1984 and in the period immediately following, Case began writing new songs, taking different routes. "I was constantly writing songs and trying to unravel some of the mysteries of music. I'd go into coffeehouses and play…." He formed the all-stringed instrument quartet, the Incredibly Strung-Out Band, with Victoria Williams, Gurf Morlix, and Warren "Tornado" Klein. "We were the world's formost interpreters of Blaze Foley material," says Case, referring to the band's intentional, below-the-radar vibe. "We didn't really do many gigs in clubs…we mostly played in people's houses and in the back seats of cars."

It's true that Hiatt and Burnett had started to "unplug" themselves well before it became a program on MTV. But Case pulled his crowd from a younger, hipper crowd than Hiatt and Burnett's people, who were mostly '70s folkie holdovers. Although Case himself is a Baby Boomer, having come up through the punk clubs, he had a different kind of cred. Theoretically, Case had an edge with his new audience, carrying the leather-jacketed crowd from his Plimsouls days with him. But he remembers the transition back to folk music as a rocky one.

"After headlining places with the Plimsouls, I was back to making $50 a night at the Anti Club [a legendary L.A. punk rock venue]. When I first went back to playing solo, I felt like I was reinventing the wheel. A lot of people came with me and a lot of them didn't.

"At that point I was bashing away. It's an old songwriting axiom, but I wanted to learn how to show, not tell, and I didn't really have any teachers. I went to Bertolt Brecht and Song of Songs in the Bible for lyrical inspiration." Case continued to fine-tune his songs before recording his solo debut with Burnett in the producer's seat. "T-Bone became a teacher," he says, "and he was a great editor." It was Burnett who helped to round up the L.A.-based

Case strikes a chord on the streets of San Francisco

musicians and session cats (including Hiatt, Roger McGuinn, and Van Dyke Parks—"they were heroes of mine") who played on Case's 1986 Geffen debut, *Peter Case*. It was a wonderful, jangly, folky record, and Case, with his new then-wife, Victoria Williams, emerged a new artist with a collection of songs so enthusiastic they sounded as if they'd burst forth in one tumble. Pictured in a rumpled, Depression-era suit against a rural backdrop, Case also lent a look to the burgeoning new school of folk. The music's disciples would go on to build their own acts around traditional, Appalachian, and country songs, clad in vintage clothing, carrying dusty banjo and accordion cases bought from the pawn shop.

Case provided the nucleus of songs for the record, culled from childhood memories with bits and pieces of Americana thrown in—"A Walk in the Woods," "I Shook His Hand," "Small Town Spree," and "Three Days Straight" among the best of them—which, besides the beginning of a back-to-basics

peter case

*The man with the blue postmodern
fragmented neo-traditionalist guitar:*

by Denise Sullivan

I saw Peter Case perform his songs throughout 1988 at the Sacred Grounds Cafe at Hayes and Cole Streets, behind fogged-in windows, among candles and friends. When *The Man with the Blue Postmodern Fragmented Neo-Traditionalist Guitar* came out in '89, it rarely left my turntable. I knew that having witnessed one of my favorite artists work out his songs in a coffeehouse across the street from where I lived would be a rare experience.

At the time I owned a small record store in the Haight, and Case came there twice to play his songs for me and the 30 or so people that could cram into my store. The shop had to close, and I moved to Atlanta, but I made sure to take my Case (a CD this time) with me. "Poor Old Tom"and "Entella Hotel"reminded me of San Francisco, even though they were about a side of life there I never knew. But I missed home so much I could romanticize even the seediest things, like a long-gone place on Broadway called the Garden of Earthly Delights.

In 1990, I met the man who was to become my husband, and one of the first things he said to me was, "I hear you like Peter Case."A mutual friend had set us up—"You'll get along great—he likes Peter Case, too"—and he was right. When we would put on *Blue...Guitar* (on cassette) it was usually on long car rides when we could listen to it straight through. And the whole time I'd be thinking how many times this record has made me happy; in fact, how it has actually changed my life.

sound, was an experiment with the percussive sounds of the day; a precursor to trip-hop, at the time Case dubbed the new sound, "tribal folk."

A couple of other songs were cowritten with other artists, like "Old Blue Car" with Williams and Marvin Etzioni. "You end up writing different kinds of songs when you cowrite, and that can have its positive and negative effects," Case says. "But it seems sometimes the heart songs aren't cowrites—they're generally the humorous or philosophical songs. With cowrites, it's not good to say who wrote what."

Collaboration is something Case continues to do, but he writes the bulk of his material on his own. In later years, he would cowrite a novelty song about a cosmic simian, "Space Monkey," with John Prine. He's also collaborated with Tonio K., Billy Swan, and Tom Russell, but he declares, "You're better off alone if you're going to pour your heart out."

By the time 1989's *Man with the Blue Postmodern Neo-Traditionalist Fragmented Guitar* came out, Case had perfected his trademark songs about drifters and losers, as evidenced in "Poor Old Tom"and "Entella Hotel,"songs whose characters were partly based on Case's reminiscences of his days and nights living on the streets of San Francisco, where he had returned to woodshed new material at coffeehouse gigs. This time out, he stuck exclusively to a traditional roots-rock sound accompanied by his own acoustic guitar and harmonica. For the L.A. recording sessions, David Hidalgo of Los Lobos, Ry Cooder, David Lindley, and Heartbreaker Benmont Tench were all enlisted to pitch in on what turned out to be a high-water mark in acoustic rock for the time. The record, though not a commercial breakthrough, was critically well-received and seemed to hasten the movement toward more rockers, particularly younger ones, unplugging, as acoustic appearances and extended acoustic sets became increasingly popular features in rock bands' live acts. The album earned Case a mention in *Rolling Stone* by Bruce Springsteen, who said Case was one of the few songwriters he was listening to at the time (although Case is not particularly an acolyte or fan of the Boss).

Following that high, however, Case experienced a period of "artistic confusion."Feeling label pressure to record a follow-up album with the commercial potential to match the critical acclaim of its predecessor, the ill-fated *Six-Pack of Love* turned out to be Case's final album for Geffen in 1992. The combination of record company interference, an unsympathetic producer in Mitchell Froom, and material conceived under duress netted a sonic disaster. "I think five of the songs are among some of the best I've ever written, and five are some of the worst." True enough. Case still plays "Beyond the Blues," the best song from the sessions, to great effect in his live set. "It was a really dark time for me,"he recalls. "If I was ever depressed in my life, that was the time."

Case got his reprieve from the record label grind with a new marriage and started a family. In the down time following *Six-Pack*, as he recovered from his unhappy alliance with Geffen, in what was turning out to be a pattern for him, when the going got tough, he turned to folk music.

He recruited producer Marvin Etzioni, and the pair recorded in Etzioni's living room. *Sings Like Hell* was a take-no-prisoners self-released 1993 album of traditional songs and personal favorites. "I just played songs I'd loved through the years," Case says of the spare but perfectly rendered versions of "Lakes of the Ponchartrain," "Rovin' Gambler," and Jesse Winchester's "How 'Bout You,"—all which fit well into the Case bag. The covers album brought him to the attention of the prestigious Vanguard label, which was experiencing a rebirth of its own; *Sings Like Hell* was subsequently reissued by them, and it's where Case's recordings find a home today.

Case says the homemade album helped him regain the focus of his own songwriting and provided the inspiration for the new material that comprised the return-to-form *Torn Again* (1995), a collection of originals played in his percussive style, at times accompanied by a band that included multistring instrumentalist Greg Leisz, bass legend Jerry Scheff, and Nashville drummer Don Heffington. The album craftily intertwined songs with personal themes—love, family life, growing older, giving up vices—with tales from the fictional world where his cast of drifters and dreamers dwell. He reunited with the production team of J. Steven Soles and Larry Hirsch from the *Blue Guitar* sessions, which may account for *Torn Again*'s warm, familiar sound.

The album's opener, "Turnin' Blue," has the lyrical core of a pulpy Jim Thompson novel; "Baltimore," a semi-autobiographical tale about street hassles, effectively weds the careless pop of "A Million Miles Away," with the tense subject. "Workin' for the Enemy" returns to the territory Case walks well—the beat where "Sonny" and "Linda Lou" survive the daily drama of "livin' on the edge." On similar turf, two mindless, directionless vagabonds, "Punch & Socko," duke it out for stature in their picaresque world. Case's ability to weave traditional, word-driven story songs with ones with pop hooks is one of his strengths.

"As my songs got stranger and more original, they sounded wrong to me," he says of the melodies that emerged on *Torn Again*. "They're right, but they're wrong by any sort of definition because they're new.

Full Service No Waiting-era Case: "It was the record I'd wanted to make for a long time..."

"When I get inspiration that gives me enough energy that I think I'm going to write a song, there's something in there that's always true. But when the technique and craft of songwriting gets in there, a lot of times it'll screw it up. I'll miss the point. But I keep going back to those things, because if there was something in there that originally gave me the impulse to do it, there's something in there that's true and I have to find out what that is."

Perhaps it was the impulse toward artistic truth-seeking that gave Case the energy in 1995—in the middle of his solo acoustic renaissance—to reform the Plimsouls, the band he had broken up more than ten years before. "I just went for it," he says. "You just gotta do things. There was unfinished business with the Plimsouls, and it still seemed like there was a lot of life in it. There was incredible energy in it when we came back." The Plimsouls were not only one of rock's more energetic bands, they were also one of its most unpredictable. They've been called everything from a garage band to a bar band to a power-pop band to an R&B band to a mess, but the bottom line was, they rocked.

"I love the Plimsouls, and we could blow the roof off a place and all that kind of thing, but at the end of it all, there's a lot of things that weren't coming through, particularly any sort of lyrics! It was a real rocking band, but it was kind of a blunt instrument too," Case says. In 1997, he set out to make the great lost Plimsouls record with original members Eddie Muñoz and David Pahoa plus drummer Clem Burke (original drummer Lou Ramirez sat out the reunion). They went into the studio, cut some demos, and took the show on the road. A version of the sessions was eventually released as *Kool Trash* (Shaky City, 1998).

"I got a lot out of it. I wish we would've made a great album, because that's the one thing I still haven't done with the Plimsouls, but I made some mistakes putting it together again. But it was really good for me physically. It woke me up…I was really out of energy in a weird way, so it kind of revitalized me. I was depressed, I guess. I weighed about 40 more pounds, I had this huge beard, and I was really angry all the time. And then I started the Plimsouls and about halfway through it, I'd adjusted and got back into the whole thing. It was like I found some brand new legs. The Plimsouls is like a Dionysian, submit-to-the-force kind of thing. I try to bring as much of that kind of vibe as I can to what I'm doin' now." So that was the good part. But as with the Plimsouls Mach I, there were also some bummers. Would he try it again?

"I don't know if I could stand it. There's no reason to break up a perfectly good band twice, you know what I'm saying? So we'll never break up again, but we might do something again. We always could. You know what…it was really hard. It was like picking up where we left off in good and bad ways. We'd have the same arguments, the same ridiculous things happening, the same incomprehension, and then I finally realized…time's infinite and all that kind of shit, but I really wanted to focus. I remembered why I broke up the Plimsouls. It all came back to me and I wanted to go solo again!"

Back to his primary vocation as a singer-songwriter, he went in and made *Full Service No Waiting* with producer Andrew Williams. "When *Full Service* came out, it was the record I'd wanted to make for a long time and I finally got to it. I wrote all the lyrics to that album in one big burst. I was hearing the music sorta in my head and I wasn't really writing it on the guitar and putting it together. It was all done from stories and words and a typewriter. As I typed the words, I'd hear the melodies in my head. Eventually I'd pick up a guitar and put it together."

Full Service No Waiting is home to some of Case's greatest latter-day solo songs—refining the spirit that has coursed through his songs from the beginning. Whether it's in the song itself, in love, or in some higher source, there is a faith that abides and guides each note and word. His voice, more mature, is stronger than before and his playing equally impressive on "Crooked Mile," "Drunkard's Harmony," and "Still Playin'." Seemingly inspired in large part by events from his youth, almost all of the cuts are in the "heart song" category he refers to—whether it's the sweet reminiscence of "On the Way Downtown," the spin on bad timing in "Until the Next Time," or the spiritual side of being blind drunk in "Drunkard's Harmony."

"The day I was finished with that record, I started working on the next one. I was out at Cape Girardeau Missouri, visiting some older people in the family. I ended up at a Pentecostal church, and there was a band of guys playing. They were all in their 60s and they all had rockabilly haircuts, but they were playing in a band at a Pentecostal church, and they were a really weird band! You just don't ever hear anybody playing like that, and I started talking to these guys, and it turned out they *had* been rockabilly, and they used to play at this place called the Flying Saucer in Cape Girardeau. So I started working on a piece about this band and this place and these people, and it went on and on into a whole lot of different songs and areas, but I ended up shelving that whole thing and writing a whole other batch of songs."

Most of the songs on *Flying Saucer Blues* were written just before they were recorded. Bridging the divide between his train-whistle harmonica, chug-a-chug-a finger-picking style, and his love of rock and roll, Case pulled in the music vets and friends he'd used on previous albums, like guitarist Greg Leisz, percussionist Don Heffington, bassist David Jackson, and producer Williams—players who can handle just about anything that's thrown at them.

He plays his usual brand of incisive folk-rock on "Paradise Etc." and "Black Dirt & Clay," songs in which he continues to ponder his past—from East Coast kid to California musician and seeker. There's only one of Case's signature wordy pieces, and it's a funny one: He says "Two Heroes" and its cast of colorful Hollywood characters is based on a true story. The folk-blues-boogie-with-horns, "Cool Drink O' Water," the smoky cabaret number, "Lost

Time Line

1954	Born in Buffalo, New York
1973–75	Arrives in San Francisco, begins street singing
	Meets Jack Lee while busking on a San Francisco street corner
	Joins Lee's pre-punk pop band, the Nerves
1980	Forms the Plimsouls
	Plimsouls' debut album released
1984	Plimsouls break up
	Solo debut McCabe's Guitar Shop, Santa Monica, CA
1986	Solo debut album, *Peter Case*
1989	*Man with the Blue Postmodern Fragmented Neo-Traditionalist Guitar*
1993	After three albums for Geffen, regroups with the home recordings, *Sings Like Hell*
1995	Signs with Vanguard label for *Torn Again*
	Re-forms Plimsouls
1997	*Full Service No Waiting*
1998	Plimsouls' *Kool Trash*
2000	*Flying Saucer Blues*

in Your Eyes," and the old-fashioned Mexican folk melody of the spiritually motivated, "Cold Trail Blues," added deeper shades to his acoustic-based music.

"I grew up listening to '50s rock and roll—Fats Domino, my big sister's record collection—that's deeply ingrained in me. 'Lost in Your Eyes' comes from that, and 'Coulda Shoulda Woulda' sounds like the Buckeroos or the Beatles to me. I wanted to have a kind of really down but happy song. I don't know what happened, but the songs on this record have a little deeper groove than on the last record. The return-to-rock vibe was a bit of rebellion. The whole time I was generating these bigger, word-driven stories, I'd be listening to *Rubber Soul* and thinking how simply elegant those songs were," Case says. "If you put on *Rubber Soul*, you think if you listen to that for a couple of days you could sit down and knock out ten of those yourself—it seems so natural."Not by coincidence then, in the summer of '99 Case performed with George Martin and an orchestra at the Hollywood Bowl. "I got to this big sound stage and there was no one there except George Martin, and he says, 'Come on over to the piano, Peter.' It was cool, you know. We just sat there and sang."

But for now, it's back to the folk haunts where Case first learned his trade. "This year it will be 100 to 120 nights on the road," he reckons. "There's a following of people who are really into [singer-songwriter music], and they're not an easily identified cultural group. There are kids, people who are into No Depression, older people—people who were there for the first Newport Festival—rock and roll fans, and people who somehow got into it recently." It's true, a Case audience is not easy to peg, although one thing they share is their rapt attention while he's playing. Case's ability to pick out complex folk melodies (born from a love of English folkies like Bert Jansch and the Incredible String Band) and place them alongside classic American structures, his unique phrasing and astoundingly resonant voice—which is rarely, if ever, out of sync with the lyrics—combine to make Case a commanding presence on the folk stage.

It would seem that Case has once again retreated into making masterful singer-songwriter records, but he also can't resist keeping his hand in a variety of complementary projects. Between records he's curated music for an exhibit at the Getty Museum in Los Angeles; organized a various artists tribute record to his childhood hero, Mississippi John Hurt; hosted singer-songwriter night at the revived Santa Monica folk club, the Ash Grove. His songs have been covered by other songwriters—like Alejandro Escovedo who cut "Two Angels" and Robert Earl Keen Jr. who picked up on "Travellin' Light"—and he teaches songwriting to aspiring writers and performers.

"Songs are used for all sorts of different things; you can write for an audience and also for one person. There are all sorts of different uses for them besides just to fill out your pop album. I come from a background of people who just sang songs in the neighborhood. Victoria Williams is like that, and I'm like that, and Jack Lee is like that—though he didn't think he was like that. Where I grew up there were songwriters and none of them are famous, but the people who really influenced me in that way were people who were always around. They would move me and other people around them, prolifically writing songs. They are the equivalent to Southern outsider artists, where a guy just paints weird things in his backyard. I don't feel like having a pop career anymore. There's a possibility that something like that would happen, but it's kind of over—it was over before I even knew it. But the thing I've been into and I've stuck with is songs—trying to put together some sort of whole picture, a world that would make sense if someone wanted to really get into it. That's all I'm trying to do, I guess.

"I was really flipping out when I was a kid. Music was such a life raft—the guitar and singing especially. I clung to it for my life, really. And I learned everything from it, too. It's just like a means for me to keep sane. For a million people it's like that."

Still trying to make sense out of things, Case brings it all back home. "My father just passed away, and after that, I went to Texas, and my son was playing me some music he made; it blew my mind. I've turned a corner. I'm right in the middle of the beginning of the end, you know what I mean? It's shocking, but it's kind of great. I'm pretty happy, even though a lot of things are really ridiculous."

Recommended Recordings

Plimsouls...Plus (Rhino, 1981)
Old-school Plimsouls at their garage-band, power-pop best. "Zero Hour," "Hush, Hush," and "Now" draw from British Invasion to roots-rock.

The Man with the Blue Postmodern Fragmented Neo-Traditionalist Guitar
(Geffen, 1989)

An important record in the resurgence of acoustic singer-songerwriter
music in the late '80s and early '90s. Some of Case's all-time best songs
live here, like "Poor Old Tom," "Entella Hotel," "Two Angels," "Hidden
Love"...come to think of it, all of them; with David Hidalgo, Ry Cooder,
and Benmont Tench sitting in.

Peter Case Sings Like Hell (Vanguard, 1994)

A back-to-basics living room recording of originals and traditional folk
songs, it's a good introduction to unembellished, traditional music for
rock fans. Folk and blues fans will also appreciate the richness of Case's
delivery.

Full Service No Waiting (Vanguard 1998)

Case's second studio release for Vanguard, this late '90s recording shows
him at his mid-career finest, especially on the story "On the Way Downtown," love song "Until the Next Time," and troubadour's anthem "Still
Playin'."

13

U. UTAH PHILLIPS

"I think Utah is the shit."
—Ani DiFranco

"**S**omething everlastingly true about riding freight trains is that it's boring," says U. Utah Phillips. He would know. Among other disparate and curious credentials, he is a songwriter, a poet, a storyteller, a peace activist, a broadcaster, a collaborator with Ani DiFranco, and a card-carrying member of the Industrial Workers of the World—a Wobbly. And, for five decades, he has worked in the tradition of humming, strumming rail riders like Woody Guthrie and Ramblin' Jack Elliott, whose cars pulled them west and whose politics leaned left. Phillips, however, was never part of the '60s folk revival— he barely even knew it was happening. Then, just as now, he stood apart from the pack of folkies and singing hobos. "I think that the romance gets pounded out of you after the fourth or fifth try, because those empties, they ride rough when there's nothin' in 'em, and I had to ride 'em for 1,000 miles squatting on my heels because you couldn't sit down without getting pounded to death. The jolly hobo singing with his guitar? You can't hear anything! Too loud," he exclaims.

No one would dare describe Phillips as a jolly hobo, although he'd make a damn good Santa with his head of gray hair, great gray beard, and gentle manner. It's the middle of a November day in Nevada City, the one-time gold mining town near the Sierra foothills, and Phillips is dressed in coveralls, a red plaid shirt, red bow-tie, and felt fedora; he looks the picture of traditional mining town resident and iconoclastic codger. Within minutes of walking the downtown promenade, he settles inside his cozy farmhouse, up the road a piece. "Three years ago, Nevada City had a downtown barber shop, a hardware store, a movie theater, and a drugstore. Those have all been upscaled, mainly by the landlords, who wanted to make more money—mainly boutiques, wine shops, and so on, so there's not a lot of reason for the people who live here who need those services to go into town. We all love Nevada City, but people go to Grass Valley or to Brunswick, one of America's great shopping cities, for their services."

Phillips first discovered the area in the late '70s, and he and his wife have called it home for over 20 years. He has made it his business to know his history, not only of the Sierra foothills region, but of the people and regions he visits about once a month in other parts of the country, guitar in hand, as a traveling raconteur—recent congestive heart failure and continuing treatment notwithstanding.

"Brunswick used to be a beautiful lake, with an island in the middle and a dance pavilion where the big bands played; people could go down on the trolley car—Brunswick Basin. It's all been 'dozed in. Now there are four shopping centers there."

Time Line

1935	Born Bruce Phillips in Cleveland, Ohio
1947	Family relocates to Utah
	Serves in Korean War
Late '50s	Meets his mentor, religious pacifist Ammon Hennacy
'60s	Works as an antiwar activist, children's guitar teacher, and state archivist in Utah
1968	Makes first run for Senate in Utah on the Peace and Freedom ticket
1979	Starts appearing on the folk circuit
	Moves to Nevada City, California, where he lives today
1996	Collaborates with Ani DiFranco for the first time, reaching an entirely new generation
1997	Awarded Lifetime Achievement Award from the North American Folk Alliance
1998	*Heartsongs: The Old-Time Country Songs of Utah Phillips* earns a Grammy nomination for Kate Brislin and Jody Stecher

If that sounds about as radical as "they paved paradise and put up a parking lot," that's just one side of Phillips and his interests. Another side has an abiding belief in the power of people to organize and overcome. It's a well-formed worldview, and he's extremely powerful in its articulation; it's contagious! It's a streak that goes way back in his 64-year personal history.

Born Bruce Phillips in Cleveland, Ohio, in 1937, Phillips' family relocated to Utah, that bastion of the Mormon church, in 1947. His father owned a movie theater that premiered the classics of the day and featured live entertainment, his mother worked for the Congress of Industrial Organizations (CIO), the union group that ultimately merged with the American Federation of Labor (AFL). His upbringing had a two-pronged effect on the young Phillips; he loved the arts, but perhaps more significantly, when Phillips' mother insisted that the ropes that segregated blacks from whites in her husband's theater come down, the Phillips clan made Utah history. But victories over racial segregation weren't enough to keep the young Bruce in Utah. He started running away from home, and after one final unsuccessful escape to Yellowstone by freight train, he was called to serve as a soldier in the Korean War. He went, finding some solace overseas as a ukelele player in the canteen band. It was an instrument he'd learned as a kid, and he had honed his skills strumming around campfires during his rail-riding years.

He returned from the war, like so many veterans, feeling angry and dispossessed; he hopped the rails again in an effort to find a place for himself, hoping to literally pound the feelings out of his system. It didn't work. But something happened during that time overseas and in those bumpy cars. Phillips experienced an awakening of sorts: He decided that he would never take orders again; that he would become his own governor.

Back in Utah during the late '50s, Phillips found a mentor in Christian anarchist Ammon Hennacy, a religious pacifist and labor organizer who was contributing to the Catholic Workers House. Hennacy, perhaps best known for his fasting in protest of prisoners awaiting execution, ultimately died of a heart attack on a protest line in 1970. By then he had already been a cofounder and overseer of the Joe Hill Houses of Hospitality (named for the martyred Wobbly organizer, songwriter, and subject of many songs himself, the most famous of which is "I Dreamed I Saw Joe Hill Last Night").

"Ammon told me I had to learn to become a pacifist to save my life, just like an alcoholic has to learn to go into the program to save his life," says

Iconoclastic codger U. Utah Phillips

Phillips. "I found out from Ammon all that takes is courage. Courage is the principal virtue, because without it you can't practice any of the others." It was also Hennacy who contributed to Phillips' conversion into a political or topical songwriter; when Phillips speaks of him, it is with the gravitas reserved for people whose lives and work have profoundly affected or changed one's own.

the chords of love and pain

170

In 1968, Phillips ran a serious Senate campaign in Utah as the Peace & Freedom candidate. "We took 600 votes. I took a leave of absence from state service to do that, and when the campaign was over, my job had vanished. And I couldn't get work in the state anywhere. That's why I'm sitting here right now. I had to leave Utah.

"Ammon told me, 'Some people learn things the hard way, and you're one of them.' I've never forgotten it. After a long period of rubbing against the world from place to place, I realized what Ammon was up to; there are more fundamental changes that need to take place before the ballot box works."

Nevertheless, Phillips plans to run for president again in the next election on his own Sloth and Indolence ticket. "I always run, and why not? Because I always win. When I'm not in the White House, it's a stunning victory!"

But, say, if he were elected…

"I wouldn't do anything. I'd say if you want something done, get together and do it yourself. I'm not the boss—I'm not gonna tell you what to do. Anarchists are some of the most organized people I know, because you gotta learn to be your own government."

In whatever so-called down time he has, Phillips works at his craft, fashioning stories set to music. "I work at the trade rather than at the industry. The trade means I own what I do, I make the creative decisions, and it's all very low level. The notion at the trade level is that you want to make a living and not a killing—live decently, be able to take care of your debts, and take care of your health insurance—nothing more." He collects his thoughts, songs, and what he calls "bits of doggerel and miscellaneous and unidentifiable trash" for presentation on a wild ride of a weekly community radio broadcast, *Loafer's Glory,* "the hobo jungle of the mind," addressing topics from labor and black history to baseball, Christianity, and communism. Additionally, since 1990 alone, Phillips has released six CDs: among them, a collection of stories from hither and yon, *The Moscow Hold,* and *The Long Memory,* traditional and original labor songs recorded with longtime pal Rosalie Sorrels. In 1998, multi-instrumentalist folk duo Jody Stecher and Kate Brislin earned a Grammy nomination for their album *Heartsongs: The Old-Time Country Songs of Utah Phillips.*

"Utah phoned us up four years ago—he'd had a dream we were singing one of those songs," says Stecher. "Sometimes you hear a songwriter's song and you think, 'that's so and so's song.' You hear Utah's songs and you think they've always existed. You don't feel his stamp, instead it feels like it came out of the earth. The craft is almost concealed, and they sound like folk songs." Brislin continues, "I felt like what he gave us were some gems, and what he asked us to do was to make settings for them, as if we were making a piece of jewelry to set off his incredible songs. He paints pictures and tells stories in song very, very well."

Ani DiFranco also created a musical landscape, albeit of a less traditional variety, for Phillips' spoken word on 1996's rhythm- and sample-inspired *The Past Didn't Go Anywhere.* "The way I see it, Utah has so much to say that this album could easily have been two weeks long," says DiFranco in the album's liner notes.

"She had pirated a recording of a concert I did in Ithaca, New York, and listened to it while she was traveling," says Phillips of his initial contact with the renegade folk singer. "[She] wrote me a letter saying, 'I want my audience to hear these stories. You don't have to do anything, just lend me live concert tapes.' So I put 'em in a box—some of them had been underwater—and I sent about 100 hours of those things to her, and I didn't know what she was going to do until it showed up in the mail. And I was stunned. I liked it. Some of my old comrades and political people didn't like it, and I just had to tell them, 'Well, it wasn't made for you, surprise!' But it really did work. And what she said in that letter, and what really sold me on the idea of working with her— I think she was 22 at the time—I can quote: 'Not that there's anything wrong with your performances as they stand, but I am aware of the vertigo a young audience experiences when the music stops and they're left at the precipice of words and ideas.' Now anybody gonna say that, you're gonna work with them, see? I would trust Ani with anything of mine. Her instincts are so keen."

The pair followed the first successful experiment with 1999's *Fellow Workers,* for which they assembled a band and recorded the process live. The experiences Phillips had working with DiFranco put him in touch with a generation of politically aware young adults, some of whom he spent time with recently at a three-day conference of peace activists in Minneapolis.

"There were 400 people who attended that conference, 300 of whom were under the age of 22. I don't believe this whole rap about Generation X— these were committed people; they had been peace watchers in East Timor— had seen people killed. They had been to Cuba, they had been arrested in the

Utah and fellow worker,
D. I. Y. diva, Ani Di Franco

forest in Northern California, and they were there to study nonviolent direct action. The conference was getting elders and youngers together, and it really went beautifully.

"At the Old Songs Festival (5,000 middle-aged, inveterate folkies in Albany, New York) some of Ani's audience showed up. Here are these people, some of whom are leathered, spiked, pierced, and it's sort of off-putting to the old folkies, but by the second day, they're all dancin' and singin' together. So it goes both ways .

"Everybody knows something I don't know. Whether I like 'em or not, the only way I'm gonna find out what it is, is to ask and to really listen, really pay attention. I made myself that way—not my school and not even my parents. It was an act of will somewhere around the age of ten when I realized I was responsible for my education and I still am. If I'm in the hospital overnight for an angioplasty, I want to know what it's like workin' on the night shift, year after year, from the night shift nurses. I want to talk to the janitors. It's an endless source of fascination being on the planet, being alive, being around other people. I guess one of the reasons I took over my education was I realized one of the most valuable things I was born with is curiosity, and I didn't want anybody to take it away."

In that spirit, curious minds want to know: What does the "U" in U. Utah Phillips stand for?

"I was gonna ask you; I thought you might know," he counters. "I've been trying to figure it out for years. Anybody has an idea out there, write me a letter and tell me. I don't know how it got there, it's just there. It could be Ubiquitous, it could be Underwear, it could be Unitarian, it could be Union or a Ubiquitous Unitarian Unionist. Or 'Uh'…I like 'Uh.'"

Recommended Recordings

The Past Didn't Go Anywhere (Righteous Babe, 1996)
Ani DiFranco accompanies Phillips on contemporary samples and sounds created especially to fit Phillips' brand of timeless, personally political stories.

Loafer's Glory (Red House, 1997)
A collection of stories devoted to wandering, culled from the best of Phillips over the last 30 years. He's accompanied by Mark Ross on guitar.

14

RAMBLIN' JACK ELLIOTT

> "He sounds more like me than I do."
> —*Woody Guthrie on Jack Elliott*

"I like being known as a storyteller, as much as I enjoy being known for the music part. I want to be a well-rounded entertainer, and I want to give $10 worth for a $5 ticket. Or I'd like to give them $40 of entertainment if they paid $18 for the ticket…" says folk music's Ramblin' Jack Elliott in his inimitable style. However, these days, and on this day in particular, Elliott has little time or patience for giving anybody a bang for their buck or even making records, although he's experiencing what can only be described as his biggest career high in nearly 50 years of making music.

"I won a Grammy and I won a Bammie all in the same week," he says. "I never cared about that stuff—I never even watched them on TV. But it's kinda nice to have around…it makes a nice decoration for the house and the cats like to rub up against them."

Elliott idolized Woody Guthrie and learned from him; he went on to inspire Bob Dylan and Mick Jagger. He once performed a private audience for James Dean. The great contemporary folk and rock voices, from Emmylou Harris and John Prine to Tom Waits gathered to pay tribute to his legacy on the CD *Friends of Mine*. But none of the awards nor all the names in showbiz can compare to the things that really mean something to Jack: his guitar, his old cowboy stories, and his knack for telling them.

Elliott makes his home in the North Bay, on the California coast's quiet seashore, with his fifth wife, Jan Currie, also known as Ramblin' Jan. (Jan passed away in early 2001.) But ever since his mid-'90s award-winning streak he hasn't been able to spend much time there. His spare, flat-pick acoustic guitar and story-songs kept coming back into favor. And so as he's personally

174

become less and less concerned with the business of music and more concerned with the stuff of his life—Jan, his boat, his cats—damn if tomorrow he doesn't have to hit the road again, this time with Tom Russell, Dave Alvin, and Chris Smither for a two-week Monsters of Folk tour. He's not looking forward to it. He's happy just to be sipping a cup of coffee, eating an egg salad sandwich, "walkin' with his baby by the San Francisco Bay," to quote from his theme song of sorts, Jesse Fuller's "San Francisco Bay Blues."

"I'm worried about getting a cold and not having enough clean clothes. I've got one day off to do laundry. If I carry enough clothes for ten gigs, I can't lift that much in a suitcase in an airport, and I hate airports, and I don't like traveling by airplane, and it's 14 airplanes in 15 days," he says, agitated. "I've been really stressed ever since I've heard about them wanting to do this tour. The only thing is, the guys, the monsters themselves, developed a kind of inner-monster-menstrual-cycle. We pump each other up. We've developed a kind of feeling of brotherhood that will give us this feeling of mutual strength to keep us going through the moments where we tend to get tired." He draws a deep breath. I've met Elliott on a number of occasions, and never once have I seen him this worked up. He vents about the round-robin format in which the songs will be presented on tour.

"I didn't plan it that way. I always think of round robins as being kind of corny and folk festivalish. In a round robin you can never get too cranked up. Usually, I'll get better and better if I'm on stage for 40 or 50 minutes, but if you're just sitting there and your turn comes up once in every four, that means I'm only doing one motor of a show. I'm only performing 20 minutes instead of 80 minutes. And I've gotta be sitting on the stage the whole goddamned night. That's work. That's tiresome. Sitting there in a chair, looking at the people for all that length of time. And then when I do sing, it's harder to sing because I'm not working a flow. 'Oh, it's my turn…'" he says, mockingly, like he's stoned.

"The entertainment world is like a fantasy-world thing," he continues. "It's like seeing the solar or lunar eclipse. It's a wonderful show in outer space. Most people don't know if there's any water on the moon or any heat on the moon. They think of it as a cold place—so many thousands of miles away. So it is with performers. They fly in and fly out. And they come in a bus or a limousine or a private jet plane because they're supposed to. And if they come in a beat-up Dodge van that's full of holes and rust, people don't want to know about that. They want to know you came in a bus. A bus is good. Well some [musicians] *are* good, but they don't have a bus. Some of them are bad and they've got a bus. Who's this Lee Ann Rimes? Got a Peterbilt. A fleet. She's got a Peterbilt motor home. I saw a picture of it. I just want one Peterbilt truck," says Elliott.

I quote from singer-songwriter Nick Lowe, who said that what musicians should really get paid for are the 23 hours they *aren't* on stage—all that driving and eating all that bad food is the work, not the hour onstage.

"No, that ain't work—but I don't want to keep doing it. I'm interested in record-making to the extent that I would like to do one that would make me some money. Because I need the money. But before this, I never even tried to bother to learn how to make a record that will sell and if it does sell, how then to obtain the money that they owe me? Let alone, what about all the money that they owed me from before that I may never collect? I'd rather spend my life tuning an old truck engine or paintin' boat bottoms with poisonous paint." Surely this talking down of the troubadour's life he's led for 50 years, that he learned by following Woody and ended up passing down to Bob is an abberration, as if he's been temporarily possessed by the spirit of an anti-folksinger.

"I'm the anti-*Christ*!" he shouts.

"I went to a rodeo when I was nine years old with my parents at Madison Square Garden, and my uncle Dan had some kind of a plan that he was going to buy a wild horse and have some local person in Connecticut break and train the horse and he was going to use the horse as a saddle horse. That plan never came to fruition, but I was totally turned on by the wild horses and whole rodeo scene," says Elliott.

"When I was 12, I started reading Will James' books. My father's nurse, Mrs. Malone, came from Minnesota," he says, emphasizing the long *o* for effect. "She gave me this book called *Lone Cowboy—My Life Story* by Will James. It was his autobiography. I started reading more Will James books and going to rodeos every year and, finally, when I was 15, I ran away to join the rodeo in 1947. I worked as a groom for Colonel Jim Eskew's Rodeo. He was a Texan, but he had his headquarters up in New York state in a place called Waverly. That was where they kept all the bulls and steers and horses when they weren't on the road."

From young buck Elliott Adnopoz to Ramblin' Jack: "I was totally turned on by the wild horses and whole rodeo scene."

So how did the young man who would go on to make his living on the road survive that first time out on his own?

"I didn't survive. They were paying me $2 a day. I had to eat one hamburger and one malted milk, which was my daily fare. I didn't get too much extra to eat. That kinda kept me alive for ten days at the Pittsburgh Gardens, an indoor rodeo in Pittsburgh, Pennsylvania. From there we went to the ranch, where we were paid $5 a week. They had a cook that fed us flapjacks, beans, and potatoes. And very good coffee," he says.

As yet, the young Elliott hadn't picked up a guitar, but there was a key moment on his first road trip that would forever change his path.

"Haven't I ever told you this story before? I've told it to millions of people. So for the millionth-and-three time, I will tell the story about the rodeo clown, Bramer Rogers, who played the guitar and sang and recited stories and poems and entertained all us rodeo hands in between shows. We'd put a quarter in his hat. That was the first time I'd ever seen anybody busking."

"When I got back to my parents' house to resume my high school studies, I started playing the guitar, as I was missin' them cowboys. I started listening to some country stations. They didn't call it country then, they called it hillbilly music. My favorites were Roy Acuff, Jimmie Rodgers, and Ernest Tubb." But Elliott says he felt like the odd man out, as his burgeoning love of country music and cowboys was at odds with his urban environs. "I didn't like New York, and couldn't wait to get out of there. When I was walking around in cowboy clothes, people didn't appreciate it, and they let me know about it. Basically taxi drivers were particularly rude and insulting. They'd yell, 'Hey Tex.' They were amazed to see anybody in a cowboy hat in New York. They don't believe there are cowboys. They don't even believe there's a West. They actually don't think there's anything out there beyond New Jersey. Many of them have never been to New Jersey or Ohio.

"I can see it in the clear eyes of the young people of the West who've never been east of the Mississippi or have never been to New York—they have an innocent look about them—New York is hard to believe unless you've been there," he says. "But I knew I had to get out. I actually took an entrance examination for Colorado A&M, which had a rodeo team. That would've really been my choice, but I was involved with a girlfriend who was going to school in Vermont, and it seemed like it would be better to keep in touch with her, so I went to the University of Connecticut instead. Of course she immediately fell in love and got married and I never saw her again."

But by then, the University of Connecticut had become his home, although he admits he didn't do well there. "Mostly, I was studying how to sail a 26-foot whale boat. But I was studying geology, chemistry, anthropology, and English. I got an A in anthropology and an F in geology because I couldn't understand the rock identification, which is one of the most important parts of the geology final examination. And chemistry I thought I'd take because my dad was a doctor and I loved horses, so I thought I'd be a veterinarian, but when I was unable to go to chem lab, I flunked out of chemistry, so that wrecked my medical career. But I didn't care too much about it; I was having fun sailing those 26-foot boats and learning to ride a 1942 Indian motorcycle."

"Buck" Elliott debuted on the Greenwich Village scene in the early '50s. He was still in his 20s when he went in search of the man who would become a friend and mentor, Woody Guthrie. Certainly by that time, Guthrie and his politically motivated music had signaled the kind of protest music that would infiltrate folk and rock throughout the '60s and beyond. Once Jack found him and literally moved his way into the Guthrie household, the pair traveled together and Elliott picked up everything he could—even the way he carried himself—from the grand master of American folk music. He played with Guthrie during those years on one of his final cross-country road trips. When Guthrie's health began to fail him, Jack generously did his best to cover up his friend's disabilities. By mid-decade, Jack moved on to Europe, preaching the gospel according to Woody as he busked across the continent. He returned home in the early '60s in time to join the Greenwich Village folk scene, which was in full swing. Elliott's legend preceded him. It was at that

Time Line

1931	Born Elliott Adnopoz, Brooklyn, New York
1947	Runs away to join the rodeo
1951–54	Meets Woody Guthrie and tours with him
1953	Begins performing in Greenwich Village
1955–59	Travels through Europe
1961	Meets Bob Dylan
1975	Tours with Bob Dylan's Rolling Thunder Revue
	Continues to perform solo but takes a break from studio recording
1996	*South Coast* wins a Grammy Award for Best Traditional Folk Album
	Receives the Bill Graham Lifetime Achievement Bammie (Bay Area Music) Award
1998	Receives National Medal of the Arts Award
	Friends of Mine, with Arlo Guthrie, Tom Waits, John Prine, Nanci Griffith, and Emmylou Harris
1999	*The Long Ride*
2000	Documentary film, *The Ballad of Ramblin' Jack,* directed by Elliott's daughter, Aiyana

time he met the young Bob Dylan and the pair formed a friendship, partly based on their mutual Guthrie fascination.

From then on, it was a troubadour's life for the singer and storyteller, who packs his guitar like a cowboy packs a six-gun. In the '70s he did a turn on Dylan's Rolling Thunder Revue. Still enamored with the cowboy's life, Elliott moved westward, although he kept up his touring schedule. And he rambled. As Elliott begins talking about this section of his life, it sounds like he's memorized a speech or is reading from a script. But soon it's revealed he's on one of his patented rambles, with no breaks and very few pauses; any and all interjections from his listeners go unacknowledged.

"I lived in Aspen, Colorado, which isn't really the West. It's sorta like a village in Connecticut that got mislocated. It was a fun place for awhile. And I even said hello to John Denver a couple of times on the street—somewhere in like 1974 or '5. I was at a party with John Denver once and it was very, very nice. I like John Denver.

"I spent little bits of time in parts of Texas. The whole West is inundated with Easterners. The cowboys are like the Indians of yesterday. They've been routed out, shoved out. The government don't want 'em to exist. They're making it difficult for ranchers to exist because the beef prices are kept so low that ranchers have to sell out—can't afford to even keep ranching anymore. I think buffalo meat is probably healthier to eat than beef ever was, anyway. Oh yeah, less fat. You don't get it very much. I don't eat much beef anymore either. Most of the times I eat in a restaurant and order a New York steak it's terrible. I'm so disappointed with the way they cook in restaurants I can't hardly eat any food in restaurants anymore. Our local grocery store has the worst meat. Some of it's from [a famous ranch], which sells good beef, but I don't like to eat it. Sometimes I get a hankering, but it's very seldom I'm satisfied with pleasure."

"I cook you good steak sometimes," his wife, Jan, pipes up.

"It's not your fault, honey, it's that oven or that goddamn grocery store. I'm kind of in favor of the cattlemen, but I never go to McDonald's or anything like that. The cattlemen are pretty much wiped out and that means the cowboys, too.

"When I was reading Will James' books—he wrote those books in the '30s, and he was strongly influenced, copying the artwork of another cowboy that came before him, Charles M. Russell, who went out to Montana in the 1880s and saw the West was a dying thing and that the cowboys and Indians were both being shoved off the land and there were changes going down and it wasn't going to last forever. He painted all those pictures to kind of depict it as it was. If he hadn't have done it, we wouldn't have that graphic representation of what those people were like and how they lived and how they looked.

"Will James wrote about 30 novels in a row—big sellers—and he made a lot of money and he bought a ranch in Montana—it was his favorite place, having been born in eastern Canada. He went west at the age of 15 to be a cowboy. One of his books, *Smoky the Cowhorse*, was made into a movie, and he went to Hollywood and tried to get into the movies but he couldn't speak well enough. Or they didn't like the way his voice came across on tape. Or they didn't have tape in those days, but on the soundtrack or whatever. So he never made it as a Western movie actor, although he worked as an extra in a lot of Western movies, just riding in the background, like a lot of cowboys did. He had that experience. Then he married a girl in Reno. I think they got married in Sausalito, actually. They lived in Reno, her dad lived in Reno, and he was real friends with her dad and another guy and they called themselves the Three—it was a club. And whenever he signed one of his paintings, he'd sign 'Will James' and the year, and like a Roman numeral three or just three ones, meaning he was a member of that club, the Three. His first writing and illustrating was in the *Sunset* magazine. Wrote an article when he was laid up in the hospital, injured from trying to ride a buckin' horse in Nevada with his friends. On a bet. A horse called Hackey. And he was then probably about 30 years old and he was injured, hit his head on a railroad track. He was laid up in the hospital for about three weeks, and one of his friends came to the hospital and said, 'Bet you can't write an article,' and so he wrote an article called 'Buckin' Horses and Buckin' Horse Riders,' and that was his first attempt at literature. Before this he was only a sketcher, mostly in pencil, sometimes in color. His friends criticized his bad use of color a lot and said, 'Why don't you go back east to Yale University art school, and study how to mix color?' And he did. He took 'em up on it and he went to Yale and studied for about six months. And hung out in New York and became a literary lion. You know, everyone was havin' him at their parties, and he enjoyed a lot of that stuff—he was always a big drinker. Anyway, when they made *Smokey* a movie, he ended up in Hollywood and he ended up drinking himself to death at the age

continued on page 184

the ballad of ramblin' jack

by Denise Sullivan

early in *The Ballad Of Ramblin' Jack,* Aiyana Elliot's Sundance festival award-winning documentary about her father, folksinger Ramblin' Jack Elliott, there's a vintage clip of Jack wearing a psychedelic purple tie-dyed shirt during an appearance on the Johnny Cash Show.

"I really liked that shirt. Don' t know where it came from or where it ended up. All of my beautiful clothes have either been lost or stolen," says Elliott. "Probably mostly stolen by fans. I wish I had it back now. I don't know where it is. Somewhere, somebody's got it." he says.

Sartorial splendor aside, Ramblin' Jack Elliott is notable for being Woody Guthrie's one and only protege and as such, inspiration to the young Bob Dylan. Born Charles Elliot Adnopoz in Brooklyn in 1931, at 14, Jack ran away from home for the first time to join the rodeo. For the next 50 plus years, he pursued the life of a hard travelin' cowboy singer and folk song interpreter as well as a buckin' bronco riding, American Indian studying, sea faring enthusiast of all things adventurous and American—the stuff we read about but few of us actually do. Aiyana's film attempts to put all the disparate and sometimes broken pieces of her father's life back together and by doing so not only creates the definitive biography for her dad but accidentally shapes her own autobiography. By combining existing Elliott and Guthrie family footage, film shot on the road with her father over the last couple of years and live performance clips, the film cuts across the special interest area of folk music and takes on universal subjects like family and the attempt to find a sense of place and identity for one's self.

Though Aiyana's parents split when she was a child, she has happy recollections of her time spent with Jack thanks to the efforts her mother Martha went to toward keeping the pair in touch. "Those are some of my best memories of my dad—driving in the Land Rover and telling stories. A couple of times in my childhood, my mom would send me out for a week or two with him to go off on the road on some shows. I think I was kinda hoping, going back out on the road with him, to recapture some of that."

"I didn't go into it wanting to talk to Jack about personal things and I don't think we actually do," explains Aiyana whose name, according to Jack, is Native American for a flower that blooms forever.

"I really felt I was just trying to get an interview with him. When that became difficult the subject shifted so it was an intuitive process that led us," she says. Interviewing Jack can be frustrating because he tends toward the tangential so Aiyana wisely went with the flow and let her dad do what he does best: ramble, which after all, is how he earned his nickname.

"I love hearing my dad talk about it all....in that way I'm probably opposite from him. I'm highly focused on whatever I'm doing and not very good at taking the side road, or seeking things like that out. My dad has a way of being very intimate with all kinds of people—strangers, with audiences—and exposing himself. I think I picked up on that from him. Just the idea of relating to an audience and storytelling and trying to tell it in a dramatic way, I got that from Jack," she says. "I think both my parents have pursued their interests to an extreme degree in spite of the consequences—though they aren't stable or economically viable things to do. I think that my parents both instilled some pretty good values in me."

Aiyana's mother Martha Elliott, Jack's second wife, currently lives in Mexico works with indigenous Indians. "My mom worked with me to try and accept Jack, keep a good friendship with him, maintain a relationship with him and encouraged me to do that. Also, I had a step father who was very supportive of me and helped me appreciate my dad." Aiyana's stepfather, Jerry Kay, also appears with his fond recollections of Jack in the film.

Jack's first wife, June Shelley is also interviewed and given due credit for providing him with the impetus to head overseas in the '50s where the pair traveled together, helping Jack make to his name a folk singer before returning to New York at the height of the Greenwich Village '60s folk revival; by then, his legend preceded him.

Elliott's third and fourth wives are not interviewed for the film even though Jack has another daughter, Maggie, by his fourth wife, Polly. "They were kind of footnotes. They were short marriages and Patty, certainly if you talk to June, was kind of a rebound marriage," says Aiyana.

There is however a remarkable amount of home movie footage thanks to the Elliott clan who would appear to have celluloid in their blood. Jack's father, Abe Adnopoz was a home movie buff. Jack's brother David Adnopoz also held a camera back in the day and he too is interviewed in the film alongside a number of Jack's friends and peers in the folk scene like Pete Seeger, Kris Kristofferson, Odetta, Dave Van Ronk and Arlo Guthrie; Elliot's new bride, Ramblin' Jan Currie also appears. Plenty of television footage was available to Aiyana as was an existing movie, *Ramblin' Jack In Texas*. For someone as mobile as Jack, it's ironic that there should have been a camera charting his every move.

"My father was definitely not a good cameraman—panning too fast or suddenly jumping from one subject to another, at a party, showing these elderly relatives standing around, trying to get it all in, using up only two dollars worth of film," says Jack.

"I think some of the footage he shot looks great," says Aiyana of her grandfather's work. "I never really knew him. It's exciting to me that he's one of the cameramen." Though it may not have been her intention to bring the Elliott family story full circle, Aiyana succeeded in creating a moving piece of family history as well as a document of American music history by recording her father's travails.

"Aristotle said the point of theater was to bring out catharsis. The films I like the most and have responded to in my life have made me feel a lot. Everyone I worked with was trying to find things in the film that would make people feel something and I think that's what led us into the murky waters we ended up in," she says.

Jack says he's very proud of his daughter's work; from a young age, he recognized "she was connected to the cosmos." Yet, there are some scenes he has difficulty with, in particular one in which he's shown walking with a limp due to an impending hip replacement. "I'm not real entertained by that scene." Nor does every frame of the film show Jack in a favorable light. He has no regrets.

"I wouldn't trade that life—I guess not," he says. "I still wanna keep doin' it too. I have to get a new hip so I can ride that bronco. I've got one more buckin' horse in me."

of 50. He died in 1942. He was born in 1892. So he was one of my prime cowboy heroes. And I read about three quarters of the books that he wrote: *Cowboys North and South, The American Cowboy, The Driftin' Cowboy, Lone Cowboy—My Life Story, Big Enough, Clint Spears—the True Story of a Cowboy*

Rodeo Contest, Scorpion, Sand, Cow Country. They're starting to be reprinted now. Ian Tyson wrote a beautiful song about Will James which I have recorded, although I missed out on one of the verses. Ian is also a big fan of Will's and a collector of Will James literature and art. We have a friend who's an Indian who teaches poetry, writing, and he's a rodeo coach at the local high school in southeastern Montana. His name is Hank Real Bird. He's a Crow Indian. I asked him if he'd ever been over to Will James' ranch,'cause he lives near there. He said, 'Yeah, I go over there a lot of times. I drink the water just to see if I can learn to write the way Will wrote.'"

And that's a wrap. It can be exhausting taking it all in, but that's why people have been going to Elliott for all these years—to listen to him tell the stories and pick a few songs on guitar in between them. He is the keeper of hundreds more rambles just like it, and I'd like to hear another. I ask about his affinity for the buffalo, but Elliott isn't ready to leave the James ranch.

"It's certainly the old-style way to do it. A lot of ranchers are mechanized. They use jeeps and trucks and have rubber-tired vehicles and it's not the same as going horseback." And with that, he picks up the thread of the buffalo.

"Bison, buffalo, the white buffalo…. The Indians said that a white buffalo was going to be born, and it was going to mean a hell of a big thing to the Native American people when a white buffalo was born. A white buffalo was born the year I got this sewn on my jacket," he says, pointing to a white-on-black embroidered buffalo patch. "I think it was about four years ago."

"Ted Nugent tried to buy it," says Jan.

"I sincerely hope that's true—that it's supposed to mean something good for the Native American people—that they receive some blessing from the Great Spirit and from God and from the great white father," he laughs. "They've been totally ripped off, you know, just kicked out of their country and off their land.

"The buffalo are a lot bigger than they look. I don't get to visit with the animals that often, but I do get to a ranch once in awhile. We go ridin'. I used to go to a ranch in Wyoming years ago, but my friend sold the place. I've been to a ranch in Texas a few times down in South Texas. And up in Montana. We visited the hometown of the largest ranch in the United States in Oregon. We didn't get on the ranch, but we met some cowboys from the ranch and had a few beers and traded stories with them for several hours."

After a 26-year hiatus from studio recording Elliott recorded *South Coast,* which won him his first Grammy Award for Best Traditional Folk Album in 1996. "I didn't think I ever wanted to go in the studio again," he says. He followed it with the collaborative project, *Friends of Mine.*

Arlo Guthrie, son of the late Woody, was an obvious choice for the *Friends* project; Jack's known him since he was four years old. Elliott also cut songs with Guy Clark, Tom Waits, and sang with Emmylou Harris and Nanci Griffith as a trio.

"Kris Kristofferson and Willie Nelson were on the list, but they got real busy working on other projects and couldn't come. I invited Bob Dylan, but he never answered." Yet Elliott wrote "Bleecker Street Blues" for the album, an open letter to Dylan, which sprang to the page a year earlier when Elliott heard the news that the folksinger, ten years his junior, had been hospitalized with a heart condition.

"I was trying to reach him because I don't know how to reach him through the normal channels…it's over the bridge and past the atomic guard station.

"He's sorta making a big comeback. I like that. I like that album that came out [*Time Out of Mind*]. I like it better than some of the other ones. I haven't even heard all of Bob's albums; although I am a fan, I'm not an avid fan. I think he's an amazing, beautiful talent. But as a person, I don't know him at all. He's a very strange person. My father was a Gemini, my brother was a Gemini; I can't get to know Gemini. They have more than one, more than two personalities."

"I'm a Gemini," says Jan.

"I don't know her either," says Jack. "She's always there, she's very consistent. I don't know a Gemini like her. She's very steady. I think of Geminis never knowing where they're at. Even Bob tries to explain it by saying he feels very strongly one way in the morning and feels very strongly a different way in the afternoon. But he's a very good speaker of the English language. I even liked that thing he did on the Grammys…" he says, referring to an appearance during which Dylan spoke at length and was especially articulate, "because in the last five years he's appeared to be drunk or asleep or stoned or totally out of it. You don't know where he's at or what he's on."

Elliott's been quizzed excessively by Dylanologists about his relationship to the folksinger. The facts, insofar as they are known, is that Dylan derived a lot of his early ideas from Jack about how to be a folksinger, how to

*Ramblin' Jack: Still a rover
50 years into his career*

walk, talk, and live the life of the hard traveler. By mythologizing and rein-
venting himself, like Elliott, the practiced persona effectively became his
persona. "I've been known to copy people too," says Elliott. "I copied Woody
a little bit. A whole lot."

"I like hanging out with musicians," he continues. "The great, the near
great, and the not-so-great. Some of the greatest musicians are very humble, and some of the worst musicians are egotistical assholes. Sometimes
the two go hand in hand.

"Like I know Doc Watson. I arrived at a gig in Kansas and I heard Doc and his son rehearsing in a room next to mine. I was just gonna take a shower and I didn't have my boots on, but I went in the hall and knocked on their door and I said, 'Hey, keep it down in there!' They said, 'Jack!' and they opened the door. Doc is blind, but he knew my voice through the door. That's a nice feeling."

I tell him his old friend, folksinger Odetta, said the recent resurgence in folk music can be attributed to "troubled times." To what does he attribute the rekindled interest and celebration of his music 50 years into his career?

"That was an obvious, good way to answer that question—as if folk music depends on troubled times—because when times are troubled, people are more receptive to the honesty of folk music. People having a hard time existing are more sympathetic to stories about people who have to struggle to survive. Whereas when everyone has five cars and three TVs in the house and a roof over their head, a lot of them get so removed from reality, they don't want to hear about it or even remember it. That would be the logical answer—a good answer. But the '80s were also troubled times and folk music wasn't doing very well then, so why was *that*? I don't know. I don't follow booms and I don't follow folk music. I don't care about it. I just play guitar."

Elliott pauses, as if to reflect on his answer, removing his omnipresent cowboy hat and stroking his thick head of hair. "Lucky I've still got hair? I'm lucky I still have a head!"

Recommended Recordings

The Ballad of Ramblin' Jack (Vanguard, 2000)
> This is the original soundtrack to the documentary film Aiyana Elliott made about her father. The 20 selections included are odds and sods, rarities, and duets with Dylan, Guthrie, and Johnny Cash—as well as songs that became Elliott classics, like Jesse Fuller's "San Francisco Bay Blues," Tim Hardin's "If I Were a Carpenter," and his own trucker anthem, "Cup of Coffee."

The Best of the Vanguard Years (Vanguard, 2000)
> This is a reissue of the 1964 Vanguard album, *Jack Elliott*, and 13 previously unreleased tracks, including "I Never Will Marry" and "Ranger's Command," still in Elliott's live repertoire.

who wrote
the book
of rock?

Ike Turner
The Crickets
Wanda Jackson
Ike Turner
The Crickets

r o c k & r o l l p i o n e e r s

Wanda Jackson
Ike Turner
The Crickets

t o state the obvious, without the early experiments of rock pioneers Ike Turner, the Crickets, and Wanda Jackson, rock and roll as we know it today would simply not exist. Think about it: Were it not for rock and roll's founders, early inventors, innovators, and rulebreakers, what would rock and roll be except for maybe a catalog of moon, June, and spoon pop songs with the tempo cranked up a few notches?

As yet, no precedent has been set for when one must retire his or her rock and roll shoes. Certainly, the last century's heritage blues artists were among the first to set the pace for performers in their latter years staying active in the business. Muddy Waters, Mississippi Fred McDowell, Lightnin' Hopkins, Screamin' Jay Hawkins, Brownie McGhee, and so many others demonstrated they could prove it all night, well into their twilight years—bluesman John Lee Hooker still rocks the house in his 80s. And all of them had a profound influence on rock and roll. There's just no telling yet the exact lifespan of the average rock and roll artist, because among those still living, a good number of them are still rockin' their lives away. Chuck Berry, Little Richard, and Jerry Lee Lewis, the triumvirate of rock's surviving founding fathers, are still performing as they near their 70s and 80s. Somewhere between the ages of 50 and 60, the members of the Rolling Stones, the Who, and a smattering of bands from the second generation of rock and rollers, for better or worse, still see fit to get their ya-yas out from time to time on the live circuit. Bands who came alive in the '70s, like Peter Frampton and Cheap Trick, enjoyed career renaissances as a wave of nostalgia for rock's most reviled decade took hold in the late '90s and early '00s. And even a handful of mainstream English and American rock-of-the-'80s bands like the Go-Go's, Human League, and Culture Club have come back around to touring and recording; others have never stopped. It seems there is no age limit when it comes to a guy strapping on a guitar. Women rocking into the ages tell a bit of a different story, but as we will see, that's changing. As long as there are high-profile career artists like Tina Turner and Cher working well into their 50s and 60s, we should expect to see more women growing old gracefully in the rock arena.

Wanda Jackson is not only a female rock and country pioneer—without question, the Queen of Rockabilly—but a rock and roll rulebreaker, period. She invented a vocal style that was unheard of for her time in the late '50s—not to mention by a teenage girl—with her series of *whoops, woos,* and *grrrrrs.* Her imaginative and hardcore rockabilly sound is best heard on her earliest sides, which also happen to be some of the all-time most memorable songs in rock and roll: "Let's Have a Party," "Mean Mean Man," and "Fujiyama Mama." Her wild, homemade fashions were also a bold stroke at a time when dowdy was the operative word for Southern guitar-wielding gals and pop vocalists.

With encouragement from Elvis Presley, Jackson abandoned the country repertoire she learned at the feet of her mentor—Western swing and honky-tonk kingpin Hank Thompson—to pursue rock and roll. By the '70s, she heard a call to sing gospel and surrendered her rock roots, but the '80s found Jackson headlining European rockabilly festivals; by the '90s, she was back in U.S. clubs on a regular rotation. "I'm working more in America than I have in 10 or 15 years, and that's exciting to me, because I get to do mostly rockabilly, but I get to do some of the country things and some gospel. It makes me happy to do all three," she says, still sounding like the spunky young gal she used to be. Certainly when she performs these days, it's with a girlish enthusiasm and a measure of chutzpah, embracing her return to the rockabilly life with a boatload of gratitude. In the process, she's witnessed a sustained, worldwide revival in the music she helped to invent. Since reestablishing her career in her late 50s, Jackson, who's now in her early 60s, has no intention of quitting just yet. Health problems have slowed her down a teeny bit, but not to worry: "I never take a break for that long," she says. These days Jackson, 63, and her husband and manager, Wendell Goodman,64, spend close to half of the year on the road.

Also returning to the recording and touring fray after being sidelined for a number of years is rock and roll piano and guitar innovator and soulsonic force, Ike Turner—although his reasons for sitting it out were quite different from Jackson's. A short prison term had something to do with his absence, but more obviously, it was his well-publicized errant behavior as the other half of the Ike & Tina Turner Revue that soured the general populace on his persona, and in turn, left him in disgrace to the point where his earliest musical contributions were becoming discredited. This is a man who is usually cited by the history books as the one who laid down the first rock and roll recording in 1951! Like Chuck Berry and Jerry Lee Lewis—among others whose bad-boy legends often eclipsed the valuable contributions they made to a formative rock and roll—Turner's extraordinary role in shaping not only rock and roll but in nurturing and discovering its talents, has been grossly overlooked in the face of his more uh, colorful, personal story until fairly recently. His boogie-woogie piano style is often imitated, but his overloaded sonic experiments on the guitar are his contribution to the nascent rock sound and has figured large in rock music as the decades wear on.

My own interest in Turner developed with a childhood fascination with the Ike & Tina Turner Revue during its late '60s and early '70s heyday. Thanks to their many daytime, prime-time, and late-night televised appearances (and our household's one copy of *Live at Carnegie Hall/What You Hear Is What You Get,* selected from the Columbia Record and Tape Club), the Turners' edgy music was completely accessible to me, and I was hooked. Tina's earth-pounding voice and presence, the cool dances and costumes she and the Ikettes cooked up captivated me; as it turns out, Ike was responsible for cultivating most of what we came to know and love about their visual and musical presentation (reportedly against Tina's judgment). The Turners' music was one of my earliest palpable connections with rock and roll's raw power and the visceral response it was capable of delivering. Tina helped to sustain my interest in the group's musical legacy with the publication of her autobiography, *I, Tina*, in 1986; a harrowing tale, but one in which the soul power of their music was never lost in the telling. Ike would have his own outrageous autobiography published in 1999, *Takin' My Name Back, The Confessions of Ike Turner.*

Having seen the renewed Tina perform just before her miraculous comeback in the '80s, by the '90s, I was glad to say that I had also seen Ike, now 70, although his return to stages has been greeted with a lot less fanfare. For anyone still having difficulty reconciling the alleged disparity between the man and the music, the late rock journalist Robert Palmer summed it up perfectly when he wrote of Ike: "Art is art, and great rock & roll is great rock & roll—no matter what kind of maniac is playing it."

Those lucky enough to have witnessed early gigs by Buddy Holly and the Crickets or to have seen their late '50s television appearances would probably tell you that they, too, verged on the maniacal. Yet ironically today (although only on the surface), Holly and the Crickets represent everything that is wholesome and innocent about early rock and roll. Certainly, Crickets Jerry Allison and Sonny Curtis are two of the more gentlemanly fellows in music you'll ever meet, but as for rulebreaking—well, let's just say that as the writers of some of the earliest and most undisputed entries in the rock and roll canon—"Peggy Sue," "Not Fade Away," and "That'll Be the Day," among others—they broke all kinds of barriers when they took this previously unheard music to the top of the charts in the late '50s. The night I went to see the surviving Crickets play in 1997 with Nanci Griffith, it was a hard sell to convince any of my friends that it would be worth seeing the band (its members hovering around 60) play the rock and roll that made Holly and them famous 40 years ago. I was happy to report that the Crickets' music didn't die the day Buddy did, nor did it fade away (as any fan who's heard the Grateful Dead or Patti Smith pay homage will tell you). The Crickets' music lives, in no small part due to the words and work of Curtis and Allison, who still bear the torch of the music they made with Holly. It probably goes without saying, but without the songs of Holly and the Crickets, there would be no such thing as the Beatles, whose principals, John Lennon and Paul McCartney, were avowed fans. And there isn't even a close second in how the Beatles changed the face of rock and roll (well, actually there is—Bob Dylan—but you get the idea).

Without the influence of rock's earliest innovators—those who were willing to put their reputations on the line as respected gospel, country, and R&B acts by busting out of the boundaries that their original music had designated for them—there would be no rock and roll. If no one had been willing to break the established rules way back when, Pete Townshend would probably have never smashed that guitar; Iggy Pop wouldn't have emerged from his post behind the drum kit of the Iguanas to become the godfather of punk rock; Johnny Rotten would never have spit-sung his profane lyrics; Kurt Cobain would've remained just another mixed-up kid from Aberdeen, Washington. Wanda Jackson, the Crickets, Ike Turner, and their most dangerous peers—now sexagenarians and septuagenarians—paved the way for others to rip it up for rock's first half century. May they all rave on well into its second 50 years.

WANDA JACKSON

"I never kissed a bear, I never kissed a goose
but I can shake a chicken in the middle of the room...
let's have a party!"
—"Let's Have a Party" as sung by Wanda Jackson

fresh from an appearance at Elvis' birthday bash at the L.A. outpost of the House of Blues in 1995, the King's one-time girlfriend and first lady of rockabilly, Wanda Jackson, stepped onstage at Bimbo's in San Francisco the next night to sing him "Happy Birthday, Baby," one more time.

"That drive was pretty hard on me, but I'm so glad I could be here tonight to sing for y'all," says Jackson, who at 63 sings nearly as tough and girlish as when she scored a Top 40 hit in 1960 with "Let's Have a Party," the song that became her signature tune.

That night was a party all right. The sold-out show, billed Women of Rockabilly, drew young and old—some dressed in Western gear, others like '50s cats and kittens and some just as plain old squares. But they'd all come to dance—to Jackson, her backup band the Cadillac Angels, and support act Rosie Flores' fiery rockabilly boogie. There were even dance lessons—for the squares.

Both Flores and Jackson appeared to be having a great time; they obviously have a genuine affection for each other. "Rosie calls me Queenie and I call her Filly. She's my girlfriend," says Jackson. Flores is Jackson's rightful vocal heiress, having perfected that rockabilly "hiccup" and those high "woos" that Jackson made so famous with songs like "Fujiyama Mama" and "Mean Mean Man," which she performed to perfection that night. The event would not have been possible without Flores—the well-respected and highly competent roots-rock artist and singer-songwriter who plays the heck out of her guitar and also includes a fair number of rockabilly standards in her own set—and roots artist Jann Browne. In 1990, Browne invited Jackson to record

"I Forgot More" as a duet with her; it helped Jackson get her feet wet again. In 1996 Flores coaxed Jackson out of rock and roll retirement to join her on two songs for her album, *Rockabilly Filly*, and the pair played a few tour dates; they continue to trade material and sing duets. It was the first time Jackson had performed in rock clubs since embracing Christianity in the early '70s. And now, for the first time in 40 years, Jackson is touring America's clubs as a headliner. Once again, she's a rock and roller with a full concert schedule.

"I'm a Christian, and for ten years, I'd been singing what the Lord wanted me to, but it seems to have swung back to the secular," says Jackson, at home in Oklahoma City. For several years, Jackson was earning her living by traveling back and forth to European rockabilly festivals up to five times a year, "which is really hard on ya," she says. "But as of 1995, when I did the cameo spot on Rosie's CD, interest was such we booked a five-week tour on the strength of it and I found all these rockabilly places and all these rockabilly fans that I didn't know was out there. And they didn't know if I was still singin' or dead or what, you know?"

Jackson made her country singing debut in 1953, when she was still in high school. After a stop in the church choir, she landed her own radio show on KLPR in Oklahoma City. Country star Hank Thompson caught one of the broadcasts and immediately took an interest in the young singer. With his help, she signed to Decca and immediately scored a country hit with "You Can't Have My Love," a duet with Billy Gray and Thompson's Brazos Valley Boys. "I learned to yodel because I loved Hank Williams, Hank Thompson, Jimmie Rodgers, and Rose Maddox," says Jackson.

She first became exposed to Western swing and got her first guitar between the ages of four and twelve, while her family was living in California. "I identify with the West Coast—I always have," she says. Her family returned to Oklahoma after the war. "I have no ties to Nashville. I didn't really fit in." By 1955, she was on the road touring with Thompson and opening shows as a country act for Elvis Presley.

Jackson's look—in contrast to the buckskin-jacketed and cowboy-booted gals working in country music at the time—was all spangles, low necklines, and spaghetti straps. Admittedly, she liked the stir it caused, although she didn't do it to be titillating. She was just rockin' her own style. But her exotic look, combined with her feisty growl and tendency to holler, was all too much for the less-adventurous Ernest Tubb and his conservative vision of the Grand

Ole Opry. "I was *asked* to join the Grand Ole Opry, but I stayed on with Red Foley in Springfield, Missouri," she explains. After that fashion-forward event, she chose never to go back. Her rebel spirit was more appreciated at Foley's show, *Ozark Jubilee*, which, lucky for her, also delivered her to a nationwide television audience.

In 1956, with her friend Elvis' encouragement, the young Jackson ditched her country leanings for a more contemporary sound, the new rock and roll. The pair spent afternoons listening to records at Elvis' house, and, for a short time, dated. Although Jackson at first had doubts about whether she wanted to go for it, once she made up her mind, she became the first female rockabilly artist to continually score hits on the pop charts. Her father helped to boost her confidence. "He said, 'Well, you can do any song you want to do—just rear back and see if you can't get some of that sexy growlin' in there.' So I tried it and I could do it—and I liked it!" Capitol Records had the bright idea to market her as "The Female Gene Vincent" (although they were always careful to include a country B-side, just in case). Well, be bop a lula, the girl struck gold.

"I didn't have any women to draw from. Nowadays, everybody tries to sound like, say, Reba or Wynonna. I didn't have that option. So I took Hank Williams and Hank Thompson and Little Richard and Elvis, and it came out Wanda Jackson," she told the *Chicago Sun-Times* in 1999.

Rockabilly was all about the party, and Jackson was the belle of the ball; she proved it with the trilogy "Let's Have a Party," "There's a Party Goin' On," and "Man We Had a Party." "Tongue Tied," a song that belongs in the pantheon of great rock and roll songs featuring s-t-t-t-uttering, and her table-turning take on "Riot in Cell Block Number Nine," which takes place in a women's prison, reach some of her lesser-known vocal heights.

"I always said, I'm not really a songwriter, but I knew the type of songs I wanted to sing and I didn't have a lot of choices, so a lot of times it was better that I just wrote it." "Mean Mean Man" was one of those. "The really good songs are just bursts. You've got the pencil and here it comes and you could write two at one time; work on one and get an idea for another one, then go back to the other one. It really is inspired." Jackson's own compositions also include "Savin' My Love" and "Rock Your Baby." During the '50s and '60s, she was supported by a crack band of mostly California-based musicians like

*The young Wanda Jackson broke the
rules on vocals and in the dress code.*

Merle Travis, Joe Maphis, and Buck Owens at turns on guitar, and keyboard pounders Big Al Downing and Merrill Moore on piano.

"My daddy traveled with me before I was married, and he did the booking he could and took care of the business. I have an old ledger of his from when I first went on the road in 1955. I'd been recording for two years already, but I had graduated from high school, and I had a couple pretty good sized hits in country music and was ready to go on the road, and I was making $50 a night when I started working with Elvis. And I had more of a name throughout the whole country than he did! Not for very long, but in the very beginning," she says. "Dad and I would drive to Dallas, which is maybe 200 miles from here, and I'd get paid $25 maybe $30, and then we got up to $50 and then you start seeing $100, $150, and then $300—it was very gradual. These days, especially in Europe, I make like a five-digit salary, so I'm kind of making up for some lost time."

Although she had an impressive run from '56 to '61, the well eventually ran dry for Jackson and her rockabilly cohorts. "At the time, some spirit in me was kind of crushed. I kept recording, but I couldn't get a hold of any fresh, new material." But Jackson didn't retreat, instead, she shifted directions. "I couldn't get played in pop or R&B, so I went back to country," she says. In the middle to late '50s and on into the '60s, if you couldn't sing rock and roll, then you just didn't work. Everything had gone to Top 40."

She continued to have country success in the '60s, beginning with her 1961 hit, the self-penned "Right or Wrong." That same year she met and married her husband and business manager, Wendell Goodman; the couple have traveled together and made their home in Oklahoma City ever since.

"I met Wendell in my home—I was still living with my mother and dad, because my father traveled with me and I never did move out on my own. My best girlfriend Norma Jean, the singer, and Wendell had been, oh, dating for a short while I guess. Just a few weeks really. She brought him over to my house and I got to meet him and it was only about two months later that she was offered a spot on *The Porter Waggoner Show.* She had to move to Nashville, and when she left she said to me, 'Take real good care of Wendell.' In October of that year I told her, 'I just can't take care of this guy unless I marry him.' So that's when we were married. And we had her blessing of course—she's still best friend to both of us.

"For one thing, we were very much in love, but love has to be more commitment than just saying, 'I'm in love with the guy,' explains Jackson of her 40-year union with Goodman. "After we'd been married probably a year, he learned enough about my business to take over the booking and some managing, and we've been together ever since the beginning."

Jackson explains there was a period in the early '70s when she and Goodman weren't sure if they were going to make it together. "Well, our marriage was not on very good ground. We loved each other, but as it happens with couples you just…well, drinking, that way of life, on the road, here today gone tomorrow, come home, catch up on a little bit of stuff, and leave again. It was a little too much probably for any marriage, but we were kind of at our wits' end. It's hard on guys—their ego, their wife is the well-known one, and they're taking a back seat. Wendell had never had to share a girlfriend, and here all of a sudden he had to share his wife with the whole world and all these fans. And that was a lot of our problem. He was jealous, he couldn't help it. That's when things were starting to get bad.

"I suppose we were both from the era where divorce was something that had a bad reputation in those days. To me and to Wendell, divorce wasn't an

Time Line

1937	Born in Maud, Oklahoma
1941	Receives her first guitar
1954	Tours with her mentor, Hank Thompson
	"You Can't Have My Love," a duet with Billy Gray and the Brazos Valley Boys, charts Top 10 on the country charts
	Decca recording years begin
1956	Crosses over to rockabilly at the urging of Elvis Presley
	Signs new contract with Capitol Records; records for them for 18 years
1960	Scores with the Top 40 single, "Let's Have a Party"
1961	Self-penned "Right or Wrong" Top 10 country hit
	Marries Wendell Goodman
1966–70	Songs such as "Tears Will Be the Chaser for Your Wine" and "A Girl Don't Have to Drink to Have Fun"occasionally chart on country radio
1971	Reenters the Baptist church with her husband
	Records sacred music
1984	Returns to singing rockabilly on European festival circuit
1995	Returns to U.S. rockabilly circuit with help from her friend, neo-rockabilly artist Rosie Flores
1999	Hometown of Maud, Oklahoma, honors her with Wanda Jackson Day; renames Main Street after her

option. We got married to be together, and we work very hard at being to-gether, because naturally the world tries to pull you in so many different directions. We went to church one morning simply because our kids made us promise that we'd come hear the preacher or something, but it was that morning that God just spoke to both of our hearts, individually, at the same moment, and I just turned to Wendell and I said, 'Honey, there's somethin' that I've gotta do,' and he said, 'Me too.' So we went into the Baptist church. We'd both been church members most of our lives, but it was never anything real in our life. From that moment on, it became real to us. Before a couple becomes Christian, it's head to head combat: Who's gonna be the power here in this marriage? It's like a constant battle. But as soon as you both yield your life and make the commitment to Jesus Christ, he becomes the center, and we both yield to that. So then, it's not the two personalities clashing back and forth. If we have decisions to make, we pray about it, and we do whatever God wants us to do, and then all of the jealously, all the fightin', all the arguin', all the drinkin'—everything, it was just lifted out of our lives, because of Christ."

Somewhere along the way, she says, she felt country music changing, and that's when she made the switch from country to gospel. "I just found myself wanting to sing the gospel songs. I even left Capitol Records in order to sign with a company that specialized in gospel music, but as soon as I did that, they sold that company to a big conglomerate, Dot Records, and it just really got bad, and so I had to leave them too, as it turned out. For ten years my fans didn't know what I was doing or where I was [she was appearing only at church functions]. I wrote a lot of the gospel things that I recorded, but then when I got back into the secular field, music had changed, and I felt like the way I wrote was too old-timey. I see now, it really wasn't. But I just kinda stopped and thought, 'I just can't write this kind of music.' That happened to Hank Thompson, too. He said, 'I just don't hear the chord things they're do-ing these days,' and he stopped writing for a long time, too."

In 1984, Jackson was invited to Sweden to record some songs and to go on a three-week tour. "And the album took off and was very good—I think it was voted the album of that year in Scandinavia. And then doors began to open in Germany and Belgium and France, the Netherlands, Denmark, all these places. They have a lot of rockabilly festivals over there—that's what I do mostly.

"People still love the simplicity, and there's room for both in the business." Jackson says listening to records by Tanya Tucker and Ricky Skaggs in the '80s recharged her interest in contemporary country music. "I worked with Tanya in the '80s somewhere along the way. I could see, 'hey, she's a rock singer—she's a rockabilly.' And then Ricky Skaggs, who's basically very pure country, I got a couple of his tapes and began listening. From that point on, I began to really enjoy country music again."

Today she finds no problem with reconciling the genres in her act. "A country audience loves 'Let's Have a Party,' 'Fujiyama Mama,' 'Rockabilly Fever,' and all these things. The rockabilly audience also likes 'Right or Wrong,' 'Big Iron Skillet,' and songs like that. That's why I'm so happy that I can still work and that my health is good and that people still want to see me perform. I'm just grateful for that every day."

Jackson was preparing to leave for another string of dates around the U.S.—what she calls Grand Ole Opry-type shows: family-oriented, no bars, no dancing, just a concert atmosphere. "I still only do one concert a night. I don't do music for dancing as such. Those days are over for me. And I hardly ever do the exact same show as I would in a country venue as I would in a rockabilly. Of course I have to do my hit songs in both of them, so that keeps it mixed up," she says.

She'll also begin her next recording project. "I'm doing rerecordings and about four cover tunes, songs like 'It's a Heartache,' 'Have You Ever Seen the Rain,' and 'Queen of Hearts.' It's for a German company." Jackson had some early overseas career success with her recording of "Santo Domingo," a No. 1 hit in Germany and a hit in the bordering countries in 1965. "They call it an evergreen song, we call them standards. And so I always include that in my shows, especially on the European continent. They sing along and hold the cigarette lighters and the flashlight things and that's neat to see that, to hear the young kids sing 'Santa Domingo.'"

She's also going to recut some of the old songs for the German market. "They have us come in and rerecord so you have a fresher sound. They also want me to record all of my German titles in the German language. Now, I'm not really looking forward to that. It was the hardest work I've ever done in my life, but I was young. When you have to sing phonetically, it's very difficult. The words come fast and furious and there's all these funny markings

The recharged Wanda Jackson: "That's neat...to hear the young kids sing..."

around a word and I have to try to remember how you say it. But it's a challenge and it doesn't hurt me."

Jackson maintains a handful of friendships with people from her past—like Hank Thompson. "He was my mentor and I'm his fan and we work together occasionally. And Norma Jean. I just spoke to her today. She was opening in Branson and called to tell me all about it. I never did have a lot of close friends in the music business because I never lived in Nashville, I just stayed in my home of Oklahoma City. So my social life was friends from here, and I just didn't make long-lasting friendships with the people I worked with in the business.

"Elvis and I didn't purposely stay in touch, but I did see him a couple of times in the middle and late '60s in Vegas," says Jackson. She spent a period in the desert town working the show rooms herself. "He came to the room and met Wendell and our friends. And I was so glad that Wendell got to meet him. He didn't stay long—about 15 minutes—but he got to visit with us. And then I saw him again in one of the hotel lobbies playing the Wheel of Fortune or something, and I sat down and talked to him."

But sitting down isn't really Jackson's forte. She has her memories, sure, but she isn't about to quit now. "We're nearly always out on the road half of the time. We kind of slowed down a little bit the last year, and I've taken five weeks off already this year. We've slowed down mainly because we're in another business with our son in Oklahoma City, so when we're home, Wendell has to wear two hats. We have our office there, the Wanda Jackson Enterprises office, and a window tint and alarm business. We're a franchise. We own three—two of them are up and running. So if Wendell has to stay and work, we'll just book some weekend things. Of course our kids have their own families and we have four beautiful grandkids and they're used to our lifestyles," she says, referring to herself as the Rock and Roll Grandma.

"Sixty really isn't old anymore, especially when you're in this business and working with young people. That's what's been exciting to me, the rock and roll, rockabillies, whatever you want to call it. Fifties rock is kind of what I like to describe it as. Maybe 10 percent of my audience will be my age, but mostly it's the young adults, 20s, 30s, 40s."

"I have things that I've had to take off for—oral surgery, that was my last five weeks off. I'm having some of the implants, so you have to take off at least two weeks, and you can't wear your bridge, so I'm kinda indisposed there for awhile," she laughs. "And that's kind of an ongoing thing. I've never had particularly good teeth. But I've started singing an hour or two or a day to get my voice back in shape."

Although for most of her professional life, she's shunned the rock and roll spotlight, judging by her '90s performances, it would appear that Jackson is right back where she belongs. "It's a pretty heady trip, people esteeming me so highly. I'm getting my strokes."

Recommended Recordings

Right or Wrong (Bear Family, 1992)

Tears Will Be the Chaser for Your Wine (Bear Family, 1994)

> *Right or Wrong* is a four-CD box set covering Jackson's career from 1954–1963; *Tears Will Be Chaser for Your Wine* is an eight-CD set, filling in the years 1964 to 1973. Clearly, it's all the material you need on the first two decades of Jackson's recording career.

Vintage Collections (Capitol, 1996)

> As an introduction to the career of Jackson, this collection is the one, as it focuses on her late '50s/early '60s country and rockabilly heyday on Capitol. Contains the greatest hits: "Fujiyama Mama," "Right or Wrong," "Let's Have a Party," and 16 more.

16

IKE TURNER

"He's been in a mess but, God, he's also been refreshed." —*Little Richard on Ike Turner*

these days, rock and soul legend Ike Turner's reputation as the demand-ing, abusive husband of Tina Turner has dimmed his distinction as a founding father of rock and roll music and innovator on piano and guitar. But Turner is back to reclaim his legacy. He's just been invited to perform two shows with East Bay bluesman Joe Louis Walker, and although he's only ever worked as an iron-handed bandleader, Turner's humbly taking a back-seat for this ride down the comeback trail.

"This is the first time I ever played with anybody in my life, other than my own show. For a fact, I've never even walked up to sit in with no band," says Turner, ensconced in a hotel room in Mill Valley, California in 1997.

Walker handpicked Turner to contribute to *Great Guitars*, a collection of collaborations with blues greats like Gatemouth Brown, Bonnie Raitt, and Buddy Guy. The weekend shows at Mill Valley's Sweetwater were a warm-up for a larger-scale tour planned for later in the year.

"I'm so high-energy, and Joe reminds me of where I should be, a little slower. When I be playin' I get all hyped up. He's more laid back. I learned a lot from working with him—learning to relax, rather than being so tense," says Turner.

Tense is probably just one of the words that spring to mind when one thinks of Turner, a commanding and demanding presence during rock and roll's formative '50s. As leader of the Ike & Tina Turner Revue, the most suc-cessful R&B crossover act of the late '60s and early '70s, fellow musicians have said he asserted cruel, dictatorial control as a bandleader. But today, Turner sounds relaxed—loose but together—having gotten his life back on

205

Turner at the controls in the '70s

track after his wife Tina left him in 1976, allegedly because of his abuse of drugs, alcohol, and her. His life spun out of control after that with his continued substance abuse, and ultimately, he found himself incarcerated on drug charges in 1990.

"When you doin' drugs man, it's a downhill, it's a total destructive thing. When you start, it's OK. You think it's OK, and the next thing you know you start livin' for the next. I can only talk about crack, cocaine, uh, whatever," he said in the documentary *Tina Turner, the Girl from Nutbush*. He was interviewed for the film during his early '90s stay at the California Men's Colony. "When you start, it's fine, but then, man, after three or four times, you start getting up in the day and the first thing you start looking for…you not looking for a plate to eat, you looking for more drugs. You start training yourself self-consciously man; you're not livin' for nothing else but the drugs."

Following that career low point, which landed him in the joint shortly after the publication of Tina's autobiography *I, Tina*, and shortly before the release of the film *What's Love Got to Do with It*, Ike was predominantly known as the drug addict, ruthless taskmaster, and abusive husband portrayed in the book. Today, at 65, he's enthusiastic about the prospect of hitting the stage again. He's returned to performing periodically with his Ike Turner Revue and with his wife Jeanette, a country singer. He's working on getting his name cleared and so far, he's staying clean and sober. The only dark cloud in his life these days is his emphysema. "My voice go out pretty fast. I didn't know I had it till a year after I stopped smoking. That was when it came forward. Maybe I should start smoking cigarettes again," he laughs.

"I'm going to play guitar with Joe on a few of his songs, and then I'm going to do something I never did on stage before. I'm gonna play piano. I consider myself a piano player, not a guitar player, but the world knows me as a guitar player." He says he's had a great time rehearsing, freestyling on some of the old riffs that inspired him. "It started bringing back stuff I used to do with Sonny Boy Williamson and Muddy Waters. All the songs started coming back to me, songs I haven't played in 40 years, like 'Rocket 88.' I haven't played that song since we recorded it."

"Rocket 88," a galloping piano number, is commonly acknowledged by rock music historians to be the first rock and roll record. Sung by Jackie Brenston and credited to the Delta Cats, it's actually Ike and his Kings of Rhythm who rocked and rolled through the R&B number devoted to the joys of ridin' along in an automobile. The song was cut at Sam Phillips' studios in Memphis in March of 1951, became an instant hit, and remains a classic. It's said to have inspired Little Richard to bang on the keys. It's clean and it's simple, but at the same time its grooves are dirty and raw. And it speeds along like the neat Oldsmobile in its title. In essence, it's rock and roll, and it's earned Turner a place in the Rock and Roll Hall of Fame and Museum as the music's founder.

I watched Turner perform the boogie-woogie piano number with the ease and grace of a professional who'd never been locked away, strung-out on drugs, or had his name disgraced. He was enraptured, and so was the audience. Like the proverbial guy who'd been lost, Ike Turner, too, had been found. It wasn't the first time the piano had saved him.

Growing up in hard times in Clarksdale, Mississippi, fatherless and at the mercy of abusive town elders, Ike tells the story of what motivated him to learn the keyboard as a young boy in the 1930s.

Time Line

1931	Born Izear Luster Turner in Clarksdale, Mississippi
1939	Inspired by Pinetop Perkins, asks mother for a piano
1951	Cuts "Rocket 88" with the Kings of Rhythm; song credited to Jackie Brenston and his Delta Cats
1956	Hooks up with Anna Mae Bullock when he hears her sing in an East St. Louis club; rechristens her Tina Turner
1960	Duo's first single, "Fool in Love," hits Top 40 and goes to No. 2 on the R&B charts
1962	Marries Tina
1966	Ike & Tina Turner Revue tours with Rolling Stones in U.K.
1972–73	Records solo LPs *Blues Roots* and *Bad Dreams*
1973	"Nutbush City Limits" last Ike & Tina song to chart in the U.S.
1976	Tina leaves; Ike & Tina Turner Revue officially finished
1986	Tina's controversial best-selling autobiography *I, Tina*, published
1990	Convicted on possession of cocaine charges
1993	Portrayed by Laurence Fishburne in the film *What's Love Got to Do with It*
1997	Tours as a sideman with blues guitarist Joe Louis Walker
1999	Autobiography, *The Confessions of Ike Turner, Takin' My Name Back*, finally published

"I looked through the window of the pool hall and saw Pinetop Perkins play piano. I had never saw a piano in my life before. I'm sure they had one at church, but I didn't even notice it. Boy, when I saw Pinetop playing that piano—man, that fascinated me to death, I wanted to play the piano so bad. I went home and told my mama I wanted a piano. She told me if I passed to the third grade, she would buy me one. And boy, when I got to the third grade, I got home and she had me a piano sittin' there. That started my musical life." Young Ike continued playing with some informal tutelage from Perkins, which is how he learned boogie-woogie.

As Turner matured, he played in bands, first with the Tophatters, then forming the Kings of Rhythm until one day, he accidentally landed in the production and talent scouting business. As the story goes, Turner was a known kid around Memphis (the Tennessee music city being just across the Mississippi border) and was observing a B.B. King session at Sun. When the musicians went for a break, Ike started fooling around on the piano, and Modern Records' Joe Bihari caught him. He was so impressed with what he heard, he dragged Turner into the session in progress and later signed him up as a talent scout.

"They bought me a car, a '49 Buick, and told me to go and find people all over the South. We went to churches and pool halls, and I'd get names. Then we would record'em playing with Howlin' Wolf and little Junior Parker in their living room and give them a bottle of whiskey or $5 if they had a piano and would let us record there," he explains. Bihari was accompanying Turner on the jobs with an early-model portable recorder that they jerry-rigged to mic the musicians individually. Ike often wrote the songs for the unknowns ,who would go on to record them. This was also around the time he was beginning to experiment on electric guitar, plying its whammy bar and bending and distorting notes that would challenge the likes of Sonic Youth's Thurston Moore's today. Critic Robert Palmer described Turner's guitar playing as "violent manipulations," "savage," and "gonzo." Add "manic" and "frenzied" to the list.

Ike is also credited for early recordings with Muddy Waters, Little Walter, Howlin' Wolf, Elmore James, and Sonny Boy Williamson. But his notoriety would always be associated with the discovery of the young singer from Nutbush, Tennessee, Anna Mae Bullock, whom he met at an East St. Louis nightclub, Club Manhattan, in 1956. Little Ann, as she was known, got up her nerve one night, grabbed a mic, and started singing along with Ike at his regular club date.

"I knew Tina was a great singer, but she was an even better performer," he says. Eventually, the pair recorded Ike's song and their first hit by accident, when Art Lassiter, the singer it was meant for, missed his session. Anna Mae was sitting in and offered to lay down a scratch vocal for "Fool in Love" that could be lifted off and replaced by Lassiter's at a later date. The genius of the cut ended up being in her ability to sound out a vocal arranged for a man, but her additional although reluctant guttural shouts of the song's signature, "*hey, hey, hey, hey, hey*" didn't hurt either.

"That's why she's straining so on that record, howling like that, because I had it in the key he would sing it in. I played the tape at the Imperial where I was working, and all the kids said, 'Man that's great, put it out.' Dave Dixon, a disc jockey, said he would send it to Juggy Murray at Sue Records. He did, man, and boom! the damn thing was a hit," explains Ike in *The Girl from Nutbush.*

Ike perceived the cut to be his last shot; he'd been working as an underpaid professional for at least nine years by then. Because of his experience of having gone uncredited on "Rocket 88," along with outside pressures to come up with a snappy name, he slapped his name on the song and copyrighted the moniker Ike & Tina Turner. He choose the name "Tina" for Anna Mae because it sounded "jungle," he says, referring to his longtime obsession with queen-of-the-jungle caricatures in old movies.

"Fool in Love" hit in 1960 and sparked a chain of hits here and overseas. Of course, the aforetold prelude, the middle of the story, and its aftermath have been well documented—in particular in the Turners' respective books: the first wave of success in the late '50s and early '60s; the overseas acceptance and prominent tours; the '66 Rolling Stones tour; the return chart run in the late '60s and early '70s; and the ultimate breakdown in relations in 1976. Ike launches into his version of the couple's story and the allegations that surrounded the breakup without much prompting.

"With the whole business, the whole thing, I have no regrets about our relationship. Of course it was blown completely out of character. I'm not denying the times we had our ups and downs, but I'm very proud of the way I raised my kids and the life that we had. I'm very demanding as far as what I want to hear where a song is concerned—the way I want it. In her telling

I, Ike: Turner on the comeback trail, late '90s

them her thoughts about me being demanding, I think they took that and put it into our personal life. That's the mistake that she made. I think the mistake that *I* made was during the time I was doing drugs, I was encouraged by an attorney to sign a contract with Disney to not sue them." He was unhappy with the deal he cut regarding the use of his name and likeness in *What's Love Got to Do with It* (in which Laurence Fishburne turned in a performance of Turner that would forever demonize Ike—although Turner concedes it was fine acting, himself having coached Fishburne on the sly one afternoon).

"Later on, when I got sober and clean and clear, I found out I signed away my right to sue them if they portrayed me in the wrong light. Everything was totally exaggerated. I even stopped interviewing on stuff like that, because it's not a good feeling. They did what they could do to make money. They didn't think about destroying someone's life. They've made it really hard for me," he says. Yet Ike, just like Tina, has every intention of moving forward with his life.

"I love Tina, but I don't like her today. I'm not jealous or envious or nothing. I'm glad that she's gone on. But the Tina that I know was more earthy. She done forgot where she came from. When I hear her talk on TV, the accent she's using, everything is phony. She looks down on America. She was born in America! Tennessee! When I see her, man I'm gonna tell her, she's got to come back down to earth, man. You can't forget where you came from."

If even half of what he said/she said is true, neither Ike nor Tina will be forgotton anytime soon. Regardless of all that, their musical legacy endures: *Hey, hey, hey, hey, hey.*

Recommended Recordings

Workin' Together (Liberty, 1970)
> Considered an all-time classic in the vast and disarrayed Ike and Tina catalog, *Workin' Together* is also their best known album. That's in no small part due to the inclusion of "Proud Mary," the Creedence Clearwater Revival song in which the Turners succeeded in doing a rare thing—they took a great song and made it better.

I Like Ike! The Best of Ike Turner (Rhino, 1994)
> Showcasing over 20 years of Ike, the set collects his sides from "Rocket 88" on through tracks with the Kings of Rhythm, with some obscurities and rarities recorded with Tina and others.

Nutbush City Limits (United Artists 1973)
> One of the Turners' classic albums, it captures them toward the end of their collaboration but stilll in fine form on the title song.

17

THE CRICKETS

"In fact, the guitar lick on 'That'll Be the Day'
made me want to learn to play."
—*Paul McCartney*

"When someone like Paul McCartney says, 'If it wasn't for the Crickets, there wouldn't be any Beatles,' I say, 'Excuse me, I'd like to hear that again,'" laughs drummer Jerry Allison, on tour with the Crickets and folksinger Nanci Griffith in 1997.

As Beatles fans know, it wasn't only in name that Buddy Holly and the Crickets inspired them; the spare, early rock and roll sound and McCartney's vocal hiccup recalled Holly as well. And the Beatles first-ever demo was "That'll Be the Day," cut when they were still the Quarry Men.

"Every year in London Paul does a celebration around Buddy Holly's birthday—Holly Day—and we go over and occasionally do a concert. He produced a record for us a few years back. He's a good guy," says Allison. McCartney in fact purchased the Holly song catalog, which means that a portion of song royalties belong to him; however, the songwriting Crickets still get their share. But a number of the Crickets' contemporaries from the early rock and roll era haven't been so fortunate. Contracts being as they were, the artist wasn't always protected, and as the stories go, unscrupulous types (in the case of the Crickets, it was manager and producer Norman Petty) often claimed their unrightful share.

"I was real lucky in that we did get our names on the songs," says Allison, who penned "That'll Be the Day" and "Peggy Sue" (originally titled "Cindy Lou," but renamed after his wife at the time, Peggy Sue). "We did have a manager that was a little, uh…like Buddy and I wrote 'Not Fade Away,' and I didn't get my name on that song, which has been a real sore spot with me," Allison says. Understandably, since the song has been one of the most covered songs

213

in rock and roll. "It is!" he agrees. "It's on the Rolling Stones first album—so that always made me feel bad. Buddy and I wrote that in the studio, and we didn't know anything about publishing and royalties, and Norman Petty put his name on it as the third writer, and he'd never heard the song when we recorded it! But at least I got a third," Allison says of the song that's been covered on record and in concert by bands from the Grateful Dead to Patti Smith and Los Lobos. "When Linda Ronstadt recorded 'That'll Be the Day,' we made some nice royalties on that," he continues. "The Beatles' first recording of it

Time Line

1936 Buddy Holly born

1937 Sonny Curtis born

1939 Jerry Allison born

1956 Holly awarded Decca Records contract, cuts "Blue Day, Black Nights" and "Love Me" with Curtis and Bob Guess

Holly and Allison begin performing as a duo

1957 Holly and the Crickets drive from Lubbock, TX to Clovis, NM to record "That'll Be the Day." Band awarded contract with Coral/Brunswick

"That'll Be the Day" charts at No. 1

Crickets do their first national tour

1958 Holly goes solo and relocates to New York

Crickets continue to record and tour until the early '70s

Allison and Curtis pursue solo careers

1959 Holly killed in plane crash

1977 Original Crickets reform for Paul McCartney's Holly Days celebration and continue to appear there every few years

1986 Buddy Holly inducted into the Rock and Roll Hall of Fame

1988 Crickets album *Three Piece* released

1997 Crickets album *Too Much Monday Morning—With Guest Nanci Griffith*, released

Tour with Nanci Griffith

In style with the Crickets (left to right):
Jerry Allison, Sonny Curtis, Buddy Holly

is on the *Anthology*, and I was real pleased that they'd done that. We were real lucky. A lot of people got cheated out of everything."

"I think we've been more fortunate than most," says guitarist Sonny Curtis. "Not that we haven't run into a few sharks along the way. But still, we were fortunate enough to get that business straightened out in the beginning, and I've been very, very protective of my songwriting through the years; it's taken care of me."

Curtis wrote "Walk Right Back" for the Everly Brothers, and "I Fought the Law," another one of rock's foundation songs. Although the Crickets recorded it, it became a hit for the Bobby Fuller Four. Curtis recalls what he thinks are some of the best renditions of the song. "The version by the Clash of 'I Fought the Law' is *one* of my favorites. I don't know if you ever heard Hank Williams Jr.'s version of that. It's my favorite. I know he's country, but he really rocks it. It's just so good. The first version, of course, was the Crickets', from *In Style with the Crickets*." Curtis reels off some more: "I loved 'More Than I Can Say,' by Leo Sayer, which we wrote. Anne Murray's version of 'Walk Right Back' I really liked. And Nilsson's. I don't think Harry actually released it, he just did it on a TV show or some project like that, but it was a really good one." Curtis also wrote the super-sweet theme for the *Mary Tyler Moore Show,* "Love Is All Around." "That was sort of a fluke deal that happened to me as a rock and roll songwriter. I believe a group called Hüsker Dü or something like that did it, and Sammy Davis Jr. had a real good version." Agreed on both counts.

The Crickets themselves have rarely been seen on television or video; the only moving footage you'll ever see are the same bits used over and over again. "There weren't that many shows to be on at the time," explains Allison. "I think we did *American Bandstand* four or five times, and Dick Clark had a prime-time show—we did that a couple of times, but there's no footage of it. We did two Ed Sullivan shows, and that's still around, and one *Arthur Murray Dance Party*—we did 'Peggy Sue' on that. Dick Clark owns that footage now. It's funny to look at. People on the show were all dressed in ballroom gowns, and the announcer said, 'And now we have some rock and roll *specialists,* the Crickets!'"

The band played a particularly raw and raucous "Peggy Sue," unlike the recording. "It was miked pretty poorly, and the people just kind of stood around," says Allison. The drummer first got inspired to play the new sound when he heard rock pioneers Little Richard, Chuck Berry, and Etta James; he started playing drums in the fifth grade after hearing jazz drummer Gene Krupa.

Once Allison and Curtis met up with Holly in 1956 to cut some country songs for Decca Records, it was only a short time until they formed the Crickets proper. But "That'll Be the Day" was rejected by the label, and Allison and Holly formed a duo in the interim; the pair once opened for Elvis Presley. Yet it wouldn't be long before the Crickets would make their historic drive from their home in Lubbock, Texas, to Clovis, New Mexico, to cut a rock demo of "That'll Be the Day" with producer Petty. It's the song that launched their rock and roll career for real in 1957. "It seemed like it took forever, but things moved pretty quick," says Allison, who was only 17 compared to Holly's 20 at the time. "Looking back, it was awfully overnightish," he says. "It was hard to believe at the time. When we first went to New York, all we did was spend all day just looking up at the big buildings. It doesn't seem like 40 years have gone by since then."

Sonny Curtis rockin' toward his music's
50th anniversary

The Crickets and Holly parted ways in 1958, when Holly moved to the
Big Apple and continued to tour with the rock and roll revue tours popular
at the time. It was on the way to one of those package shows with the Big
Bopper and Ritchie Valens in 1959 that the trio were killed in a plane crash.
"We miss him every time we play. He was a good friend," says Allison.

The Crickets continued as a group after Holly's departure and long after his death. Curtis kept his hand in writing songs and releasing solo records. Allison has a place in the cult-rock kingdom under the recording name Ivan with his single "Real Wild Child." And the Crickets still get together at least once a year for special events; they've been known to play the odd oldies revue, car show, and state fair.

Throughout 1997, the Crickets (who also include one-time Crickets bassist Joe B. Mauldin and pianist Glen D. Hardin) were on tour with Griffith, accompanying her on songs from her *Blue Roses from the Moons* album; they did a set of Crickets songs during the show. Curtis had been friends with Griffith at home in Tennessee for nearly ten years. When Griffith chose to record "Well All Right," for the *Not Fade Away* Buddy Holly tribute album, "She called Sonny and asked him to play guitar, and I sort of weaseled my way in," says Allison. We all got to be friends."

Allison and Curtis keep the same pace as contemporary touring acts on the road, although they aren't necessarily up to speed with the music. "There's a lot of songs out there—contemporary heavy-metal rock—that feel good," says Allison, somewhat apologetically. "But I like the Little River Band, even although they aren't that current." Yet he emphasizes that the guys in the Crickets don't belong to any real or imagined pioneers of rock club; the only pal they keep up with from the old days is rockabilly's Buddy Knox. "We mostly hang out amongst ourselves," says Allison. The Crickets' latest record, *Too Much Monday Morning—With Guest Nanci Griffith*, was released in early 1997 in England, and Allison says he hopes to see its appearance on these shores. "I'm not sure who's going to put it out…it's not Decca or anybody. It might just be Cricket Records," he laughs.

Recommended Recordings

The Chirping Crickets (MCA, 1957)
> The Crickets' debut includes the Allison and Curtis–penned "That'll be the Day" and "Not Fade Away," among others on this historic disc.

The Crickets—Still in Style (Bear Family, 1992)
> The most extensive Crickets collection in existence. As with all of the Bear Family sets, it's usually more than one will ever need from an artist—but it's good to have it.

beyond the fringe

Spiritualized
Julian Cope
Ann Magnuson
Spiritualized
Julian Cope
Ann Magnuson
Spiritualized
Julian Cope

maverick. Eccentric. Iconoclast. Freak. Crackpot. Weirdo. Julian Cope, Ann Magnuson, and Jason Pierce of Spiritualized have been called all these names and more. But what would rock and roll be without artists like them? Cross-dressing Little Richard was one. Leather clad Gene Vincent was, too. Musical geniuses like Phil Spector and Brian Wilson are often found in this category of music, where the so-called crazies dwell. These people are possessed and driven by the spirit of their art—to the point where they often forget to check themselves before unleashing their prolific genius on an unsuspecting public. They are rule-breakers and risktakers. If you don't like what they do, they know someone else will, although they probably won't find a corporate sponsor or benefactor, nor a guarantee that they'll attract an audience of more than one. "They are the outsiders—even to people with underground sensibilities," John Waters once said of his filmmaking heroes, the iconoclastic Kuchar brothers; the same applies to rock and roll's mavericks.

The legendary Syd Barrett of Pink Floyd, Roky Erickson of the 13th Floor Elevators, and Skip Spence of Moby Grape all found themselves at one time or another in the chapter titled "Loony." Whole books have been devoted to brilliant genius in the face of personal demons. And certainly funk is a genre that, seemingly more than any other, supports an outsider faction: Just look at the influential and commercially viable careers of Sly Stone, George Clinton, and Prince, all of whom at one time or another have been referred to as stone freaks.

Are these artists fueled by drugs? At times yes, specifically here in the cases of Julian Cope and Spiritualized. Are they divinely inspired? Well, if it's not alluded to directly in the lyrics, and it often is, it can certainly be read in the notes. Is their I.Q. off the charts? You bet. They are truly iconoclastic in that they aren't at all interested in existing doctrine.

Some might argue that Julian Cope, Ann Magnuson, and Jason Pierce are simply willfully eccentric as opposed to legitimately off the hook. Either way, it takes a strong character to explore the emotional depths of expression they reveal in both their songs and performances. It is with great privilege that I've watched the artists who've allowed the light to shine on their personal, spiritual, and artistic dilemmas without reservation.

I don't know what any of these artists would or wouldn't do for money. For many artists, as in our society in general, money is a closed subject, but Cope, Magnuson, and Pierce don't allude to having paid a price for their choices. They are simply grateful to be doing what they are doing (and if they aren't, they don't complain about it).

In the late '80s and early '90s, Ann Magnuson was the voice and lyricist behind the surreal, shrewd, and almost parodic rock band Bongwater; she simultaneously conducted an amazing journey in Hollywood films and network television. Prior to that, she hosted a club night in downtown New York—a precursor to the alternative club nights that thrive today. Yet her public profile (or lack of one) remains a conundrum.

Hailing from West Virginia, Magnuson is the picture of an arty urbanite. She has a keen mind and an extraordinarily quick quit, fueled by ideas from pop culture and its attendant casualties. She describes herself as an unapologetic feminist. Her real-life experiences in show business inform her stage shows such as *You Could Be Home Now, The Luv Show,* and *Ann Magnuson Sings Pretty Songs.* In her stage work, she is an inspiring, courageous, and honest performer. Accompanied by a rockin' band, Magnuson's shows combine cover songs, originals, monologues, and audience participation. *Ann Magnuson Sings Pretty Song*s was the third in a trilogy to chronicle the large life and times of a woman of the '90s who came of age in the '70s. Magnuson is acutely—sometimes painfully—aware of her past and present, which she channels through her characters' inner dialogues, often portending a brighter future for them. Or her. Semi-autobiographical, part pop psychology and 100 percent rock and roll, Magnuson's approach is entertaining while managing to stay intensely and personally political. Like artist Karen Finley, Magnuson is not afraid to poke fun at things like self-empowerment, recovery, and spirituality—ideas and concepts that captured the public consciousness in the '80s and '90s; at the same time she embraces those movements' timeless and inarguable messages. She entertains on topics like grief and loss accompanying death (specifically AIDS); the national health care crisis (specifically women's health); dysfunctional families and relationships; and spirituality or the lack of it. A lesser talent might run the risk of sounding didactic, maudlin, or even offensive. But Magnuson delivers her polemic with a brilliant actor's sense of tragicomic timing, aided by plenty of glitz and glamour. On all subjects, she isn't afraid to say out loud what many of us are afraid to even think.

Her television and film work (*Anything but Love*, *The Drew Carey Show*, *Caroline in the City*, *Clear and Present Danger*, *Making Mr. Right*, *The Hunger*) pay the bills, but she chooses her roles carefully. She says that in each role, a bit of herself is revealed. The Magnuson I talked to didn't seem to bring along her caricatures from TV, nor was she the icy rock goddess she sometimes played in Bongwater or the amiable gal pal she projects in her stage shows. At the end of our conversation, I ended up liking her, but she didn't make it easy; at times I was so frustrated I felt like shouting the old game show question, "Will the Real Ann Magnuson Please Stand Up?" But the great thing is, she doesn't really care what you or I think. And that's what's great about her.

On the other hand, although it may sound like a cliché, talking to Jason Pierce of Spiritualized is more like talking to a friend or a fan than a musician keen to scratch another promotional interview off his list. OK, so that makes him either a really good actor or a genuinely nice interview, but either way, Pierce spoke to me at length in rambling, disjointed passages—not so much telling stories as riffing on a variety of subjects, much the way his music shape-shifts from song to song, sometimes even within a song. It's a style that can drive some people crazy.

The honest, often unwieldy sonic mess of Spiritualized captured my imagination because the music felt like a perfect fit for me; it's the best thing to have sprung from the millennial music trend of cutting, pasting, scrambling, and leaving what sticks and works on the brain like meditation. The bonus is that instead of coming out pure metal machine music, Spiritualized has a heart pulsing through every painstakingly delivered word and note.

The band is part of the time-space continuum that includes avant garde composer Karlheinz Stockhausen and jazz maverick Sun Ra, but they are neither an experimental nor a jazz band—they are a rock band that distill the essence of the past masters into their own future trip. "The future is now—it's happening as we speak," says Pierce. A fairly sane-sounding quote from someone with a reputation for insanity. Or is it? Welcome to the world of Spiritualized, where everything up is down. Particularly live, the noise can be so insane at times—so deafening—that if one listens close, the quiet spaces in between are quite possibly the closest thing to sanity you'll ever find.

Julian Cope is another in a long line of eccentric English musicians, writers, and thinkers—he happens to be all three; after a long period of self-discovery, he may've proven himself to be, as they say in rock and roll, positively god-like.

Cope is a good talker, and in hindsight, our conversation came at what seems to have been a huge creative juncture in his life. He had just rediscovered the German experimental-psychedelic-progressive rock he sought refuge in as a teenager—Krautrock. And so, he explains, it was his duty to write and publish *Krautrocksampler*, a free-form remembrance and guide to the music. As Cope reclaimed his musical roots, his own creations started to take on deeper, multicolored hues.

In 1995, his last album for a U.S. major label, *20 Mothers*, was issued. He and his wife of 16 years, Dorian, and their two daughters were living near the British Isles' sacred sites in Avebury; they had planned to move even closer to the mysterious standing stone sites in the area. Cope is the author of *The Modern Antiquarian* (1998), a cartographic guide to the sacred sites of England, and is working on its sequel. In the '90s he recorded a couple of Moog music records under the sobriquet Queen Elizabeth. After years as a celebrated user of drugs, he's given up the harder substances and remains extraordinarily prolific as an author and recording artist. For further insight into the mind and madness of Julian H. Cope, aka The Arch Drude, I fully recommend his autobiographies parts I and 2, *Head On* and *Repossessed*. As Cope would say, *"Awlright!!!"*

Unclassifiable artists are notoriously misunderstood. That's partly why I've presented the Cope and Magnuson pieces in the question-and-answer format. Although the Q&A has its detractors, in many cases, it can be a crucial vehicle toward preserving the artist's integrity. Often, words taken out of the context in which they were spoken have been known to intensify reputations which are already largely misbegotten.

I feel particularly empathetic toward the artists here who, as they approached middle age, were still moving and growing and changing, relentless in their efforts to have their voices heard—even at the risk of appearing foolish or awkward. It is to these artists and others like them to whom this book is dedicated. They are the brave souls who in the face of everything life tosses at them—from adventure to adversity to ecstasy—are willing to test new boundaries, scale new heights, break traditions, and reclaim what's good about the tried and true. Pressing on, sharing their findings with us, they let the freak flag fly. Right on.

18

"Sometimes I get a feeling about someone, an artist, writer or performer: a feeling that they have more than talent, they have Wisdom....
I've had that feeling for some time now about Ann Magnuson." —*Ron Rosenbaum*

"This is my happening and it freaks me out."
—*Ann Magnuson*

h ow was the show with the Tindersticks last night? [Magnuson sings the song on the Tindersticks album *Curtains*.]

Oh! It went really, really well. I actually sang with them once before in New York. The tour manager told me it was the first time he ever saw Stuart [Staples] blush on stage.

Does he have a crush on you?

No, no, no. Apparently he'd never sung live with anyone, and for that particular song, "Buried Bones," I dress and act appropriately for that character...and that's what happened.

Were you a fan before you sung with them?

I got a call from Jeff MacDonald of Redd Kross, and he said they were looking for me. I don't know if this was the beginning of anything, but you never know.

Are you spending a lot of time in L.A. these days? I think of you as a New York person.

Well, my work keeps me here, but I really live in New York. Once the supermodels took over, it felt like it was time to get the hell out of Dodge. My band is here in L.A., but I try not to venture west of Vermont [Street] while I'm here.

How did you find the people in your band?

Kristian Hoffman helped me put together the band. A couple of years ago, when I did *The Luv Show*, I made the record first and the live show came after. So I thought I would do it the opposite way. So after we get the live show together, we'll make a record. Jonathan Lea I knew from his band, Jigsaw Seen. I knew DJ Bonebrake played vibes, and I wanted vibes. I needed a backup singer, so I got Renee From Paris.

Is the show at all like You Could Be Home Now *with set, costume changes, and personal elements?*

That was very personal. It's a bit like that. I have one costume change, but this is a band. In *The Luv Show* I had a sort of alter-ego; things were heightened and pumped up a bit, but not that much. It was basically about chaos. And it was at the end of a tumultuous love affair for me.

So you've worked things out and you're going into the next phase, which just happens to fall during the late '90s millennial mania. Is Pretty Songs *the final chapter?*

There's only one end to the story, and that's six feet under; the story ends at Forest Lawn. Actually, my end of the millennium show will be next.

Are there some therapeutic/cathartic elements to doing a show like this?

Absolutely.

People are often critical of self-referential stuff these days.

I used to care, and that's a waste of time.

By singing "pretty songs" and imagining the world as a nicer and kinder place, is the show one big—and I hesitate to use the word—affirmation?

Yeah, yeah, and no reason to be hesitant about using the word. To tell you the truth, on one hand, I'm not the biggest fan of art that is just a replacement for a shrink's couch, so that's why I like to be more indirect, and I like to gussy it up with baubles and bangles and bright shiny things. First and foremost in my mind is entertaining. That's been my therapy—to get on up there and not so much dump on everybody, but to celebrate the absurdity of it all and create a camaraderie. In this show, I play characters, but it's hard to explain. I start off the show with a ten-minute poem called "What Is Pretty" and then there are cover songs and originals and conversations with the audience. If *The Luv Show* was about getting in bed with Satan, then this show is about getting closer to God. What we discovered in *The Luv Show* is that the devil's a lousy lay.

Did you see The Devil's Advocate?

No; they offered me a role, but I thought the part was so hateful. They wanted me to play the shrewish woman that was the wife of one of the law partners. In my opinion, that is the female equivalent of the Stepin Fetchit role. Those shrewish characters are just as bad as 'Yes, Massa, I be gettin' that for you real soon.' Do you know how hard it is to turn down that kind of part—the exposure and the money? But I would've felt like I had taken my soul and everything that I believe in to the core and dragged it through the mud and left myself without a shred of dignity. I don't mind playing comic characters, but my brain gets in the way when it comes to that stuff. All of the actresses auditioning were whispering to each other, 'Can you believe how hateful this character is?' But I feel for the actors that do these parts to keep food on the table.

Living in the belly of the beast must be like one big research project—your everyday life potential material for the shows. What's a typical day like, and do you ever relax?

Oh yeah, I try to go to the park everyday. In fact there's a part of the show that takes place on a trail in Griffith Park. L.A. is definitely ground zero for everything, but I have wonderful friends, a great band, and I just got a part in another movie with a good director, a big blockbuster type of thing. Lately I just have to take a lot of phone calls. And I have to write two big articles—one about bad boys, and the other is called "Ugly Like Me"—like that book *Black Like Me*—where I made myself ugly and then I had to go to Carolyn Bessette-Kennedy's hair colorist to become pretty.

I'm sick of hearing about that guy!

I know. I'm actually blonde now. I decided to keep it, but I had it redone.

*The enigmatic yet straight-talking
Ann Magnuson*

I'd like to get one of those assignments.

I know, but I never know when the next one's going to come. That's the hardest part. It's inevitably when I'm in the middle of a show.

Where do you stand on bad boys?

I'm over it. I've always had a thing for Errol Flynn. My perfect man is a cross between Errol Flynn and Ward Cleaver. I've been in a relationship for

Time Line

1978	Magnuson moves to New York's East Village
1979-81	Manages/performs at Club 57 in New York
	Begins an ongoing career as an actor, writer, performer, and musician
1983	Lands a role in *The Hunger;* sporadically appears in cult and Hollywood films throughout the '80s and '90s
1985	Role in *Desperately Seeking Susan*
1987	Stars in *Making Mr. Right* with John Malkovich
	Joins art/indie-rock band, Bongwater
1994	Lands a small role in *Cabin Boy;* the film is widely panned (though it's a must-see for Magnuson and Chris Elliott fans!)
1995	*The Luv Show*
1997	Debuts the work in progress, *Ann Magnuson Sings Pretty Songs*

about a year and a half with a tremendous, wonderful man, but we're taking a little time out. It started right after that long, tumultuous turmoil of a relationship.

What on earth made you call up the memory of Jobriath [obscure glitter rock musician from the '70s] for the show?

First of all, I love some of the songs. They're really pretty songs. And the story about his desire for stardom—he got hooked up with the wrong people, they hyped him instead of developing a fan base slowly, and in hindsight it was all wrong, He was *waaay* too out for his time. No one could believe the hype. He was dismissed and ignored and discarded—I think every artist can relate to that. That's why I had so much fun with the Jobriath character. But it's a tragic story. He became a lounge singer and then he died of AIDS.

It's like he was a little angel brought down to earth to teach people about the potential pitfalls of celebrity.

He's like a fairy figure.

He called himself a fairy.

Yes! Very good! He said, "David Bowie pretends to be gay. I'm a true fairy." At the beginning of the show, I establish the whole fairy theme in Griffith Park and the fairy comes back throughout the show.

In the show, do you come to terms with success or the fantasy of success?

Well, it's all a fantasy, and it's important to remember that. But it's important to keep the fantasy alive.

Recommended Recordings

Doublebummer (Shimmy Disc, 1988)
The Big Sell-Out (Shimmy Disc, 1992)

> *Doublebummer* takes on originals based on Magnuson's wacky pop culture dreamscapes and skewers songs by The Beatles, Gary Glitter, the Moody Blues, Goffin and King, Soft Machine, Johnny Cash, Mike Nesmith and Roky Erickson; "Dazed and Chinese" is Led Zeppelin's "Dazed and Confused" in Mandarin—wicked smart stuff. *The Big Sell-Out* tracks rock idol worship in "Celebrity Compass," flips-out Fred Neil on "Everybody's Talkin'" and tries on pathetic pop-folk on "Love Song."

The Luv Show (Geffen, 1995)

> Magnuson performed these songs live on stage in a musical theatre comedy piece disguised as a rock show. "Sex with the Devil" and "Live, You Vixen!" showcase her talent for turning her favorite themes upside down and inside out. She still plays songs from the collection, her showstopper the heavy metal "Miss Pussy Pants."

SPIRITUALIZED

Spiritualized's album, *Ladies and Gentleman We Are Floating in Space*, opens with a female voiceover echoing the album's title, setting the tone for their journey to the center of the future of rock and roll. Spacerocker Sun Ra might've taken the "space is the place" ideal to the max, but Jason Pierce and his band Spiritualized, with fuel left over from his old project, Spacemen 3, has built the perfect vehicle to take you there—there being the other world, where all people and their music reside in perfect harmony.

From the racial, planetary ideal envisioned by Sun Ra to the computer world predicted by Kraftwerk, there's always been some form of space rock—call it the science fiction genre—in music, where artists from Gary Numan to George Clinton have offered us their unique visions of the future. Sometimes the sound supports the vision, whether it's through the *woo-woo* sound of a Theremin or Moog or through what's come to be known as a "space jam." But Spiritualized, rather than singing the galaxy's praises or imagining what it might be like out there, are literally...*out there*, pushing the envelope, as they say, to the limit. Pierce sticks to his vision, whether it's through the minimalist sounds of his astrally inspired band Spacemen 3, or through the sonic assault of Spiritualized's 1997 magnum opus, *Ladies and Gentlemen We Are Floating in Space*.

As the band's captain and architect, Pierce is pleased to explain the nuts and bolts of how he built his rocket to the moon. "That's Kate at the beginning of the record," he says, referring to his bandmate and former romantic partner, Kate Radley. "She rung the studio on the phone." A simple but cool idea, a voice welcoming the listener aboard for the wild ride. It's like NASA—

a little creepy, a little paranoid, and definitely appropriate to the band's brand of tripped-out, repetitive trance rock with guitars. Pierce, also known as Spaceman, consistently drops references to the galaxy, not to mention drugs, into his songs,which has understandably led listeners and critics to place him and his work in the space rock file.

"'Space rock' is just lazy journalism," Pierce says. Besides, he'd rather not be judged as some kind of science project. Pierce simply aims to incorporate the best music into his unique visitations to other worlds. The breadth of his musical knowledge *is* alien in contemporary alternative rock music; it's simply astonishing. His creations are at once musically adventurous and trance-inducing; they never get tiring because each listening uncovers something new, lending the records to repeat listenings. Even the most cacophonous moments with guitars and effects pushed past 11 (around the nine-and-a-half-minute section of "Cop Shoot Cop" for example) have a comforting, almost psychically numbing effect. Horns and sonic boom are what Spiritualized add to its repetitive string and organ riffs, not to mention guitars, the feedback and drone variety an offshoot of the pervasive Velvet Underground influence in punk and post-punk rock. Spacemen 3's 1987 album, *The Perfect Prescription,* had a song called "Ode to Street Hassle" which was exactly that—a study on Lou Reed's epic song "Street Hassle," which quite possibly came from the Velvet Underground's study of minimalist masters like Steve Reich, La Monte Young, and John Cage, who also serve as spiritual mentors to Spiritualized. But along with the hypnotic, spacious passages copped from avant-garde composers, Spiritualized include the devotional aspects of

Time Line

1982–91	Jason Pierce and Pete Kember found Spacemen 3 in Rugby, England
1990	Spiritualized form
1991	Debut EPs released, *Feel So Sad, Run/I Want You Smile/Sway*
1992	*Lazer Guided Melodies*
1995	*Pure Phase*
1997	*Ladies and Gentlemen We Are Floating in Space*

Spiritualized fill the musical prescription to whatever ails ya.

Gospel and Hare Krishna, as well as hints of the blues, in their stash box. Call it what you will, but this lazy journalist is calling it "space rock."

Spiritualized rose like a phoenix from the ashes of Spacemen 3, the merry band of tripped-out rockers Pierce formed with Pete Kember around 1982. Drone was the dominant element driving their higher moments like "Ecstasy Symphony" and "Suicide." The band even had a slogan to define its sound:

"Taking drugs to make music to take drugs to." A dearth of percussion was another defining element of the alternately three- and four-piece 3. But by the early '90s, the Spacemen were getting restless, particularly Pierce, who formed Spiritualized with players from the final recording days of Spacemen 3. He contributed to bandmate Kember's (aka Sonic Boom) side project, Spectrum, but ultimately, the pair opted out of refilling their ℞ around 1991. Boom was going in an increasingly ambient direction—experimenting with techno-electronica and toy instrument sounds. Spiritualized went on to release three studio albums—*Lazer-Guided Melodies, Pure Phase*, and *Ladies and Gentlemen...*, mining from many of the same sources the Spacemen did: the MC5, Sun Ra, 13th Floor Elevators, and the touchstone for all the freaked-out English drug bands of the '90s, Sly Stone's *There's a Riot Goin' On.* It was the logical way to follow up what the messed up Spacemen 3 had begun, Spiritualized being only a nanometer off the original mark.

"For awhile I was into '60s music, and only hung out with people who were into '60s music. Then I had a friend who was into classical, and I got into that. I think Stravinsky is just as psychedelic as anything," says Pierce.

Ah yes, psychedelic. Drug references in rock music aren't exactly breaking news, but Spiritualized's fondness for them is unparalleled in contemporary music. Lest the *Spacemen 3* titles "The Perfect Prescription" and "Taking Drugs to Make Music to Take Drugs To" be forgotten, the album package for *Ladies and Gentlemen We Are Floating in Space* was designed to look like the insert to a prescription medication, right down to the exact dosing instructions and a pull-out designed to read like a contraindications pamphlet. The accompanying press kit was cleverly constructed to look like a medical file. Pierce says he had a great time coming up with it. "I'm not advocating use of prescription drugs," he says, "but music is also soothing—it soothes the emotions."

One of the emotions Pierce set out to soothe on *Ladies and Gentlemen* is one of rock's favorite themes: the pain of love lost. By going public with his breakup from bandmate Radley, Pierce exorcised some personal demons while providing a musical balm (or at least a Band-Aid) for anyone who might've needed more than the Bee Gees to mend their broken heart. He prefers that his own experience not be retold for the record, but the meditative "Broken Heart" and the crashing "Cool Waves," he will admit, tell it for him.

"Broken Heart" opens slowly; the keyboard begins to swell and a tender horn line tentatively enters. Pierce sings his prayer in a fragile voice: *"Although I have a broken dream, I'm too busy to be dreaming about you/there's a lotta things that I gotta do/I'm wasted all the time, I've got to drink you right off of my mind/I've been told that this will heal given time..."* occasionally interjecting the plea, *"Lord, I have a broken heart."* Soon, the proverbial yet tasteful heartstring-tugging violins enter the scene, and just as magically a big bass drum joins in to recreate the slow thud-thump of the injured organ. Listening to Spiritualized as an antidote to pain can actually be as effective as taking a tranquilizer.

For the recording of the album, Pierce acted as maestro, employing over 50 musicians to join him in the studio—from a full gospel choir to a mini orchestra. He plays guitars, piano, and a couple of other stringed instruments. Ever since *Pure Phase* he's relied on Radley for additional keyboards and Sean Cook on bass and harmonica while hiring a revolving cast of other players. Moving through musical galaxies is nothing new for Pierce—he's covered rock songs from the '60s to the '80s, from the Troggs to Mudhoney. Blending styles and musicians is perhaps his strongest suit. This time out, he added mysticism to the mix, calling in legendary New Orleans voodoo pianist, Dr. John.

"I just rung him up. I don't think a lot of people do that to him. He was immediately interested," he explains, still excited from the rush of having worked with the Grand Poobah of Mardi Gras piano. When Dr. John and Spiritualized were both on the road, coincidentally following each other from city to city, the timing was right for some live collaboration. In New York, the Night Tripper joined Spiritualized onstage for a long-winded rendition of "Cop Shoot Cop," the 16-minute free-form journey through space and sonic dissonance that Dr. John also played on the album. And on the nights the good doctor can't turn up, well, there's always the possibility of Neil Young and Crazy Horse. Having already done one tour together, Pierce says he finds Crazy Horse simpatico with his own corral of uniquely qualified musicians. There are nights when he claims he could tell their "Like a Hurricane" was becoming more and more Spiritualized. "Just as our songs became more and more like Crazy Horse," he says.

Pierce has no problem connecting with the like-minded in rock—the legends *get* him—even if, like the more obscure work of his spiritual mentors, the general populace have yet to appreciate Spiritualized's truly mind-expanding and marvelous sound.

*Spaceman Pierce delivers
one of his sonic devotionals.*

"Nobody remembers how many stars *There's a Riot Goin' On* got when it came out," he says. "We hope to make music that's timeless like that.

"Dr. John and I were having a conversation about the whole idea that there's 'good music' and 'bad music,'" Pierce explains, outlining the obvious distinctions. "You can't really come out and say that…because I think all music touches all people in some way."

There is good music and there is bad music. Perhaps there is even an ideal musical universe that exists beyond the one in which we are currently exiled. Spiritualized is the mothership connection to that place in space. But for the time being, Spiritualized is also good medicine for the here and now. Spiritualized is good music.

Recommended Recordings

Spacemen 3: The Perfect Prescription (Glass, 1987)
   Listening to this druggy, droney, and mesmerizing album is like taking a trip in itself. Its minimalism and repetition explores sonic territory that Spiritualized would mine later, while also incorporating aggression, noise, a refreshing naive pop spark and a cover by the Red Krayola— in other words, something for everyone.

Spiritualized: Ladies and Gentlemen We Are Floating in Space (Arista, 1997)
   If it gets better than this, then be prepared to bow down to Spiritualized, the new gods of space rock. Horns, sonic boom, repetitive string and organ riffs, free jazz, orchestration, and even a full gospel choir combine to make this among the greatest, most timeless rock records of the '90s.

J U L I A N   C O P E

julian Cope was barely 20 years old in 1976—a stone freak with a passion for the music of '60s holdovers like the Doors and Love and a sophisticated ear for Krautrockers Can and Faust—but by the end of that year, he'd gotten turned on to the Modern Lovers, Patti Smith, and Television. Like so many of his generation, he says, "Once, I heard this stuff, there was no going back." So, inspired by the D.I.Y. spirit that had infested London, he started his own band, which ultimately became the Teardrop Explodes.

As the neopsychedelic band's frontman from 1978–83, Cope belonged to a group of Northern mavericks who set off the second musical revolution to come straight outta Liverpool in 20 years. With his dusky voice and unpredictable behavior, Cope quickly established himself as a strong-willed, charismatic performer with an apocalyptic vision. But after only two studio albums, the Teardrops exploded. Ten years later and with the beginnings of a solo career already behind him, Cope recounted those dizzying years in his 1994 memoir, *Head On*. By that time, he'd already released a load of confusing solo albums, including *World Shut Your Mouth* and most notably, *Fried*. Although still dabbling in neopsychedelic sounds as a solo artist, Cope himself was drowning in hallucinogens, and his music and image reflected his experimentation—sometimes for better and sometimes, worse. On the album cover for *Fried*, he appeared to be crawling naked, shielded only by a tortoise shell. The image set off a feeding frenzy in the British press and solidified his reputation as King Loony. Even his record company began to have their doubts about him, although they allowed him to persevere with less than sales-record-breaking recordings, like *St. Julian* and *My Nation Under-ground*. And oddly, perhaps to spite them, he independently released experimental/improvisational home recordings like the superb but difficult to track down *Droolian,* and *Skellington* , which further fueled his mythology. In 1991, he reorganized for *Peggy Suicide*, his first in a three-part series of albums devoted to endangered Mother Earth. It was around the time he was recording the second, *Jehovahkill,* in 1992, that he says he accepted his purpose on earth as a Gnostic, truth seeker, storyteller, and modern-day mystic. In 1994, vanguard label American Recordings picked up *Autogeddon,* the final album in the eco-terror trilogy; *20 Mothers,* a celebration of all things familial, quickly followed. The records were the death knell (or a godsend) to Cope's 20th-century career in the major label recording arena, although ironically, they include some of the high points in an extensive catalog of excess—proven to be key to his musical and personal development.

In 1996, the techno-and psych-driven album *Interpreter* was the culmination of Cope's introspection and explorations of ancient spirituality, mysticism, and sacred sites. The erratic behavior and bitterness he purged in his autobiography now behind him, for part two of his life story, *Repossessed* (published in 1999), he took a more subdued (although by no means entirely sane) view of his life and career. Inspired by the writings of Lester Bangs and John Sinclair and the recordings of Sly Stone and Burton Cummings (!) Cope retraced his trip to the edge of madness and back again. When I spoke to him in 1995, he was in rehearsals for an upcoming American tour.

You haven't been to California in a really long time.

I'm not coming to San Francisco. I'm living by the Arthurian principle, which means that I have to avoid fault lines.

Is that really true?

Yes! I'm affected by cosmic effervescences.

But you say in your notes on 20 Mothers *that you were going to put all end-of-the-millennium psychoses aside, that it's going to be an easy ride...*

I'm trying to put it aside as much in my songs as I can, but unfortunately it still manifests itself in my everyday life. Because I'm livin' on the fumes of the Mother Earth at the moment, it's hard going to America, and it's hard go-

The Teardrop Explodes before the final explosion in '83.

ing to London. I'm not being a prima donna. I'm going to attempt to do as much as I can. The whole point of the poet or the artist or whatever you want to call him is that he has a duty to get his message to people. So I know that I have to come and say these things.

The thing that strikes me about your book Krautrocksampler, *is that you are the ultimate fan, yet I never really heard the influence in your work till recently. Were there subtle traces of it in your music before?*

Yeah, I think there's always been traces of it. The Krautrock influence was so fundamental to the Northern post-punk thing. It's extremely prevalent in the Teardrops. You wouldn't really hear it because it was so fundamental to the Teardrops' sound that you would think that it was just our sound. Everything was very Krautrock influenced in attitude, but not a lot musically, until I went solo. The difference is, is that in the old days, if you consider my trip as a diagram, it was a narrow, upward-facing arrow going at about 45 miles per hour. Now I'd say the same arrow is about two feet wider, so it's really fat, but

Time Line

1957	Born in Deri, Wales
1978	Forms an early band in Liverpool; scenesters Ian McCullough, Pete Wylie, and Budgie all pass through
1979	Teardrop Explodes forms
1980	Teardrop Explodes debuts with *Kilimanjaro*
1983	Teardrops disband
1984	Marries Dorian Beslity
	Solo debut album, *World Shut Your Mouth*, released
1989	Writes part one of his autobiography, *Head On*
1991	Explores England's standing stone monuments and sacred sites
	Daughter Albany born
1994	Daughter Avalon born
	Head On published
1995	*Krautrocksampler* published
1998	*Modern Antiquarian* published
1999	Part two of autobiography, *Repossessed*, published

it's going at five miles per hour. And that's the difference. Now I have a voice that covers more of the spectrum. In Britain I recently did *Top of the Pops* a couple of times and I wore a Neu! T-shirt. That was my way of saying, 'I'm going out to 20 million people and they're all going to know about Krautrock.'

I suppose I hear the Krautrock influence in the darker side of the Teardrop Explodes, but then I never thought of the Teardrops as a very dark band.

No! We were quite the opposite. I think we were an offendingly light band. I'll tell you what—the story of Krautrock is a really spiritual one. Imagine these people as young kids, sort of 16 and onwards, suddenly coming to psychedelic music via America and Britain, six months late. But at the same time, they were just coming to terms with the fact that all these atrocities had been performed on their land by their parents and their parents' friends. However touched by the world you are, multiply that by how you would feel if just down the road, 50,000 people were killed. To keep people in Berlin, because everyone was leaving, the West German government started to give people grants to stay. So all the freaks stayed there and spent their money on synthesizers and drugs and taking acid. The weirdest music in the whole of the world was made in the '60s and early '70s, 96 miles inside the Eastern Bloc by Western musicians. It was really weird.

I see why it was worth documenting.

I thought it was up to me to write the book, because I have the time to do it and I'm capable of doing it. It's shadowy and it shouldn't be shadowy. Krautrock is symbolic of the underground and the occult and everything that is underneath, and it's my job to bring it out to people.

So for now, recorded music and your books are the way you get your message out there, rather than touring?

Yeah, which is fair enough.

You say the way you were raised helped you deal with contradictions in life from a very young age. Is that how you reconcile releasing your songs about vegetarianism, green politics, preserving sacred sites, and love of family, through notoriously sleazy music business channels?

Oh, completely. I think what I always thought was that as I got older it would become easier. But what I found is that whatever state it gets to, it's never easy for me because however easy it is, I put barriers in the way. When Mahatma Gandhi came to Britain in 1947 in the worst winter of the '40s wearing a sari, he said later that he arrived like that because he knew the British were so pompous and so worried about decorum that they'd have to get Mr. Gandhi indoors and seen to quickly, even although he was a real spanner in the British works. And that's the way that I have to be seen. That's why I dress bizarrely. Everything that I say is true, and I don't mean that everybody has to believe it. But I feel that it has to look that bizarre as well because that's the way that I'm being told [to dress]. It's not easy for me to walk down the street because I look too ridiculous, but that's obviously the way that it's meant to be. People like Sly Stone always came over in a big family way and I want to be the white version. I want to look as ridiculous as those black guys got and I want to look for a bit of that grace. If I have to become a Stardust Cowboy to be that, then I'm gonna be. It's like George Clinton in the early '70s. He was full of incredible, stellar wisdom and he imparted it through Funkadelic. That's why I quote him all the time now on my records and on my adverts. The reason I do that is that true wisdom comes from the most unlikely places. See what it is, I've kind of fallen in love with the world, and the world radiates so much light at me, and I look at everybody and go, 'fuckin' hell, you just look amazin',' and I fall so much in love with that life and it reflects on me.

The songs on this album seem to be specifically about the people and things that make you feel that way: "Wheelbarrow Man" is about sibling love, "Try Try Try" about motherly love, "Queen/Mother" about Kurt Cobain and Courtney Love. That wasn't happening on your other records quite as intentionally, was it?

    I always use a different voice. Sometimes the voice speaks to one person and sometimes it speaks to a lot. Even when the songs are specific, as soon as you put them out into public domain, they lose their specifics. I shoot stars out to everybody that I know and everybody that I don't know. When I put out a record or a book now, I just hope that I'm going to make those connections, and I do.

And the strange phenomenon you're into, the stone circles and sacred landscapes you speak about in interviews and fan club correspondence—it's just as important to get those ideas across?

Yeah, because it's part of the whole. Everything in my trip is a holistic thing. Some of it's very left field and some of it is right in the center. I believe that we formerly had collective magic that we used in a community way. I think that the collective magic in 3,000 B.C. in Britain made large stone circles. The stones were so big no one can even imagine it now as magic—because it was a communal effort. But at the same time, we are in the middle of a very high technological magic that we don't even accept. If archaeologists, using the kind of ideas they use now, in 5,000 years discover car culture, they really won't believe that we could have driven at 80 miles per hour on the motorway with very few collisions. If you think about that in a rationalist way, it doesn't really make sense. But we think that it can't be magic because we can do it. That's what I term the whole Fordism, the car culture. So we still have that collective magic, but we've applied it to technological pursuits and we fall victim to thinking in a technological way so we can't get back to our magical selves. So that's my job, to let people know about it.

Sometimes, people who represent outsider, underground, and fringe interests end up with a loony or freak tag. How do you cope with that?

For my first 11 years in music, I served an apprenticeship to understand what it would be like when I was on the trip. I've been on this trip now for five years, but because I suffered at the hands of the press all the time with things like when I put *Fried* out—imagine putting *Fried* out in 1984, when everybody was in haute couture and I was naked under a turtle shell? I'm so used to being utterly slagged just for being who I am. It makes you so strong that you no longer even react to it, you merely act. You can throw it off.

The other side of this whole discussion is that you drive a car, and you obviously have a phone and fax. I'm staying in Tunbridge Wells, where the new-age travelers want to live off the land, yet they are tapping into water supplies and waste disposal systems that the town's people pay for—more of those contradictions.

The thing is, that's why on *20 Mothers* it says, 'Better to light a candle than to curse the darkness.' I think you've got to start somewhere. You have to confess to yourself, 'What am I guilty of,' and then say, 'I'm guilty of all these things that I can't get 'round.' I'm not pointing fingers at anybody, other than everybody. I'm pointing the finger at myself. I'm not like Sting, saying, 'You're all wrong,' I'm saying, 'We're all wrong.' Cynics will always say, 'You're not perfect, so you're not in a position to comment,' and the thing is, that is the greedhead's way of stopping people from getting anything changed. I believe that I can be 90 percent wrong, but it doesn't matter, because if 10 percent of me or even 5 percent of me has got a little grain going, 'This is right,' then I've got to act on that grain. That's why I say on 'Ain't No Getting 'Round Getting 'Round,' *I need to get to London and I need to get there fast but my car is a polluter and it's messing up my future and there ain't no getting 'round getting 'round."*

If you ever came to California again, you'd find a lot of people who share your beliefs—you might enjoy trading ideas with them.
I know that I would, but you'll have to solder up that fault first.

When it comes to songwriting, do you think to yourself, "Hm…I want to address this issue of the car and the role it plays in our society…"?
No! No! Nothing like that. It's nothing to do with me. It's a gnostic odyssey. When I say that I have vision and clarity and lyrics pass through me, I mean that. Before I recorded "Upwards of Forty-Five Degrees" off *Jehovahkill*, I have notes in my journal from that time where I believed that if I didn't quickly record it I was going to die—so I obviously believed that it was high knowledge. And I know that because one of the lyrics, *'To penetrate the diamond, the pituitary gland gets torn on its axis and frees,'* is exactly what happened to me. It did. It's how my third eye opened. The reason I write so many songs now is that it has nothing to do with me, but it's a huge, tumultuous tidal wave of white gooey cosmic light.

And it just kind of comes out in one spurt and there's no going back and playing around with it?
Not really, because I'm not the interpreter. Maybe I'm the translator, but I'm not the interpreter. Have you heard the Lou Reed lyric, *'Between thought and expression lies a lifetime'*? That's bullshit. That's an intellectual truth, but intuitively it's not true. When stuff comes out of the heavens, it comes directly through you, and words describe your interpretation.

The solo Cope and his customized mic stand

Maybe it's a stupid question, but could you ever conceive of going back to song-writing as you knew it?

That would be like saying…

Could you go back to eating meat?

…Eating meat, or could I go back to having the TV on when I wasn't watching it. Like I can't even have the TV on when I *am* watching it. I can't take that amount of information anymore. I'm primed to take in information in precisely the right amounts.

Where do you get your information in a given week?

From books, from people, and from walking, because I'm walking on the sacred landscape and a lot of my vision and a lot of my fuel is just through walking.

Things like films, music, other art forms…how do you gauge how you will take it in?

Well, with a lot of modern music, I don't even make an effort because psychically, I can't deal with records that are made in an atmosphere of hopelessness, so I usually deal with things through recommendations. I don't watch films a lot because I can't take that kind of generation of energy. But occasionally, we do watch a film. My wife watches films, but I just can't take it. I mainly spend a lot of time under the stars, you know. And that's the way my information is picked up. Like I'm an aerial. Can I tell you something? Where we live is a sacred landscape. It's the central sacred ceremonial area of the Neolithic culture who inhabited the area from the top of Sweden to the Iberian Peninsula from 3,000 B.C. to about 1,500 B.C. And the central ceremonial area was at Avebury, and we live four miles from there. In four weeks we move two miles closer. But that's why I go there and I walk every day because it's sort of Avalon. All the great mystics have written about it and spent time there. It's a kind of Blakian landscape, and I suppose that's the reason my music and my everything sounds the way that it does now. The music is more extreme than ever, really. This last album I wanted to make was a pop album, but it's still pretty wild soundin'.

You encourage your fans to stay in touch and interact with you.

Yeah! The weirdest thing about this last tour that I did in Britain was that I did three-hour shows, and I had a walkway so I could get right down to the front row, and it was just phenomenal because there was so much physical contact. I was neckin' with women and guys all the time. The audience was moving in waves like in a very different way to any shows I've ever done in the past. It was like a real physical show, and I thought, if you treat women like goddesses, they respond by acting that way. And if a woman comes up and treats you like a god, you walk taller. I just figure, something clicked on that tour where everybody felt bigger and better and I believe in it more than ever now.

I like that you're such a big champion of the underdog.

I appreciate the underdog, who is a frog about to turn into a prince. And I appreciate it that everybody moves me up to the next notch. So I figure that it's absolutely my job to champion the underdog; if I don't do that, then I'm full of shit.

Recommended Recordings

Floored Genius: The Best of Julian Cope & the Teardrop
   Explodes 1979–1991 (Island, 1992)
Floored Genius: Volume 2 (1983–1992) (Dutch East, 1994)
Leper Skin—An Introduction to Julian Cope (Island, 1999)
   Any or all of these collections would be a fine overview of Cope's super-sonic psychotic pop milieu as they cover his many guises: From straight-ahead chart pop artist to unpredictable, psychedelia-drenched experimentalist.

Skellington (Zippo, 1990)
Droolian (Zippo, 1990)
   Both of these albums are difficult to come by but well worth seeking out, as they far exceed any of Cope's major label-supported studio recordings. Made in spare acoustic style (in the case of *Skellington,* in one and a half days) Cope takes on his old favorites and unearths classics like "Out of My Mind on Dope and Speed" to great effect. Read all about it in *Repossessed.*

Denise Sullivan is a San Francisco based-freelance writer. She is the author of *R.E.M. Talk About the Passion—An Oral History,* currently in its second worldwide edition. She is a contributor to the reference books, *The All Music Guide to Rock, The Mojo Collection, The Rough Guide to Country Music* and the *Virgin Guide to San Francisco.* Beginning as a college reporter and radio DJ, she co-founded KUSF-FM's new music format in 1980 and throughout the decade worked at various music industry jobs: from club DJ and indie label publicist, to sole proprietor of an independent record store and major label marketing manager. A full time journalist since 1991, she writes about rulebreaking legends, future superstars and cult icons of rock, folk and punk as a columnist for the *Contra Costa Times;* her work can also be read in Rollingstone.com and Allmusic.com, among other papers and websites. More on her work, her likes and dislikes and direct contact can be found via her website, www.denisesullivan.com

sources and acknowledgments

friendly and thoughtful editors originally assigned most of these collected interviews; the versions contained here grew out of those stories. They are reprinted courtesy of their original publications or noted as follows:

Camper Van Beethoven appeared in the February 9–15 2000 *SF Weekly* as "Happier Campers: Why the Members of Camper Van Beethoven Are Talking Again a Decade after an Acrimonious Breakup." It was revised and additional material was compiled for the chapter.

Portions of the interview with Teenage Fanclub's Raymond McGinley appeared in the July 25, 1997 *Contra Costa Times* as "Fanclub's Output Builds Solid Following: Four Guys from Glasgow Crank Out Timeless Rock." The interview with the Fanclub's Norman Blake ran as a Q&A in *Addicted to Noise* as "Join the Fanclub." Additional material was compiled for the chapter.

Portions of the interview with Ray Davies appeared in the May 2, 1996 *Contra Costa Times,* as "Davies' Show Is 'X-Ray' of His Life." Some quotations and other matter on Dave Davies were originally used in the record review, *Re-kronikled, The Kinks, A Soap Opera, Schoolboys in Disgrace, Sleepwalker, Misfits,* in the December 9–15, 1998 *SF Weekly.* Additional material was compiled for the chapter.

Sparks was an assignment for *BAM* and appeared the October 9, 1998 issue as "Cool Places with Sparks." Some material was added and some was deleted for the chapter.

Portions of the interview with Charlie Louvin may have appeared in the *Contra Costa Times* during 1997, but the original was not archived. Additional material was compiled for the chapter.

Portions of Shonen Knife originally appeared in the December 8, 1995 *Contra Costa Times,* as "Shonen Knife on Punk's Cutting Edge/Trend-Setting Japanese Band Isn't Your Average Girl Group." Additional material was compiled for the chapter.

Julie and Buddy Miller appeared in the May 24–30, 2000 *SF Weekly* as

sources and acknowledgments

"Wedding Albums: Buddy and Julie Miller Are Virtual Unknowns in the Nashville Scene They Now Call Home. So Why Are Country Artists Lining Up to Cover Their Songs?" Another version of the story ran in Rollingstone.com. Additional material appears here.

The first portion of the Chuck Prophet and Stephanie Finch story appeared in the April 18, 1997 *BAM* as "Homemade Prophet." The second half of the story was compiled in June 2000 and appears here for the first time.

Portions of the Tom Verlaine story appeared in a Spring 2000 *Contra Costa Times* column, "The Show Goes On." Additional material was compiled for the chapter.

Portions of the Elvis Costello piece originally appeared in the August 30, 1996 Contra Costa Times as "Costello Still Beautiful, Hardly Useless." The concert review, "Costello's Material Clutters His Act" appeared in the October 2, 1999 *Times*. Additional material was compiled for the chapter.

A few quotes from the Talking Heads interview appeared in the Friday April 30, 1999 *Contra Costa Times* as "Talking Heads Open Up about Heyday and the End." The majority of the material appears here for the first time.

Portions of the Peter Case story appeared in the January 1996 *Acoustic Guitar* as "Case Studies: Peter Case Rediscovers the Roots of His Rock." Additional material was compiled for versions that appeared in Rollingstone.com and *SF Weekly* in 2000 and additional material was compiled for the chapter. The sidebar on *Blue Guitar* appeared in *SF Bay Guardian,* October 1993.

Utah Phillips was an assignment for the *SF Weekly*. It appeared in the November 17–23 issue as "A Hobo's Progress: U. Utah Phillips, Inspiration to Ani DiFranco and Card-Carrying Wobbly, Is Northern California's Institutional Memory of Itinerant Folk." Additional material was compiled for the chapter.

A handful of the quotations from Ramblin' Jack Elliott appeared in the April 3, 1998 *Contra Costa Times* story, "Jack Elliott Rambles Back into Vogue." Additional material was compiled for the chapter. The interview with Elliott and daughter Aiyana Elliott on her film, *The Ballad of Ramblin' Jack* was also a *Times* assignment though it could not be located in the paper's archive.

Portions of the Wanda Jackson interviews appeared in the January 12,

1998 *Contra Costa Times* as the review "Grand Celebration of Women in Rockabilly" and in various editions of my column "The Show Goes On." Additional material was compiled for the chapter.

Portions of the interview with Ike Turner appeared in the March 10, 1997 *Contra Costa Times* as "Ike Turner Mends Career after Bad Press." Portions also appeared as "Ike Turner, Phone Home" in *MOJO*. Additional material was compiled for the chapter.

Portions of the interview with the Crickets appeared in the November 19, 1997 *Contra Costa Times* as "Influential, Yes, But Crickets Don't Always Get Their Due." Additional material was compiled for the chapter.

The Ann Magnuson interview appears in print for the first time here.

The Spiritualized story originally appeared in the August 29, 1997 *Contra Costa Times* as "Band Blends Many Genres (who was the genius at the headline desk that day?!). Leader of Spiritualized Likes Stravinsky and Has Worked with Dr. John." Additional material was compiled for the chapter.

Julian Cope was an assignment for *Addicted to Noise*, though it appears in print for the first time here.

The opening quote by Salman Rushdie is from *The Ground Beneath Her Feet*, Picador U.S. A., 1999.

The lyric opening the Camper Van Beethoven chapter is from "Never Go Back," by Lowery, Segel, Krummenacher, and Pedersen, Camper Van Beethoven Music Co. Inc.

The lyric opening the Kinks chapter is from "Brother," written, arranged, and produced by Raymond Douglas Davies, Davray Music Ltd. (BMI).

The quote by Ron Mael opening the Sparks chapter appeared in the *New Yorker*, July 17, 2000.

The lyric opening the Shonen Knife chapter is from "Buttercup (I'm a Super Girl)" words and music by Naoko Yamano, Ten Fifty Music (BMI).

The quote from Patti Smith is a portion of her poem "True Music," from *Early Work 1970–1976*, W. W. Norton Company, 1993.

The lyric opening the Elvis Costello chapter is from "I'm Not Angry," by Elvis Costello, Plangent Visions Music, Inc. (ASCAP).

The lyric opening the Talking Heads chapter is from "Once in a Lifetime" by David Byrne, Brian Eno and Talking Heads, Index Music/Bleu Disque Music Co. Inc. ASCAP/E.G. Music Ltd. BMI.

The quote opening the Peter Case chapter is a portion of the poem, "Everyone Sang" by Siegfried Lorraine Sassoon.

The quote opening the Ramblin' Jack chapter is taken from Joe Klein, *Woody Guthrie: A Life.* Delta, 1980.

The lyric opening the Wanda Jackson chapter is from "Let's Have a Party," by Jessie Mae Robinson, MPL Communications, Inc. (ASCAP).

The quote by Little Richard opening the Ike Turner chapter is from Ike Turner with Nigel Cawthorne, *Taking Back My Name: The Confessions of Ike Turner.* Virgin Books, 1999.

The quote by Paul McCartney opening the Crickets chapter is from Geoffrey Giuliano, *Blackbird: The Life and Times of Paul McCartney.* Da Capo, 1997.

The quote by Ron Rosenbaum opening the Ann Magnuson chapter appeared in the *New York Observer* in November 1999.

The quote opening the Spiritualized chapter is taken from John F. Szwed, *Space Is the Place, the Lives and Times of Sun Ra.* Da Capo, 1998.

The quote from Lou Reed opening the Julian Cope chapter is from "Some Kinda Love" by Lou Reed, Oakfield Avenue Music Ltd, Screen Gens-EMI Music, Inc. (BMI).

The quote on p. 155 is from Kurt Loder, *Bat Chain Puller.* St. Martins, 1991.

I wish to thank all of the musicians, their managers and the publicists who helped to arrange the interviews that were conducted either by telephone or in person.

Thanks to all of the editors who received pitches, responded to them, assigned stories and edited them. Special thanks go to Mark Athitakis of the *SF Weekly* for his skillful editing and for coming up with the idea for the U. Utah Phillips story; to Randy McMullen at the *Contra Costa Times* for being crazy enough to give me a column and for the Charlie Louvin and Crickets assignments; and to Bill Crandall, formerly of *BAM* and now of Rollingstone.com for indulging me in general. Thank you to Hilary Hart and Cheryl Moody of the San Francisco International Film Festival publicity staff for coordinating the Talking Heads and Tom Verlaine interviews (and for all the great movies that inspire me every spring), Rick Bates for Ike Turner, and Harry Duncan

sources and acknowledgments

and Wendell Goodman for Wanda Jackson. Thank you to the contributing photographers, Jay Blakesberg, Toby Burditt, Bert Dievert, Tom Erickson, Rocky Schenck, Chuck Pulin…and especially Ebet Roberts.

Thanks to everyone at Backbeat Books especially Matt Kelsey, Dorothy Cox, and Nancy Tabor, plus Jay Kahn, Nina Lesowitz, Amanda Johnson, Julie Herrod-Lumsden, and Kevin Becketti. Thank you Rich Leeds for the cover design and Leigh McLellan for text design. Because Woody Guthrie, Elvis Presley, Emmylou Harris, Jeff McDonald, Raymond Carver, Nanci Griffith, Rosie Flores and Kris Kristoffersen were mentioned as inspiring more than one of the artists collected here, I thank them and the generosity of their spirits. I thank Neil Young—inspiration to Teenage Fanclub and Spiritualized—whose work as rock's most heroic iconoclast is an inspiration to me. Thanks to my friend and teacher Howie Klein for the foreword. I am continually and consistently inspired by the work of rock writing's past masters Kurt Loder and Mikal Gilmore; I don't see nearly enough of their printed words these days.

Loder said in his collection of articles, *Bat Chain Puller*, "Anyone who interviews musicians or other artists for a living is in a unique position to fill in some blanks in the history of their art and the culture from which it springs. I only wish that more such magazine work by other writers could be similarly compiled, rather than allowed to molder away in a warehouse somewhere." That paragraph helped give me the courage to collect these stories, to write from the heart and turn them into something larger.

Thanks to my friends and colleagues: Yvette Bozzini, Charles Cross, Jaan Uhelszki, Richie Unterberger, and Kurt Wolff. Also: Joel Bernstein, Paul Bradshaw, Peter Case, Patrice Catanio, Kate Cook, Jeany Duncan, Stephanie Finch, Ben Fong-Torres, Laurie and Bill Forbes, Stephanie Foster, Callie John, St. Jude, Alan Korn, Tom Maffei, Rachel Matthews, Erin O'Connor, Lisa Orsaba, Brigid Pearson, Chuck Prophet, Suzi Sarro, Rene Sedliar, Velena Vego, Shell White, Chris Woodstra, American Express, and the bee that stung me in the Yuba River.

There is no way I could compile a book like this without thanking my family: my parents who gave me complete freedom to listen to music, never censoring nor disapproving of it, and to my brother for listening with me and for playing and singing along on my demand—until of course he went on to make his own discoveries. This is to all of you, with love.

Jon Savage. *The Kinks, The Official Biography.* Faber and Faber Limited, U.K. 1984

Robert Shelton. *No Direction Home, The Life and Music of Bob Dylan.* William Morrow and Company, Inc., 1986.

Joe Klein. *Woody Guthrie: A Life.* Delta, 1980.

Ike Turner with Nigel Cawthorne. *Takin' Back My Name, The Confessions of Ike Turner.* Virgin Books, U.K., 1999.

Tina Turner with Kurt Loder. *I, Tina: My Life Story.* Avon, 1986.

Anthony DeCurtis, editor. *Present Tense, Rock & Roll and Culture.* Duke University Press, 1992.

Julian Cope. *Repossessed/Head-On.* Thorsons, U.K., 1999.

John F. Szwed. *Space Is the Place, the Lives and Times of Sun Ra.* Da Capo, 1998.

Bill Flanagan. *Written On My Soul.* Contemporary Books, 1987.

photo credits

p. 197 Courtesy of Wanda Jackson Entertainment

p. 202 Photo courtesy of Wanda Jackson Entertainment

p. 206 Photo courtesy of United Artists Records

p.211 ©'97 Ebet Roberts

p. 215 Courtesy of Steve Bonner

p. 217 ©'97 Ebet Roberts

p. 227 ©Rocky Schenck

p. 232 Photo courtesy of Paul Bradshaw Collection. Photo by Kevin West-enberg, 1997.

p. 235 ©'97 Ebet Roberts

p. 239 Courtesy of Mercury Records

p. 245 ©Chuck Pulin/Star File

Campervanbeethoven.com

Teenagefanclub.com

Davedavies.com

Raydavies.com

Sparksofficialwebsite.com

Shonenknife.com

Buddyandjulie.com

Wandajackson.com

Chuckprophet.com

Iketurner.com

Elviscostello.com

Annmagnuson.com

Spiritualized.com

Juliancope.com

Petercase.com

Ramblinjack.com

Tomtomclub.com

Davidbyrne.com

Talking-heads.net

Utahphillips.org

index